C ese

Edited by Liu Bingwen and Xiong Lei
with In-house Editor Tong Xiuying

Foreign Languages Press Beijing

First Edition 1990

ISBN 0-8351-2561-0
ISBN 7-119-01160-X
17-E-2479P

Published by Foreign Languages Press
24 Baiwanzhuang Road, Beijing 100037, China

Printed by Foreign Languages Printing House
19 Chegongzhuang Xilu, Beijing 100044, China

Distributed by China International Book Trading Corporation
21 Chegongzhuang Xilu, Beijing 100044, China
P.O. Box 399, Beijing, China

Printed in the People's Republic of China

Contents

Editor's Note

Editing this book has been the most rewarding task in my thirty-four years as a journalist. In my memory, at least, no work of reportage on China either by a Chinese or a foreign writer, equals this book in the broad range of people interviewed or in the depth of the interviews.

This book contains seventy interviews out of the well over one hundred that were conducted. We have tried to choose those that we thought would interest Western readers most, and at the same time would reflect the experiences of the Chinese people themselves. It is safe to say that these seventy are a representative sampling, as they come from all walks of life, ranging from a college student to a primary school pupil; from a rich grain grower in East China to a needy farmer on the Loess Plateau; from a taxi driver to a former Red Guard; from a newly-emerged wealthy entrepreneur to a kebab seller from remote Xinjiang.... In short, they are people one might come across in a city, town, or village in any part of the country.

Even more striking is the candor with which the interviewees in this book spoke. For instance, a hairstylist from Guangdong now working in Beijing and a private taxi driver in Shanghai both admitted frankly that their goals were to make money; a Moslem imam confided how he managed to maintain harmony with his two wives; an accomplished Shanghai portrait photographer disclosed that he wished to take a nude portrait before his retirement; and a woman pilot said the only regret in her life was that as a pilot she could not wear her beautiful hair long. Almost all the speakers touched on sensitive political subjects that a person would have had to have great personal courage to talk about ten or twenty years ago during the turbulent years of the Cultural Revolution.

Today, hundreds of foreign correspondents based in Beijing are writing and filing news dispatches on events as they take place in China, while, on the Chinese side, the New China News Agency (Xinhua) and Radio Beijing provide extensive domestic coverage in English as well. Despite the aforementioned, however, foreign visitors are still hungry to know more about the daily lives of ordinary Chinese people, their joys and sorrows, successes and failures, hopes for the future and dissatisfactions with the present. All the writers of this book have done their best to sound out their interviewees so that the book will live up to the expectations of its readers.

And I am convinced that the best way to know a country is to let the people speak for themselves.

Editing this book has also been a frustrating task since something of the original flavor—in particular, the individuality of the different interviewees—was bound to be lost in its English translation. We hope that our effort has not done too much injustice to the original interviews.

In this book, we have used the metric system for most weights and measures along with a few traditional Chinese units of measures in order to convey the mixture of old and new which still exists in

China. Chinese currency is called *Renminbi* (RMB), with the basic unit being the *yuan*. One-tenth of a *yuan* is called a *jiao*, and one-hundredth of a *yuan* is called a *fen*.

Finally, sincere acknowledgement is due the following people: our writers, most of whom are from the China Features of the New China News Agency; Ms. Xiong Lei, who helped edit the interviews with me; as well as our foreign experts for their assistance. Our heartfelt thanks go to them for helping to give foreign readers such an intimate look at the Chinese people.

Liu Bingwen
Beijing, winter 1989

Part One

Looking Back

Retired Cadre: Wang Zhichang

Retirement creates lots of problems.

He was called "Big Wang" by the students and faculty members of the Central Conservatory of Music in Beijing, both because of his height and also because of his demeanor, which many people associated with servicemen.

A member of the small number of the "cadres of '38," a name given to those cadres in China who participated in the Chinese Communist cause during the Anti-Japanese War, Wang was discharged from the army in 1965 and went to work at the conservatory in a civilian position as an administrator.

In 1977, when the country's college entrance exam was restored after a gap of more than ten years, he was the conservatory's admissions director, and recruited such musical talents as Chen Yi, Qu Xiaosong, Tan Dun, and Guo Wenjing. He is proud of these efforts and regards them as the highlights of his civilian service.

The retirement age is sixty for men and fifty-five for women in China. Since 1982 more than two million veterans like Wang have retired, thus creating room for younger, better educated professionals to move up.

Wang now lives with his family in a three-room apartment located on the campus of the conservatory. Three of his children have moved out, and his bedroom also serves as a study and reception room. The only modern appliances in his home are a color television and a refrigerator.

The Communist army in Shandong Province was quite a well-known fighting force during the Anti-Japanese War. I became a soldier in this army when I was seventeen. I fought the Japanese for eight years, and later I took part in the war against Chiang Kai-shek. I crossed the Yalu River into Korea to fight the U.S. troops in the early 1950s. I consider myself to be a true veteran.

I was lucky, or as the Chinese saying goes, "Having a big life." I had several narrow escapes, and there were times when bullets went through my bag or hat. It's hard to believe that I wasn't injured. I was hit by a Japanese shell only once.

In 1965, I left the army and was asked to work among the intellectuals. I became the director of the political department of the Central Conservatory of Music in Beijing. I worked there until I retired in 1982. I'd actually begun work as a political instructor at nineteen, and had been involved with politics and ideology ever since. So I was a bit sensitive, politically speaking.

The year I retired, the Party Central Committee emphasized that a leading cadre should be both young and professionally competent. I thought that I wasn't qualified in these two respects. I asked myself why I'd hold on to the position. I was sixty at the time and had just reached retirement age. I retired of my own choice.

In the early days of my retirement, I felt uncomfortable with all the free time I had. I accompanied my wife to the hospital when she was ill. I found that a man cannot do without a partner when he gets old. My wife and I were separated by circumstances for many years. Now that I'm retired, I hope to make it up to her.

When I wanted something to do, I went to help the conservatory's man who is responsible for incoming and outgoing mail. Now I think I can do a better job than he does. There is a lot of foreign mail, and they always ask me to dispatch them, not because I can speak any kind of foreign language, but many of the names are spelt in Chinese *pinyin*, which I happen to know. At the dispatching office, you meet lots of people and can converse when working. Time flies by very quickly. Although having worked as a cadre and had privileges in the past, I feel very much at ease when I'm among ordinary people.

Later, the dispatching office work was contracted out, and I was asked to join. I'd worked there voluntarily for two and half years. I turned down the offer because they offered me a salary. Another reason is that since my first granddaughter was about to born, I would have to stay home and take care of her. Besides, I just didn't want the money. After babysitting for more than two years and was just about to send my first granddaughter to nursery, my second granddaughter was born. My wife jokingly called me a qualified babysitter. She wasn't exaggerating. I did almost all the babysitting except feeding. I've four sons and daughters, and three of them were brought up by my wife. Now I've the time, and I think it's my turn to help my children, so that they can have more time to pursue their own professional interests.

Every morning, I get up at six o'clock and walk around the neighborhood for an hour as a form of morning exercise. Then I read the ten or so newspapers subscribed to by the conservatory for us old cadres. I always help my wife with the cooking. We cook Shandong style. In the evening, I watch TV until the announcer says good night.

I've been working for the revolution for fifty years. In the past, ideological work was strongly emphasized and I was sent to study for a year at the PLA (People's Liberation Army) Institute of Politics. I felt that my job was mainly concerned with people and that it was quite important. But now, I feel that I'm useless and have become somewhat of a burden. Of all the retirees, the professionals are all employed. There is a fashionable saying that "professionals have both social status and economic gains." Over the years, I had been busy helping people cope with their daily troubles and, thus, couldn't find the time to learn a trade.

My wife has done administrative work all her life, and had similar experiences to my own. She has never had a wage increase since the 1950s.

I've told my family that they shouldn't do political work. I've suffered because of my involvement, and I want to make sure that the next generation in my family will never suffer the same fate. My children have promised me not to do so. A most unfortunate thing is that my eldest daughter has had psychological troubles resulting from the chaotic Cultural Revolution (1966-1976). My other children work as a middle-school teacher, an engineer, and an information analyst.

My present basic pension is 180 *yuan*. With subsidies, I can receive about 240 *yuan* each month. Of course I can no longer enjoy all the privileges as I did as a senior cadre. The 240-*yuan*-salary is equivalent to the monthly pay earned by my son-in-law, who is a worker. I'm earning a 1950s salary but paying for

1980s consumption.

Retirement also created lots of other problems. When you were in power, you received adulation. The moment you leave, everyone seems to have forgotten you.

I thought of helping my daughter to transfer to a job nearer home so that she could have more time to do the housework. But I didn't, for fear of being suspected of taking advantage of my position. I thought she could change her job after I retired, but I was wrong. Later I learned that I'd offended some people in the past and that now they refused to help.

I'd have a larger apartment because of my rank as a division commander when I retired. During the Cultural Revolution, the radicals confiscated one of my rooms, which is still not returned to us. I've tried dozens of times in vain to get it back. The nurse we hire for my baby granddaughter has to sleep on the sofa. I understand that there is a tremendous housing strain at the conservatory now. A person is helpless when out of power.

And my feelings are shared by many veteran cadres at the conservatory. I still act as branch secretary of the Party committee for veteran cadres. We hold a meeting from time to time, and at such times, they complain of many things. The conservatory promised to give us old cadres a car, but there's still no sight of a car. The Party Central Committee has laid down a good policy for us, but its implementation is quite another thing.

Old people love to recall the good old days. And I'm no exception. The most satisfying thing I ever did was being in charge of the conservatory's personal admission and recruited many musical talents who are now having a great impact on music in China. After years of political activities, I at last did something meaningful.

I'm quite healthy except for a slow heartbeat. Now I want to write down some of my experiences. Not for publication. My children jokingly call me a "fool," saying that I didn't use my power when I had it. But I don't agree with them. Compared with my comrades-in-arms who laid down their lives in the war, I'm very lucky. So very lucky, indeed!

Former Red Guard: Xie Xialing

I was at first a "Red Guard" and then denounced and imprisoned as a "class enemy" during the Cultural Revolution.

In 1966 when China was plunged into the Cultural Revolution, which for ten years wrecked havoc on the nation, young students were mobilized as a shock force to mount attacks on everything traditional. Those politically naive youngsters, donning red armbands and calling themselves "Red Guards," were eulogized by some ultra-leftists as "the most revolutionary elements." Waving little red books of "Quotations from Chairman Mao," the Red Guards denounced state leader Liu Shaoqi, Party general secretary Deng Xiaoping, down to almost every official at the grass-roots level. They converged in the streets trying to wipe out every trace of "bourgeois extravagance" by cutting young women's permanent waves and pig-tail hairdos, stormed into private homes of suspected "class enemies" and ransacked the houses for possible evidence of "counter-revolutionary crimes."

But as time went by, many came to realize that they had been used or even cheated. Some overzealous ones went a little too far and later themselves bacame "class enemies" and suffered persecution.

Xie Xialing, now a lecturer in philosophy at the prestigious Fudan University in Shanghai, was once a "Red Guard" in the early days of the Cultural Revolution. Originally he majored in engineering, but his experience as a Red Guard changed his academic orientation and he ultimately acquired a doctorate degree in philosophy.

Dr. Xie has written a number of philosophical works which will be published soon. He now lives with his wife, who is a primary school teacher and ten-year-old son in a small red brick apartment building in the northeast suburbs of Shanghai.

This round-faced, forty-three-year-old scholar is a thinking man. His recollection of his experiences as a youth throws light on the mentality of young people during that decade of great turmoil.

What type of a person am I? It's difficult for me to explain. I'm atypical in that I'm not a typical Chinese. Most Chinese tend to accept what comes their way without complaint, no matter whether they like it or dislike it. It's supposed to be a virtue that a man or woman should have, because, supposedly, he or she will be liked by others because of it.

But I don't believe that. Our country's too many people who think this way. Yes, in some cases it leads people to altruism and philanthropy. But it also fosters servility, compliancy and obscurism. It doesn't serve to push a modern society ahead.

Furthermore, it hasn't ever been my style, even from the time I was a small child. I simply refused to be pushed around and never hesitate to speak out if I felt I was getting a raw deal. Philosophers must have this quality—good ones especially.

Sometimes life can be really tough just because you don't agree with the majority of society. I've seen and gone through too much not to know that. But I never changed my attitudes just to conform to current ways of thinking. I've never had an identity problem. I won't retreat from a position if I think I'm right. The right, sooner or later, will defeat the wrong, though sometimes the process may be agonizingly slow.

I've been to many places. Shortly after my birth in Chongqing in southwest China, I moved with my family to Shanghai. Several years later I moved to Beijing, where I spent most of my childhood, all my teenage, and part of my youth there. Then in 1968 I became a "class enemy" and was sent to a prison in the countryside. I spent nearly two years there, working on the prison's farms. In late 1973, I was exiled to a small rural town near Nantong, the hometown of my parents'. Since 1977, I've been here in Shanghai again.

During the process, I've been many things. Chronologically, I was a university student in engineering, a Red Guard, a "class enemy" in prison, a manual laborer, a high school teacher, a graduate student, and in the early 1980's a "heathen" who tried to modernize Marxism. Now I'm a doctor of philosophy and a university teacher.

In one sense, these ups and downs in my personal fortunes give me an advantage over many young scholars. Some of them can recall only faintly the recent history of China, and most of what they know comes from books. I've seen it, felt it, and have grown up with it. I've got a deeper understanding of China. You can't understand China if you don't understand China's vast countryside. You've no way to understand how China's evolved if you lack understanding of the root causes of the Cultural Revolution.

Only a dozen of years have passed since the Cultural Revolution ended in 1976, but it's dimming in the memories of most Chinese. That's understandable as few people want to recall that nightmare. But what happened is still fresh to me. I'll never forget it, not only because it was a turning point in my life but also because it was much more than a personal concern. We Chinese have an old saying that, "Past experience, if not forgotten, is a mirror of the future." The Cultural Revolution was a disaster for China. It should be closely studied in order to draw lessons to prevent its recurrence.

In the middle of 1966, when the Cultural Revolution was about to begin, I was a senior at Qinghua University. I entered the university in 1962. When I was young, it was a real privilege to get a higher education. In 1962 the competition to do so was very fierce. Even so, I found it rather easy to get admitted to Qinghua's Electric Motor Department, notwithstanding the fact that to do so required very high grades. All my family were excited about my success, as I was the Xie family's first university student.

At the time the political pressure was building up, I was completely unaware of it. At that time I was in a rural village on the outskirts of Beijing, together with several of my classmates. We'd been there since September of 1965 to "help the peasants carry out the 'Four Cleanups Movement' " as we'd been asked to. I was appalled at how destitute the farmers were, realizing how really difficult it was for them to make a living. I told myself I wanted to help them lead better lives.

The moment we arrived back on campus, I sensed something unusual was happening. Crowds of students were rushing about. Loudspeakers transmitted agitating messages. The normally peaceful and placid campus seemed changed. Instead, the atmosphere was painfully sullen and nervy and tense and taut as if something was going to explode. Soon I found out that some students were "rebelling," trying to seize power from the university's Party Committee. Although the committee refused to, at noon, students in increasing numbers started gathering around the administration building and, at dusk, the university was under the firm control of "student rebels."

Meanwhile, riots began outside the campus. Soon the Beijing Municipal Government went through a major upheavel. And, not long after this, a "working team" was sent to our university. At that time, the teacher of the "student rebels" was Kuai Dafu, a friend of mine. Yet, unlike him, initially I didn't oppose the "working team." I only went to tell them that some of their ways to control students were wrong. I was sincere, but they rejected me roughly. Moreover, they said I was an "arrant alien of the people." I was offended and outraged. But I had to be a member of the movement in the form of a "Red Guard."

Soon, I found I was at the center of the "student rebel" think-tank. It wasn't because of an innate gift for eloquence on my part, but rather because of my ability to get right to the heart of matters. I followed every phase of a situation, pieced together contradictory pieces of news and tried to figure out where the movement was heading. Through questioning, I'd interpret the underlying meanings of otherwise misleading slogans and remarks made by officials.

Yet as the Cultural Revolution advanced and I got a better view of it, I gradually became disenchanted. The more I knew, the stronger my suspicions became. In many ways it was the complete antithesis of what I thought it should be.

At first, what I'd seen and felt in the countryside made me readily accept Chairman Mao's call "to oust capitalist roaders in power in our Party." Yet, later on, I heard, and was told by friends, that those people working for Lin Biao and Jiang Qing enjoyed many privileges, some of which were even flagrantly in violation of the law. They didn't act in accord with what they preached. I was an idealist and couldn't respect a revolution led by hypocrites.

What's more, I was a city dweller, a university student, and wasn't easily fooled by lip service. I believed in democracy, decentralization, and respect for knowledge and abilities. All of those had been tarnished and damaged by the Cultural Revolution.

So I reached the conclusion that this movement was wrong and had to be stopped. I began to openly express myself, for which was promptly denounced as a "class enemy." Then a close friend of mine dragged me off to the Beijing Police Bureau. I was tried and put into prison. Ironically, about two years later, this same friend was occupying the cot next to mine!

It's said that a jailbird is a bird that cannot fly. It's actually worse than that. Under constant supervision, you can't act or speak freely. The food was poor. Daily farm labor was exhausting. What was also painful was that there were no books to read other than the works of Chairman Mao, Marx, and Lenin. I managed to get an English edition of the Chairman's works to brush up on my English.

In 1978, about one and a half year after the reign of the Gang of Four ended, universities began to resume enrollment of graduate students. At that time I was a teacher in a rural high school. I decided to apply for admission to a master's degree program in philosophy and later, if possible, for admission to a doctorial program. My plans were universally opposed by my relatives and friends. They said philosophy was politics, politics was dangerous, and danger was what one'd avoid. I didn't accept their advice. I applied and passed the entrance exams and was enrolled in the Philosophy Department of Fudan University. In 1981, I got my master's degree and, in 1985, my doctor's degree with a dissertation on Kant.

Why did I shift from natural science to philosophy? First, I like it and enjoy it. Philosophy's cerebral in nature and requires much thinking, and thinking is what I enjoy doing. I recall that as a fifteen-year-old, I'd often tell friends, "Be quiet; I'm thinking."

Secondly, China needs philosophy.

China's undergoing a dramatic change. She's recovered from most of the wounds incurred during the ten-year turmoil and is now engaged in economic development. The future of China's at stake. The more modernized a country's economy is, the better the country will be able to stand in the world community. During this process, it's essential to change people's thinking, and it's in this area that philosophy can help.

Upon getting my doctor's degree, I was invited to stay at the university as a lecturer. Now I give lectures on sociology. I enjoy it; it's especially rewarding when you find students who like to listen to your lectures. It's a two-way process that sparks my mind intensely, as I hope I does for the students. Sociology'd been forbidden for nearly two decades before it was again taught in the early 1980's. Even now, it's still not as popular as in most Western countries. Here we've no independent program in sociology, and it's only a compulsory course for students in the philosophy department.

Apart from teaching in the philosophy department, I sometimes hold seminars for anyone who wants to attend. The topics can vary from Plato's works to an analysis of the current reforms. It's my belief that every student, no matter what's his or her major is, should know something about the liberal arts and social sciences. China needs more engineers than philosophers, but it won't do if one knows everything about machines, but nothing about Plato or Kant, literature, or the Cultural Revolution. I've often raised questions and asked my students to find answers on their own.

Differing with some young scholars, I believe that making choices isn't easy. It's not a black and white situation. People and culture decide where a country heads. Chinese culture is distinct from that of Western countries, so China can't, and won't, imitate them during the process of her economic development. I think it's my duty to tell these young students to read up on history, try to get some understanding of the larger issues, and then come to their own conclusions.

It's beyond dispute that China has contributed greatly to the world's philosophical understanding. China'd many outstanding philosophers in ancient times. Their works have survived and are being studied all over the world. Yet some people, both inside and outside of China, say that China has no philosophers in her recent past or at present. I disagree. For instance, we have Xiong Shili. He's done much excellent research comparable in terms of quality to the research done by West German's Heidegger and Gadamer, and France's Derrida. Now, with more international exchanges, more Chinese philosophers will gain worldwide recognition.

I also do research work. I've just finished several books now in several publishing houses to be on the market soon. One is an expanded version of my doctoral dissertation on Kant; another is a study of Taoism. My main goal is to establish an individual philosophical system. I'm now surveying and assessing the achievements of both Chinese and Western philosophers. I hope the outcome will be a new system designed for modern socialist China.

This academic work takes up most of my time, but it's not the only element of my daily life. I like to listen to classical music. I read assiduously. I help my wife in doing household chores, and try to find time to spend with my son.

Now I'm quite content. To me, the greatest enjoyment's to do work worth doing and have the time to do it. When in prison in the countryside, I longed for this opportunity. Now that I have it, what else do I want? My principal regret is that my mother died before seeing this phase in my life. When she was dying, I was in prison and not allowed to be with her. How I wish she'd see me involved in reading, thinking, and writing.

War Veteran: Xie Zhenwu

I cannot tolerate the idea of just sitting, eating, and sleeping all the time.

Xie Zhenwu, thirty-six, was a war hero on the Laoshan front. A native of Guangxi Zhuang Autonomous Region, he joined the army in 1974. He fought against the Vietnamese from 1979 to 1984. In May 1984, he was seriously injured and blinded by a shell explosion. From May 1984 to June 1987, he was hospitalized for treatment. His wounds eventually healed, but he is badly scared, and is still blind.

At first he was extremely frustrated and pessimistic about his future. But, he decided that as a soldier, he should not give up and, instead, should continue to be a useful person.

In August 1987, the Beijing School for Blind People offered a new program aimed at helping former Laoshan Mountain soldiers who lost their eyesight. It was recruiting twenty-four blind soldiers to be students in a massage class. Xie applied and was admitted. Now he has spent a year in class and is doing well because of his tenacity.

Xie was married in 1983. His wife, the younger sister of his former platoon leader, is living in his hometown of Guangxi.

I live in a dark world. But my heart's full of hope. It's my hope that I can still be a useful person, the only thing that makes my life bearable. Otherwise, I cannot imagine what I'd do the rest of my life. I'm grateful to the Beijing School for Blind People for organizing this massage class.

When I was lying in a hospital bed, I felt hapless and hopeless. When I heard people playing ball, singing, and dancing, I couldn't have been more depressed. My body wounds were bearable. But the loss of my eyesight drove me crazy. Doctors did everything they could to restore my eyesight, but they were still unsuccessful. I often lost my temper, and cursed my bad luck, saying I wish I'd been killed in action than become crippled and blind. At other times, I'd become silent and refuse to speak to anyone all day.

My wife took care of me in the hospital. She told me many stories of disabled people who had struggled to have successful careers and lead meaningful lives. Trying to cheer me up, she encouraged me not to be so negative. I was able to overcome my attitude over time.

I often think about fellow soldiers and my former platoon leader who was killed in action. And I also have many dreams about battles I fought in. Memories of that fighting often haunt me.

I joined the army in 1974 at the age of nineteen. When the Sino-Vietnamese border war broke out in early 1979, I was a squad leader. My army unit was immediately ordered to go to the border front near Guangxi.

We pushed back the invasion of the Vietnamese and chased them into their own country. After we crossed 10 kilometers over the border, we met strong resistance. There was no road, and we had to bushwhack our way up the mountains. The Vietnamese took advantage of the terrain, planting land mines that might explode anywhere. However, our strong fire overwhelmed them, and we took over one height after another. But our side also suffered heavy casualties. When we reached the foot of the Height 008, there were only five of us left in our platoon: the platoon leader, three soldiers, and me. The order came through the platoon leader's radio-telephone to capture Height 008 as quickly as possible.

We began to climb toward the height, each keeping a certain distance from the other. The Vietnamese fired at us from their commanding position. In an exchange of fire, the three soldiers were killed. After the platoon leader asked for artillery support, a barrage of artillery fire pummeled the enemy position. Under the cover of artillery fire, the platoon leader and I got close to the top, where a machine gun was firing constantly. We hid in the bushes, unable to move further.

For a moment, the firing stopped, and the platoon leader heard a click. He knew that the enemy soldier was changing a cartridge clip. His experience told him that even a skilled man would need seven to eight seconds to change a cartridge clip. He seized the chance and jumped into the enemy's trench. He found there was only one enemy alive. There were five corpses, obviously killed by our artillery fire. Before the enemy soldier could react, the platoon leader killed him. I also jumped into the trench, and we, thus, occupied the commanding height. Before long, seven to eight Vietnamese troops began to attack from the southern side, trying to recapture the height. I fired to prevent them from getting closer, while the platoon leader requested by radio-telephone for reinforcements. Dusk fell, and more enemy troops became involved in a fierce counterattack. We were confident because we knew reinforcements were on the way. We kept firing at moving objects with automatic rifles and a machine gun. I saw that we killed at least five enemy soldiers. But the platoon leader was hit by two bullets in the chest. Minutes after our reinforcement arrived, he died. Before dying, he asked me to take his place, and to see his younger sister if I got back home. I'd do nothing but nod "yes."

We held the strategic height until we were ordered to withdraw. I was officially appointed platoon leader after we returned to our country. My platoon continued to be stationed on the Guangxi border.

I did what my platoon leader asked, and went to see his younger sister whenever I'd take time off. Gradually, we developed affection for each other and were married during the Spring Festival (Chinese lunar New Year) in 1983. At that time, there were no big clashes on the Guangxi border except for the irregular exchange of artillery and occasional enemy excursions.

But there was a lot of action on the Faka and Laoshan Mountains, two strategic points on the border of Yunnan Province.

In May 1983, my war-experienced army unit was ordered to defend Laoshan Mountain which, though under our control, was constantly being assaulted by the Vietnamese. My platoon went to the front-line, where we'd observe every move of the Vietnamese.

We were to stay there for one year. My men and I occupied small, damp tunnels called "kitten's holes," keeping close surveillance on our enemies. When they bombarded our position, we sought protection in the kitten's holes. When they tried to make a frontal assault, we left the tunnels to repulse them. Such small clashes occurred very frequently. We did this for a year. On May 22 1984, one week before we were to leave, two squads of Vietnamese troops mounted a sneak attack on our position. We beat them back three times. While I was inspecting our sentry, a stray shell exploded three or four meters in front of me. The blast knocked me down and I lost consciousness.

When I came to the following day, I was lying in a hospital bed. I felt sharp pain all over my body, and my face was covered in bandages. The shell fragments had ripped skin off my chest, arms and legs, and some had cut deeply into my flesh. To save my life, the doctors focused on preventing infection. Many skin-graft operations were performed. I was in hospital for three years until all my wounds had healed. But the doctors could do nothing for my eyes, because the pupils had been damaged.

To reward me for my service, authorities of my army unit increased my pay to a company leader's level, which is 130 *yuan* a month. As a war veteran and a first-class disabled army man, I can get paid like this for the rest of my life without doing anything. But I cannot tolerate the idea of just sitting, eating, and sleeping all the time. That's why I'm here in the massage class. I want to be a massage doctor, to use my hands to relieve the pains of other people.

I now lead a regular school life. Getting up at 6:30 a.m., I've half an hour of physical training every day. I usually jog in the same place. Then I exercise with dumbbells and do push-ups to enhance my strength. Doing massage requires strong arms and fingers. We have breakfast at 7:10. In the morning we have four periods of class, which begin at 7:50 and end at 11:50. After lunch at 12:00, we have a siesta. After 2:30 there are two periods which last until 5:45. Then we have supper. At 7:00, we have a period of self-study. We turn in at 9:30. Although blind, every one of us can take care of himself.

We have four courses: basic theory behind traditional Chinese medicine, principles of massage, including the study of collateral channels and acupoints, finger skills in massage, and braille. Next year, we will learn clinical massage therapy.

I'm fighting another battle. This time, it's in the classroom. I feel great pressure from my studies and often worry about possible failure. Because we're unable to take notes, we have to rely on tape-recorders to record what teachers say in class. Then in the self-study period at night, we listen to the tapes over and over until we have memorized what the teachers have said. As former army men, we all have the tenacity to bear hardships and the courage to overcome any difficulty. We're all very hard-working. Sometimes we listen to tapes and study braille late into the night until the wee hours.

But it seems we cannot rely on tapes all the time. We have textbooks written in braille. For me, it's most difficult to learn braille. A learner must be sensitive enough to feel all those small raised dots and determine their meaning. It's relatively easy to learn braille early in life. But we are grown-ups, and our fingers are big and rough, and not sensitive and responsive to those small dots. So in learning braille, I'm afraid I'm fighting a losing battle. Anyway I'm trying my best.

In addition to enjoying study and physical training, another great pleasure is receiving letters from my wife, who is now attending a secondary technical school in my hometown. I usually ask others at school to read her letters to me. At first, I also asked others to write my letters for me. But my wife objected to this arrangement, saying other people's writing couldn't convey my own feelings. She wants to read my own writing, even if there's only one word or one sentence. So I use a large piece of paper to write a few lines on when I write to her.

I know what my wife looks like, because we met and married before I became blind. So I can use my imagination to picture what she looks like. I've some classmates here who got married after they became blind. So they don't know what their wives look like.

I've one more year in school. After graduation, I'll go back to my hometown, and run a massage clinic there.

Ex-Government Official: Xiao Bingyuan

In the ministry you are the one people turn to for help and favors. Here, in the corporation, you've to turn to others for help and favors.

In the past two years the Chinese government has taken measures to streamline its overstaffed offices to improve their work efficiency. The most important action was taken in April, 1988, when the ministries and commissions under the State Council were cut back from 45 to 41. That means 10,000 government employees, or one fifth of the total, had to be transferred to other jobs.

Xiao Bingyuan, fifty-one, is one such official. Now working with the China National Machinery & Equipment Import & Export Corporation, he was an official of the Ministry of Machinery Industry from 1956 to 1986 until it first merged with the Ministry of Ordnance Industry in 1987 and then with the Ministry of Electronics Industry in 1988. The new ministry is now the Ministry of Machinery & Electronics Industry. Unlike some of his colleagues who were reluctant to leave their administrative offices, Xiao volunteered to join the corporation, instead of remaining as an official.

However, he does not think that the streamlining will be effective, believing that more offices will be created following the merger. But he loves his machinery and his future plan is to "find more large overseas markets for our machines."

I haven't left the machine industry since my graduation from the Shanghai Power Equipment School in 1956. I continued to work with the ministry while I studied mechanics at Qinghua University two years later. I graduated from the university in 1963. I believe I'm one of the few people who have been with the Ministry of Machinery for so long.

The old ministry had two pillars: generating equipment and metallurgical equipment. I worked with the administrative department which was in charge of the production of generating equipment. My work was to see that the production quotas for generators of different kilowatts were met. In order to do this, I deal with a lot of people in other ministries—for example, those of transportation, railway, material supply, power supply, and water supply. Since I determined how much investment and supplies they got, I was in a superior capacity with the manufacturers.

Yet, I wanted to leave the ministry as early as 1983. I knew well the advantages of working in the ministry. As a government official you've a lot of contacts and may be well informed. But the disadvantages also are obvious. Although you may have more access to leaders, you aren't really in a stable position. And you aren't your own person, especially once you become a department leader. People come to you for all kinds of things: wage raises, housing allocations, and promotions.

But, in 1983 I couldn't leave the ministry. Some very close friends had just been appointed heads of the bureau where I worked, and since I was an old hand in the office, they needed my help. So I remained to support their work. They were my friends, both before and after their promotion.

However, things became different when they

were transferred to other places. The new leaders didn't seem to appreciate too much my knowledge of the industry.

At the end of 1986, I learned that our ministry was to merge with the Ministry of Ordnance Industry. I was shocked, because the news came as a surprise to us. It seemed to me that our ministry was on the losing end. I didn't quite understand why our machinery manufacturing wasn't as valued as it'd have been. This time, I was determined to leave the government office.

I was then a department head. Leaving the government office meant I might be a loser. But I didn't want to be an official and still don't. What benefit would I gain when I became an official? Nothing. What privileges would I lose if I became a nobody? None. So I applied to join this corporation early in 1987.

At that time some 700 people in the ministry wanted to shift to the corporation, although there were only 50 places. I was told they'd give us an examination in English or other major foreign languages and test our knowledge of foreign trade and Chinese composition. I feared nothing. I'd studied English, and I'd worked with a department in the ministry which was responsible for checking the plants to be introduced in China, from which I gained substantial knowledge of foreign trade. As for composition, I'd drafted numerous reports in the past three decades, which had improved my writing ability.

Actually, I think, people like me who've a solid education and professional knowledge wouldn't mind leaving the government office or be afraid of taking an examination. But it'd be different for people without much education. Probably that's why only some 120 people applied to take the examination. The first time only eighteen persons passed. I was one of them. I came to the corporation in May of 1987. Shortly after that, the standards were lowered and more people were accepted.

I'm now a sales dealer of generating equipment. My department, with a staff of forty, is the most profitable in the corporation. Last year we were responsible for earning over US$ 70 million of the US$ 100 million the whole corporation, which has more than 1,000 employees, made.

Of course it's different working here than in the ministry. There you are the person others turn to for help and favors, while here you've to turn to others for help and favors. There you've a lot of contacts and deal with all kinds of matters, while here you've fewer contacts and you concentrate on only special items.

Personally, I enjoy working here. Here you can do what you want, without people bothering you and asking for this and that. When I was in the ministry I hardly had a moment free for myself. I really got fed up with the work there after so many years. It was bothersome. I'm no official here. For me, it's a relief. And you earn more in the corporation which is responsible for its own gains and losses. I get at least 60 to 70 *yuan* more every month than I did in the ministry, because there you get no bonuses, but here you do. Here I've the title of senior engineer, for which again I took an exam in English and came out in second place in the corporation. You can't have a title as an official, and to me the title is important.

Is the streamlining effective? To tell the truth, I doubt very much that the government's role could be reduced by cutting back some ministries and commissions. You can go to the ministry and see whether there are fewer people coming from local manufacturing plants to seek this and that. There must be some 1,000 such visitors there every day, the same as prior to the merger. We'd quite a few streamlinings before. Each time after that, some new offices were created and more people employed. That's really not right.

I didn't have to consult anyone in my family when I decided to change my job. I'm the decision-maker in my family. My wife works with the ministry's machinery research institute, and my two daughters are university students.

My oldest daughter took my advice and majored in electric generators at Qinghua University. I told her that as an electric engineer she'd play an important role, one she wouldn't be able to play if she worked in the computer sciences (although the latter's quite fashionable now).

My younger daughter is majoring in foreign industrial trade at Hunan University, which she entered in 1987. The university had only one place for candidates from Beijing and she was selected.

What troubles me now is the competition between our domestic corporations that sell the same products. In Beijing alone there are three major corporations which sell generating equipment to foreign enterprises. As we don't have the authority to coordinate our marketing activities, these corporations tend to get into "price wars," in order to make sales. They thus create a lot of opportunities to get good deals for foreign businessmen. It's really sad to see that.

But I'm interested in this work. I see a great potential in the overseas market for our generating equipment. So far I haven't made any big deals. Nevertheless, I'm confident that I'll make some big deals some day.

Part Two

In the Neighborhood

Neighborhood Committee Head:
Li Yaying

We're like a family. As head of the family, I'm constantly on the move and have constant headaches.

"Even an upright official finds it difficult to settle a family squabble," an ancient Chinese saying goes. It indicates the helplessness of the government toward those family troubles that cannot be regulated by law, such as family quarrels or friction between neighbors. And it is true. Urban residents in China tend to go to their neighborhood committees instead of to government offices for help when they have family problems.

A neighborhood committee is a self-governing residents' group whose aim is to provide them with social services. Settling family quarrels is only one of its tasks. It is playing an ever more important role in dealing with people's daily lives outside their eight-working-hours.

This is even truer in densely populated Shanghai, with its 12 million residents.

"The neighborhood committee has accomplished what the local government hasn't been able to," said an official of the Shanghai Civil Affairs Bureau.

According to him, Shanghai has over 3,100 neighborhood committees. And each one has eight to ten committee members in charge of 500 to 600 families.

Here is a story about a 60-year-old grandmother who has worked with a community committee for thirty-six years and is now head of the Liushi Neighborhood Committee in Nanshi District, Shanghai.

There's so much to say about the work of the committee. Often we describe our work as both trivial and varied: cleaning public toilets, streets and dustbins, solving disputes, and managing neighborhood telephones.

We're like a super family, with about 6,000 family members. As a head of this big family, I'm constantly on the move and have to deal with all sorts of problems. I'm often stopped in the street by someone in trouble. People can't even leave me alone when I'm eating. Often, there's a knock on my door at night. Since I've no idea when people will call, I'm always on the alert, even when I'm in the bathroom.

I'm not suggesting that people're too selfish or not polite. No. I'm just trying to describe the situation we're in. I know people come to me because they need me and most of all, they trust me.

For our part, we community workers have tried our best to do as much as possible for the residents. Two years ago, our residents complained about the lack of a kindergarten. They'd turn to no one but us since it was a quite complicated matter concerning several governmental departments. We had to find a suitable building, clean and furnish it, and hire several women to look after the children. It wasn't an easy job, but we did it.

We also set up a service network in the neighborhood. Those who work in the network are all retired workers of the neighborhood. Residents who want to have their bicycles or watches repaired can go to a neighborhood repair team which also provides such services as sharpening scissors, making keys, and repairing shoes. As a means of preventing thieves from stealing bicycles, we built a bicycle shed. A committee member's on guard in the shed at night. To help those in their late twenties and early thirties who haven't yet found a spouse, we've set up a match-making office. Now, twenty-one couples have got married.

We've also organized a group of housewives to knit cotton gloves for a knitting mill. In this way, they can make a little money.

For three years now, we've organized trips for those committee workers who've done outstanding work to go to Suzhou or other places of interest near Shanghai. We hired a bus and provided accommodations for them. The money comes from the hostel the committee has set up. With a profit of nearly 50,000 *yuan* a year, the hostel is really a bank of the neighborhood committee. All the money's used to provide social services. Last year, we bought construction material and hired some laborers to pave a backstreet in the neighborhood with concrete. During the Spring Festival (Chinese lunar New Year), we gave towels, soap cakes and pens to those residents who were activists in the committee work to show our committee's appreciation of their contributions. Every year, we hold a birthday party for the forty-six residents over eighty years old. We buy them a peach-shaped birthday cake and take color photographs of them.

Working eight hours a day like any ordinary

worker is a dream to us. We work far longer. Every morning, we're busy distributing bottled milk to residents and cleaning the public toilets. In the evening at eight o'clock, we ring a bell as we stroll through the neighborhood, warning residents to close their windows against thieves and to bring their laundry inside. During the daytime, if it rains while some residents are at work, we'll collect the clothes they've hung out to dry.

However, what we do is regarded simply by the residents as what we committee workers are supposed to do. Though satisfied with the conveniences we've provided, the residents aren't necessarily grateful. They're like spoiled children—seldom taking their parents' efforts into consideration.

In fact, committee workers're perceived as public maids and servants. Residents, it seems, are perfectly happy to ask you to do something for them because, they say, you're the head of the big family. But if you ask them to give a hand, say, in setting up the bicycle shed, they often refuse without offering any excuses.

Am I complaining? Well, at least, the residents trust us to solve their problems.

The biggest problem I have is that I can't ever get away from my work. I can't have a good rest even on holidays. During the Spring Festival last year, a woman in the neighborhood came to my house and knelt down before me, crying for help. She said she'd had a bad quarrel with her husband and that her husband wouldn't let her go back home.

There's a superstitious saying that having someone crying in your house during the Spring Festival will bring bad luck to the family. Even though I didn't believe anything bad would happen to my family in the new year, the incident was unpleasant. What else could I do except go with the woman and try to persuade her husband to reconcile with his wife?

Frequently, we pay visits to our residents. After years of work, I've visited every family in the neighborhood and know some of them quite well. People say I'm like a living computer of the committee's affairs. But recently I feel my memory isn't as good as it was. I'm old after all.

Some people believe we're unofficial authorities supervising thousands of residents. The truth is we can't give orders to the residents. Even if we did, they wouldn't obey them. On the contrary, it's the people who're the authority. They'll ask us to do something for them, but when we need help, we've to beg them. That's the difference. We aren't entitled to administrative means because we're a non-governmental social group.

Others think we must enjoy many conveniences and privileges since we've many friends in the neighborhood. For instance, they say, you can buy vegetables of better quality and without having to wait in a long queue in the early morning. That isn't the way it is. The only privilege we have is looking after other people's daily lives.

If we jump a queue, people will say sarcastically, "Look, what a good example the head's making for us!". Later, when you arrange a meeting, for instance, they won't come. Even worse, they'll dislike you because they feel you've betrayed their trust.

Unlike ordinary workers and cadres who leave the neighborhood to go to work every day, we community workers have to work the neighborhood all the time. Our activities are always under the scrutiny of the neighborhood residents. Therefore, we're always conscious of our behavior. Even our children aren't supposed to have any shortcomings.

I've five children. None of them has ever quarreled with other children. When they've been bullied, they'd just come home saying nothing about it. I know they've done this because of the work I do. Unlike their father, they never have complained.

My husband's been retired for five years. In the past two years, he's complained a lot about my work. He says that now is the time for the two of us to enjoy a "quiet and undisturbed life."

Sometimes I feel the same way. I often feel exhausted and have headaches. Work, such as resolving family disputes, has become too demanding for me. Though I retired five years ago, I haven't stopped working. People need me.

Needless to say, people hope we can solve all their problems. Some we can, some we can't. For example, we can offer little help to those who want to move into newly built living quarters. They'd go to the housing administrative office instead of coming to us.

Though the committee work is tiring and demanding, I don't regret being a community worker. As long as the residents regard me as one of their family members, I think my efforts are being fully compensated.

However, what I've really wanted to do for years is to be a statistician. I received an education in this field in the 1950s, and I think I've talent in this area, too.

I began to do community work in 1952. It was compulsory until 1958. What we did then was almost the same as what we're doing at the present. Only, we've much more to do today.

A community worker got thirty-two yuan a month before 1976. Then, we got two raises—first from thirty-two to forty-five *yuan*, and then to fifty-four. Besides, we receive a thirty *yuan* a month subsidy from the government. We earn much less than even a contract worker.

However, money isn't a problem. What troubles me a lot these days is the sleepless nights when I've problems that require me to resolve them but have no idea where to start. It's been like this for years. I'm old after all. I'm thinking of quitting my present work, but I haven't decided yet when I'd stop going to the neighborhood committee.

House Swapping Middleman:
Liu Benren

My brain holds data for hundreds of clients.

In most countries, people who want to sell their houses advertise in the newspaper. But in China, most houses are allocated rather than sold to individuals—thus the necessity for non-profit organizations in charge of swapping houses. The Xicheng (west district) House Swapping Center in Beijing is one of them.

The center has eight employees who help about 1,000 households swap houses every year. Beijing residents who come to the center have various reasons for wanting to change homes.

Liu Benren, fifty-six, has worked in the center for ten years. He holds the title of *zhuangyuan* (the very best) in house swapping in Beijing. He changed houses for 230 households last year.

An amiable man, Liu is eloquent in explaining various kinds of situations—an indispensable quality for a house swapping middleman.

People come here for various reasons. They want to change houses because their work units are too far from their home; or they aren't on good terms with their neighbors; or they want to get away from their parents or children becuase of family disputes. Some want to live nearer to or with their children or parents. Some young parents are looking for a neighborhood that has good schools for their children.

Others are anxious to leave their old houses because family members have died in them.

Last September a young man and his father came to me for help. They wanted to change their house as soon as possible, because they'd had a fight with one of their neighbors. The young man and his parents lived in a *siheyuan* (a compound with houses around a courtyard). The courtyard had only one public water tap. The young man went to wash vegetables and splashed water on a woman neighbor who was washing clothes there. They began to quarrel.

The woman called the young man a "rascal." Her husband heard her and came out of his house and joined his wife. The two men came to blows. The young man was badly beaten and since then didn't dare to come home because of constant threats from that neighbor. The police could do nothing about it.

The young man and his father came to my office every day and pleaded for quick service. In about twenty days I found a trade for them. The new house was smaller than their original one. But the family was so eager to change that they didn't have second thought.

If someone's died, the family usually want to change houses quickly, for the old home will constantly remind them of the dead which will sadden them all the time.

One early morning last December, a man living in a sixth floor flat accidentally fell to his death. He'd wanted to let in some fresh air by opening the window. But he was thrown out of the window from the bed he was standing on. His wife asked to change to a new place quickly.

Of course, nobody wants to live in a house where someone's died. Sometimes, we've to be cautious in telling the truth. Once, after a girl failed a college entrance exam, she drank poison and was later found dead in her sleeping bag. Her parents moved out of the house. Some time later, the new owner of the house came to us and complained that we didn't tell him about the suicide, which he'd learned about from his new neighbor. It turned out that in the end he was quite satisfied with the quality of the house. He'd come to us just to vent his spleen.

Most of my clients want to solve certain difficulties by changing houses. They're sincere and their demands are reasonable. But there're others who come here just to find a better place to live. They come here almost every day and wait for the right opportunity to come along. Some of them have succeeded. Someone has changed houses through me three or four times. And every house is better than the last one. I think there's something wrong with their intentions. Anyhow they're my clients. And I cannot refuse to help them.

The clients most difficult to deal with are those in commercial circles, including salesmen, shop assistants, managers, and private businessmen. Their profession is to sell and make a profit. They'll do nothing that'll incur a loss. That's also true in swapping houses. They like bargaining.

My tactic is to handle the easy clients before the difficult ones. By "easy," I mean the clients whose houses are in relatively good shape in terms of space and quality and who want to move into houses of roughly comparable quality. By "difficult," I mean those whose housing conditions are poor and who want to move into better houses. The easy ones take me ten or fifteen days. The difficult ones take two or three years. However, those who demand too much will sometimes change their minds a bit as time passes by.

Not all clients tell the truth about their houses. Most tend to exaggerate on space. Nobody can cheat me on the location and direction of houses. I've done this job for ten years, and I know the districts where most people want to live and the districts that are out of the way. As for the direction of houses, I'm referring to single-story houses. Old Beijing residents have a saying: "If you have money, don't live in an east-facing or north-facing house." Houses with southern exposure are the best, those with western exposure second. Houses facing directly east are worst, for they're cold in winter and hot in summer.

People who want to swap houses in this center are required to register first. I can judge the overall situation of the houses by what they've written and what they say. We middlemen are required to call at everybody's house, but that's quite impossible. However, I can learn more detailed information by letting clients exchange visits. The clients are very careful in inspecting each other's houses. If they are dissatisfied, they tell me what they think. Then I'll have a better idea.

One of the qualities of a housing middleman is that he must dare to point out the defects of a client's house and remind the client to be realistic. If you always say "yes and good," you help nobody.

But on the other hand, you've to be sympathetic and committed to people who really have difficulties. Last October I was asked to help in moving households from *Xidan*(in downtown Beijing) to new living quarters far away. The households had to move away to make way for the building of a commercial center. In the new community, housing conditions would be better.

But several households refused to leave for various reasons. One of them, I think, had a good reason. The old man in the family was paralyzed. His married daughter who still lived with him was pregnant. If they moved to the new place, his son-in-law, the only able person in the family, would spend four hours commuting to and from work. The wife of the old man, after visiting the new house, said she'd die there if they were urged to move.

The only way to help the family was to swap the new apartment for one that was nearer to the son-in-law's work place and of similar quality. And I succeeded. I used the same method to help other households unwilling to live in the new living quarters move to places that they liked. But for swapping houses, I'd have not succeeded in transferring the 400 households to other places in less than a month's time. Now three big commercial buildings are being built in the evacuated area.

A house exchange middleman should have a good memory if he wants to work efficiently. You get information either through client registration or through acquaintances. Most of my information comes from acquaintances. Whenever I walk in the street or ride on a bus, I'm approached by acquaintances who ask me to help them, or help their friends or relatives.

My brain holds data on hundreds of clients. We've a computer here. The district housing administration spent 40,000 yuan for it. But the computer only tells the location and the number of rooms in the house. It doesn't show the direction and quality of a house. So we've to put the computer to sleep. My brain's far more effective.

We work on a quota. Each of us is required to change houses for ten households every month. Most of us exceed that number. I made thirty exchanges for the first month this year, twenty for the second and twenty-eight for the third. Generally speaking, there're fewer clients in winter, because people don't like to move in cold weather. However, those who're anxious to change care little about the season.

Don't think swapping houses is a one-to-one deal. Actually, I often find myself dealing with four or five clients at the same time. The biggest deal I helped make involved fourteen clients. That's because A may want to move to B's place, but B prefers C's and C may find somebody else's house more ideal than A' and B's.... The chain-swapping method, I think, helps people find more satisfactory partners. Of course there're gains as well as losses among the clients.

If a family that wants to change its house has many difficulties, they cannot possibly solve them all by moving to another place.

Do some have regrets after moving into a new place? Yes. But people seldom bring the issue to our center. Before the actual change, peopel exchange visits, sometimes more than once, and they hold discussions among family members. They must sign their names if they agree to swap houses. And the paper they've signed has legal binding. If somebody changes his mind after signing, he's required to compensate for losses.

Apart from the routine work, we organize a house-swapping fair in the district every year. It's usually held in May. We also take part in such an assembly at the municipal level. It's often held in September every year. On this occasion, hundreds of people gather at a fixed location to exchange information. There aren't many on-the-spot deals, because it takes days for these people to make so important a decision. However, I think the assemblies are necessary for us middlemen because they provide us with a lot more information.

Swapping houses is a non-profit service, and it should be. If we thought about money, the nature of our service would change. In the past we didn't charge our clients. In 1980, the center bought two trucks, which were used to transport furniture and personal belongings for the clients. We asked our clients to pay only for the gasoline consumed. It turned out to be a losing proposition. And we had to sell the trucks.

From late last year we began charging our clients. They pay thirty cents for registration. If they succeed in changing their houses through our help, they pay 1.5 *yuan* for each room of the house they're going to move into. There isn't 100 percent fairness. You pay more if you move into three small rooms than if you move into two large rooms. Anyway, people today don't worry about such sums of money as long as they're satisfied with their new houses.

People feel grateful to us when they move into houses that they are satisfied with. Some send me expensive gifts, but I decline them all. It isn't that I don't recognize the good intentions. An elderly man was so grateful to me that he asked me to visit his new home and treated me to a water melon. In this case I accepted his invitation. I often receive film tickets. And before new year, people send me beautiful hanging calendars.

I used to smoke, but I had to give it up. That's because if clients know you smoke, they habitually offer you a cigarette or a pack of cigarettes when they greet you. If you don't accept, they'll think you are out-and-out refusing to help them. But if you accept and smoke the cigarette, you aren't certain whether the giver is in good health. If he is not, you might catch a disease of some kind. So I think it's wise to give it up.

Not all our clients are reasonable and grateful. Sometimes, when I arrive at the center, dozens of clients crowd around me, each trying to speak first. And they get into quarrels. And I have to raise my voice to stop the quarreling. Often, at the end of a day's work, I find my voice has become hoarse.

Not all the houses in Beijing are exchangeable. That's the biggest problem we encounter. Many houses or buildings aren't under the management of the municipal housing administration, because they've been built by various work units. And the leaders in the work units are unwilling to let outsiders live with their employees, who often enjoy some favor of subsidies from their own work units. This is especially true of housing owned by the central government and military compounds. Take me for example. My family—my wife, two grown-up daughters, and me—live in a two-and-a-half room flat owned by my former work unit, the Ministry of Water Resources and Electric Power. I very much want to move to a place near my present work unit, because at present it takes me three hours to commute to and from work. But my former work unit won't allow me to change unless I give up the flat. So I've to stay where I live. Anyway, our home isn't very far from my wife's work unit. It isn't that bad. Now people are talking about housing reform. It's said houses will be sold or bought in the future instead of being allocated. By that time, there may be fewer families who want to change houses. But the day seems far away. At least there's no indication that fewer people are coming to the center to change houses. I don't think our center will shut its door in the next couple of years.

Part Three

In the Management

Factory Manager: Zhou Qifa

I'm stubborn. Silence is my weapon in dealing with criticism.

A factory manager in China is often compared to a woman who has many mothers-in-law to please. Everything—from the employment of workers, the appointment of managerial personnel, supplies, quotas, and the sale of products—is controlled by higher-level departments. The manager of a factory works with many handicaps, without enough room to use his own initiatives.

This situation, known as planned economy, is changing with economic restructuring. In recent years, the market mechanism has been introduced in China, and the contract system is being adopted by more and more factories and enterprises. This system allows more decision-making power to those who contract to run the factory and, thus, have their own personal interests at stake.

Zhou Qifa, at the age of twenty-five, is one of the managers who take this risk. He contracted to run a county-owned distillery of 460 workers in Feidong County in Anhui Province, East China, in January 1987.

We met in his sparsely furnished office, where there are two desks, four chairs and an old telephone. Although he is thin and shy, his eyes, behind a pair of glasses, glow with confidence.

I was deputy-director of Hefei Winery in the provincial capital Hefei before I took this job. I volunteered in April, 1986, to come to this county-run distillery, which is 30 kilometers east of Hefei. At the time it was 600,000 yuan in debt and on the brink of bankruptcy. The workers had not received pay for months. Some went to Tibet and other remote areas to do odd jobs; some applied for a transfer, while others asked the canteen for free meals.

I signed a two-year contract in January, 1987 with the county administration, pledging to make the distillery yield four million yuan in output value, and one million yuan in profit and tax in 1987, which would double the 1986 quotas respectively. And in 1988, according to the contract, I should increase the figures by 25 percent.

My colleagues thought I was crazy to take such a chance. The consequences, in case of failure were formidable: I would get demoted, and would be charged a 500-*yuan* fine, plus having to repay one percent of the loss. That would mean I couldn't afford anything for at least six months. My monthly salary is eighty-odd yuan.

But I think I acted correctly. County officials granted me the authority to promote, or demote, managerial personnel; the power to increase or decrease the employees' wages and to determine bonuses and welfare funds; and the power to punish those who violate regulations. Without these powers, I wouldn't have accepted the job.

The distillery at that time was an awful mess. The most startling thing was that there was no discipline. For example, the former director had to go to the workers' homes to beg them to come to work. If they refused, he had no choice but to hire farmers who had come to buy distillers' grains as pig food.

Yet I couldn't retreat. I had to push on. I started by issuing a seventeen-article regulation and told all the employees to abide by it. I said to the workers: "An army without discipline would be wiped out in a life-and-death battle. A factory without discipline cannot survive intense commercial competition."

Soon after that, a worker was fired for theft. Another one was placed on a year's probation for disobeying his workshop head and staying away from work without authorization. The wife of the former Party secretary was also punished for reading novels while on her shift. And I had no special privileges. If I was late for work, I was fined as well.

I had to have competent managerial personnel to streamline the management. I let go two deputy-directors of the distillery, because they were not qualified for their positions. One was in charge of production, but knew nothing about business administration. The other, who was responsible for financial affairs, was not reliable. I also dismissed a workshop head I had promoted, because he smoked while working in the shop and then refused to pay a fine for this offense. These dismissals represented a different approach. In the past, factory leaders never were relieved of duties even if they were incompetent.

And I eliminated the deputy posts in an effort to reduce red tape.

Seventy percent of the 460 employees of our distillery are contract workers. Most of them were farmers. In most state-run factories, farmer-workers never can become factory leaders, and their assignments and pay usually will never be as good as regular workers. That's not right. I judge a person solely on ability and work performance. I don't care what he used to be.

I promoted a former farmer to be the head of the yeast workshop because he was able to extract much more alcohol out of raw materials than others do. Now, I've put him in charge of the operation of the entire distilling shop, and he is doing very well.

Now, the workers are paid according to their performance. Better pay for better work, less pay for less work, no matter whether you are a contract, or regular worker. We also reward those who make outstanding contributions to the enterprise. A salesman can be awarded a refrigerator if he has done a good job.

It hasn't been a bed of roses for me, of course. I've not only had difficulties but a death threat as well. A worker who was placed on probation for one year swore that he would get revenge. He threatened to kill me if he were fired. I was warned to beware of him. Naturally, I was concerned. I would get up in the middle of the night to see if my door was safely bolted. I'm young and I don't want to die. But I'm determined to carry on the reform. Several hundred workers depend on what we are doing to make a living.

Strangely enough, when the one-year probation expired for the worker I mentioned, he came to me, not with a weapon but with a self-criticism note. He promised to behave himself. He resumed working and has done well ever since. One of his sons is also employed here now.

Because of my policy in dismissing people—both workers and officials, I was nicknamed "*jupiaode*," meaning "dismissal enthusiast." Some people really dislike me, because my reform goes against their vested interests. They spread the rumor that I embezzled public funds. The rumor was so widespread that the county government sent a team to investigate. I was not frightened, because I knew I had done nothing wrong.

What do I expect to get from the contract? Nothing. All I have done is to search for a way to run this enterprise well. Chinese enterprises badly need reform.

I graduated from a secondary technical school specializing in wine making. Since I went to work in 1980, I've extensively read up on business administration. I was eager to test my theories at an enterprise that was operating at a loss. This distillery has provided me with that opportunity. I'm pleased when my reform plans prove successful. When I was deputy-director of the Hefei Winery, my plans had to go through several departments before they were adopted. But now things are different here.

Because I volunteered to work in this county distillery, my girl friend said goodbye to me. I didn't blame her. Who would want to leave a big city for a small town? And who would entrust her life to so many uncertainties? She was free to make her own decision, as I was, too.

To tell the truth, it is quite tiring to be a manager. Not only physically, but also mentally. When I wake up, I think of what I'm going to do that day. As soon as I step into my office, I have to make quick decisions to solve all kinds of problems that await me. Before I go to bed, I also recall what I have done that day, and reevaluate the decisions I've made.

I'm only twenty-five, but the toll has made me look ten years older. Yet I like the pressure and the challenge. When I leave my office for my dormitory, I always look forward to coming back to work next day.

My efforts have been rewarded. At the end of 1987, the distillery had made up its deficit of 600,000 yuan, and all the quotas stipulated in the contract were overfulfilled. Workers' wages rose by 20 percent.

How much did I get? I won't work for money. People who contract to run an enterprise usually get more than 1,000 *yuan* in bonuses every year if they fulfill their contract quotas. But I only accepted 500 *yuan*. I don't want to take more than that. I decided to accept less in consideration that I might fail in the future. I don't care that much about money. If the money I make can feed me, then that's enough.

Of course, I have disappointments. I really felt frustrated last year when my plan to build a new workshop couldn't be carried out because some farmers in the nearby villages held up the construction. The delay cost us a great deal. I turned to the county administration for assistance. I went to it several times, but nothing resulted. I can settle a dispute within the distillery in minutes, yet I felt powerless with the farmers.

The county officials promised to help, but moved slowly. They only offer you promises. They claim they support the reform, but actually they don't want to offend anybody.

What I'm looking forward to is to make my factory into a leading winery in Anhui Province. *Baohetequ*, one of our major products, has become a famous liquor in the province. It sells so well that it's difficult to get in any stores in Anhui . I am going to double the output of this liquor.

One of the biggest headaches I have now is that we are short of qualified personnel. We don't even have a brewery engineer. No good personnel, no good enterprise. To try to solve this problem, I've sent workers to other advanced distilleries to study. I've invited college teachers to give lectures to our workers. Last year, I hired forty-three high school graduates by advertising. They are knowledgeable and energetic. Yet the county labor department came to me saying that I had caused them trouble. If I continued to recruit workers independently, they said, they would be out of work.

I don't care. I'm stubborn. I do what I think is right. Silence is my weapon in dealing with criticism.

To run an enterprise can be described as either simple or complicated. If you proceed only from the interest of the enterprise, it is simple. Otherwise, with personal considerations involved, it is complicated. And, once you confront problems, sometimes they are not really as complicated as they seem to be. If you are overcautious, you'll find they become more and more complicated.

Union Leader: Deng Maohua

Although I'm familiar with union work, it hasn't been easy working as a union leader in a Chinese-foreign joint venture.

Union work in a Chinese-foreign joint venture is a headache for union leaders who are accustomed to working in a state-run enterprise. For fifty-two-year-old Deng Maohua, it's no exception.

In the Beijing Jeep Corporation (BJC), workers consider the American general manager the "boss," since he is in charge of the enterprise, under the leadership of the board of directors. Deng, like other union workers, was confused at first, despite her thirty-one years' experience doing Party and union work.

But now she understands more after four years of hard work at the BJC.

Established in January 1984, BJC, which is a Sino-American joint venture, is the largest of its kind (car production) in China. This year, it was awarded the "May First" Labor Certificate, the highest honor an enterprise can receive in China.

Everyone at the enterprise calls her "Sister Deng." She looks just what the term indicates: energetic, generous, and sympathetic.

Speaking about her family of four, her husband and two sons, she can't understand why her sons, both near thirty, have not married yet.

Working in a joint venture is quite an experience. I hesitated four years ago when I was asked to work at the Beijing Jeep Corporation. Approaching fifty, I didn't want to change my life style. I hated the idea. Besides, it was a twenty minute bike ride from my home to the corporation and I don't like cycling.

To my own surprise, I'm very proud today to work in the enterprise's trade union. The work is a great challenge, since there are no guidelines and you are on your own. It's like groping your way in the dark or wading across a river. It's this challenge that has kept me going.

With eleven years of experience as a union leader in a state-run enterprise, I'm familiar with union work. But it's not the same in a joint venture. The trade union in an enterprise is an organization performing functions of three parties: the Party, the youth league, and the trade union. I wasn't fully prepared for the union's new role and didn't know what to do.

Out of habit, I went to the workers for advice. I found they, too, were at a loss over what to do. Some had lingering fears that it was politically dangerous to have anything to do with foreigners. Many old workers were greatly worried about their retirement benefits since, they felt, they no longer were in control of the enterprise. Others couldn't understand why, after so many years of self-reliance, we'd hand over the reins to foreigners. A driver who came back from the Korean War was the angriest of all. He refused to "serve the Yankees" who had once been his enemies. The young workers, on the other hand, regarded themselves as hired hands. As long as they were paid for their labor, they didn't care. I think they consciously, or unconsciously, believed they had lost control of the enterprise.

The situation allowed me no time to take a wait-and-see attitude. I spent several days studying carefully whatever was available concerning the Party's policies and state laws on joint-ventures. I thought I was fully prepared to educate others.

Still, it took a lot of persuasion to convince the workers that they still controlled the joint venture. Some workers stressed they were only responsible for what they did. They only had to obey orders from the American boss. And nothing else.

Thus, we realized that these workers had little sense of their legal rights. They didn't know they'd participate in the democratic management of the enterprise. To some extent, their despondency was justified, for an individual worker could get nowhere without the workers' representative assembly, a mass organization under the leadership of the trade union popular in state-run enterprises. So a similar organization was needed to receive workers' suggestions and complaints and to work out solutions with management. The idea was seriously considered both by the workers, and the general manager. In February 1985, the union members' representative assembly was established, with 102 representatives.

Now with an increasing sense of participation, workers have achieved a number of things. For instance, to put into production the 213 model Beijing jeeps, before October, they offered twenty-eight suggestions and made efforts to solve technical problems. The first car rolled off the production line on September 28, 1985. The general manager said he had worked in several countries, but it was only in China that workers so sincerely cooperated with management.

But for a period, American managers were somewhat distrustful of us union workers. Because of their experience in Western countries, they believed that unions were troublesome. Whenever I went to the managerial department, they were always wary. I disliked the tense atmosphere, thinking that the trouble was that they didn't know the Chinese union well. So we tried to communicate with them through various means. We held a joint conference once a month with the general manager to report on the union's work and to solicit his response to our report. Also we sent him extracts of documents on union work as well as bulletins in which we set down our views. Gradually he became familiar with our work and admitted the union was really a great help in improving the business.

To improve communication with the American staff, we invited them to join us in gala celebrations and evening parties. We never forgot to visit their wives on International Women's Day. An American project manager once told me at a dance party that it was his happiest day in China. He brought his wife and children there, too.

As is done in a state-run enterprise, we also choose ten workers as model workers each year. In 1985, one of the ten was an American project manager. He had a big red paper flower pinned on his chest pocket, a Chinese expression of honor. And he was awarded a box of cosmetics, a cloisonne vase and a certificate of merit. He was as shy and excited as a schoolboy, saying that although he was used to getting a salary raise for remarkable work, he also appreciated this kind of award. For, he said, it meant his efforts had been appreciated not only by the boss, but by his colleagues too.

Certainly, there are times when we have disagreements with the American side. For instance, the Americans insisted on increasing the salary gap between the managerial staff and ordinary workers. Some workers couldn't accept that. Besides, there has been no such practice in China yet. Although the Americans gave in in the end, they expressed regret over the matter.

Work in a joint venture is demanding. During working hours, nobody can be idle in the workshops. Everybody has to work for his salary. They can no longer use work time to conduct recreational and sports activities, a common practice in state-run enterprises. So we had to think of activities that could be carried out in leisure time, such as collective dances, *taijiquan*, football, and boat-rowing. We also have a small band that is appreciated by music fans and dance-goers. Sometimes, I go to parties, although I don't dance well.

The union work is demanding. There is always so much to do that we have to work long hours. The union has only nine workers. Each of us has to be in charge of three or four kinds of union work. But nobody complains. It's an opportunity, I think, that gives full play to talent and allows us to develop our potential. In fact, unions enjoy much more attention from managers in joint ventures than those in state-run enterprises.

Busy as I'm as a union leader, I still find time to talk with workers to find out what problems they have. I can't say I know everybody in the enterprise, but I'm familiar with most of them. When I'm too busy to visit them, they become concerned, and come to my home to see if I'm all right.

The biggest problem we have is that there is no clear law backing us union workers. We cannot go on strike like in Western countries. We get the boss to compromise through negotiation and persuation.

I joined the Party at the age of nineteen, and all my life I have been trying to do whatever the Party asks of me. However, if it had been up to me, I'd have preferred becoming a skilled worker. In that case, I believe, I'd have become an engineer, as many of my classmates have.

Part Four

In the Office

Public Relations Specialist: Tian Ye

My greatest hope is to study public relations in the United States because the "PR" field there is well developed.

At thirty-two, Miss Tian Ye is a very active public relations person at China Global Public Relations Corporation. She serves as an account executive in the international business department in her corporation and also is a member of the U.S. Burson-Marsteller Public Relations Corporation in the People's Republic of China. Her corporation, China's largest, established a working relationship with Burson-Marsteller in 1985. The international public relations business clients she serves are mostly those channeled through the Hong Kong office of Burson-Marsteller. She has decided to make public relations her life career.

A native of Beijing, Tian Ye is vivacious, sophisticated, and outgoing.

Her husband is a sports reporter at the Xinhua News Agency. They have a three-year-old son. Their 16-square-meter-room home in western Beijing is filled with household electric appliances and modern furniture.

I've been in public relations for only one year. But I like my work. Although I don't know exactly what the necessary qualities are for a PR person, I find my present work suits me very well. It allows me to work with people with various backgrounds, including foreigners, and solve many problems on my own.

I completed my high school education at No.1 High School in Fengtai District of Beijing in 1974. My grades were very good, especially in English. Because of this, I was selected to become a teacher of English for the junior high school class at my school. I taught English for five years there until 1979 when I entered the English Department of Beijing Institute of Iron and Steel Engineering.

After graduating in 1983, I was assigned to do educational research at the Higher Education Research Center attached to the institute. My research subject required me to read extensively in educational works in English. As part of my research, I translated four foreign works into Chinese. They were *Problems Solving in the U.S.A.*, *Higher Education in Canada*, *Administration in Higher Education in Britain*, and *Educational Evaluation in Japan*.

Gradually, I became convinced that I'd change my work, because I wasn't sure whether I'd be able to achieve academic results in my research. Also, I didn't like research, because it could confine me to an "ivory tower." I wanted to do some practical work. And, furthermore, my husband objected to my doing educational research work. So I applied to the school authorities for a transfer.

At first, they denied me permission. But once I had decided, I wasn't to be held back. I tried many times and at last persuaded them to approve a transfer. I contacted two work units that were willing to employ me. One was China Electronics Import and Export Corporation, and the other was China Global Public Relations Corporation. The former was very interested, because they lacked an English interpreter and because I was the type of person they were looking for. If I work for them, they promised to give me a two-room apartment, which was a great attraction. At that time, my husband and I had no house of our own. Each of us was living separately in dormitory rooms. My husband urged me to accept their offer. But I declined it, for I thought the work there would require a lot of professional knowledge that I didn't have. There was another major reason. If I became their interpreter, I'd frequently go abroad on business. My husband often goes abroad to report on international sports matches. If both of us were away at the same time, our son's education would suffer.

Finally I accepted the offer of China Global Public Relations Corporation. Before that I hadn't heard the term "public relations," and didn't know what it meant. It was only when the corporation people gave me a brief introduction that I felt I'd do the job. I had been active in social activities during my student days. In high school I was a class monitor for several years. At the university, I also was a leader of the students' association. So I had learned how to deal with different kinds of people.

So, I became a public relations worker in April, 1987.

In the past year, I've been responsible for four large-scale PR projects, and assisted my colleagues in several others. All those projects, both for foreign and domestic clients, were successful, thanks to the combined efforts of our people. Our clients were satisfied. For me, these experiences were very valuable.

The first project was to prepare a news release for the international journalists' meeting at the hall of All-China Journalists' Associaton in July 1987. The news release, for IRRI (the International Rice Research Institute) based in Manila was to report on the achievements IRRI had made in rice research and to stress IRRI's efforts to help solve the world's food shortage problem.

Another effort was to introduce Dr. M.S. Swaminathan, IRRI's director general. He was the first winner of the General Foods Prize, awarded by the U.S. government for his achievements in agricultural research.

IRRI chose China to release this news, since China is a large agricultural country, and has attracted world attention because it has been able to feed a billion people.

The institute wanted to invite reporters from all the major Chinese newspapers, news agencies and TV stations in Beijing, as well as all Beijing-based foreign reporters to the news conference. We didn't print invitation cards. So I had to make dozens of telephone calls to invite them. This was enough to drive a person crazy, because dialing a telephone number in Beijing is an arduous undertaking. It was relatively easy to notify the Chinese media, but quite difficult to reach foreign reporters during the day, because these foreign newspapers or news agencies usually have only one Beijing-based reporter. They are out covering news during the day, and return to their offices at night. That's when I'd reach them on the phone. For two days and into late evenings, I was on the telephone.

After arranging that, I had to see that the conference hall was properly decorated, a sign-in desk arranged for, and that refreshments would be served on time. It was necessary to take care of every detail. One small error would have caused heaps of trouble. So even when I was in bed, the project was still in my mind. I was forever wondering if I'd missed something.

The last thing was to obtain a qualified English interpreter for the conference. Though I was an English major, I couldn't serve as an interpreter myself, since I'm account executive. It was impossible to get one from the Ministry of Foreign Affairs. And, furthermore, my corporation has no professional interpreters. Every time it conducts a PR project for a foreign client, it has to search for a willing and capable interpreter. This can be very frustrating when no one is available. This time it was my turn to tackle the problem. A day before the news conference was held, I still hadn't found an interpreter and was, you can imagine, upset. I at last found the right person. As it turned out, the first PR project was a success.

In October 1987, I was assigned my second project for the 1987 Beijing International Contractors' Symposium, which was held for two days at the Kunlun Hotel. My preparations began ten days earlier. I needed to get the symposium brochure and related materials printed and the meeting hall arranged as well as see to it that many other small but necessary things were taken care of. And again, the problem of interpreters cropped up. To streamline matters, the symposium organizer, China Construction Engineering Corporation, decided to use simultaneous interpretation. This requires a high proficiency on the part of the interpreters. I went on another merry-go-round looking for interpreters. Fortunately, I found four people. Yet I had to persuade their superiors to give them permission to work for us.

When I thought everything had been arranged, the Japanese contractors' delegation said, just two days before the symposium, that they wanted the interpretation to be in Japanese.

It was already late afternoon. I searched immediately for four people with proficiency in Japanese. I had to give them the symposium brochure and a list of procedures so that they'd have time to look these over. After I acquired the consent of their immediate superiors, they'd already left their offices, so, I had to go to their homes to deliver the symposium contents. When I finished interviewing the last person and got back home, it was ten o'clock at night. My husband was somewhat upset about my being late.

As a PR person, one of my greatest problem is when foreign clients make quick requests, without understanding the difficulties these can represent. They pay a certain PR fee and, thus, feel they are in the position to order you about and that you are obliged to satisfy their requests. Sometimes they make a request that takes hours, and even days, to fulfill.

Our general manager tells us that our clients are always right. We always try to do our best to satisfy their requests. But our best sometimes doesn't satisfy them—there are things that are beyond our ability or control. Clients fail to understand this.

In January 1988, China Automobile Industry Import & Export Corporation recommended us to General Motors as a PR firm. That was the third project of which I was in charge. The client asked us to obtain some special passes for some of its commercial officials so that they'd enter China without being checked by customs. This request was beyond our authority. We declined to attempt it and offered explanation. We also reported the matter to higher authorities.

Our preparations for the news conference for General Motors in the Great Hall of the People was a success. Immediately after that, GM officials had another request. They wanted a traditional Chinese lion dance at their office at the Beijing-Toronto Hotel to celebrate the occasion. So I hurriedly contacted some Beijing Opera troupes and acrobatic troupes. A lion dance requires artificial lions, performers, colored silk balls and a band. Although I spent a whole afternoon on the telephone contacting people, they all turned me down because of one thing or another. At last I contacted the Beijing Railway Song and Dance Ensemble, which agreed to perform a lion dance. Our guests were greatly entertained by the performance. But I don't think any of them realized how much time I'd spent in arranging for their amusement.

When I accepted the job at China Global, I thought I'd have more time to take care of my son. Just the opposite. When I'm involved in a project, I cannot leave my office.

At first, when I put him in the kindergarten, I

had to pick him up before 5:00 p.m. That arrangement conflicted with my work, so I took him to my retired parents living in Fengtai District, southeastern Beijing. On Sundays, my husband and I visit my parents to see our son. Since I started working in public relations, I haven't spent a single Sunday at my own home. I either go to see my son at my parents' or work at the office.

I like fashionable clothes, and my job requires me to pay attention to my appearances. Economically, things are getting better and better. Though my monthly wage is about the average of an office worker in China, my bonuses and allowances exceed that, depending on my workload. I've been able to buy five home electric applicances—a color TV set, a video deck, a refrigerator, a washing machine and a radio-cassette recorder. Of course that's due to joint efforts by both my husband and myself. Our living standard is above that of many people. But I don't have much free time to enjoy video and music, which I like very much.

Some people say that a woman journalist should change her job at the age of thirty-five because being a journalist takes too much out of a person. There's some truth in this. I feel it's the same with public relations. Up to now, my general feeling about public relations is that it's hectic and tiring. Such hectic and tiring activities can last one week, ten days or a fortnight from the start to the conclusion of a project. I think that when I'm thirty-five, or at most, before forty, I'll shift to PR research or teaching PR at the university. I'm now accumulating experience and material in my job. I consider PR work meaningful and worth doing.

My corporation has decided to send me to Hong Kong for a four-month internship in the office of Burson-Marsteller this year.

My greatest hope is to study public relations in the United States, where the field is well developed. Later I plan to write a book on the qualities of a PR person. I want to do something to help develop public relations field in China.

Interpreter: Gao Zhikai

I've a job I find challenging and very rewarding.

He is a native of Suzhou, a city famous since ancient times for its beauty and its gifted scholars. Perhaps it is owing to the erudition of his ancestors he has inherited that he showed his talent at an early age. He was admitted in 1978 into Suzhou University at fifteen and majored in English language and literature. One year before his scheduled graduation, he was a winner in a national talent-search examination, and enrolled in an advanced training course for top government and United Nations interpreters and translators. The course is conducted at the Beijing Foreign Languages Institute (now the Beijing Foreign Studies University.)

He finished the two-year course in 1983. Since then, he has been a translator-interpreter in the English Division of the Ministry of Foreign Affairs. His name may not be familiar to many, but his face definitely is, since he appears frequently on television with Chinese leaders at foreign affairs activities and press conferences. For his near impeccable skills in translation and interpretation, he has received commendations from his colleagues, international reporters, and others who know English. Despite this, he remains modest. At twenty-six, he holds the official diplomatic rank of third secretary. He has a lively sense of humor, which occasionally is accompanied by a good-natured smile.

Some say that capable people write, less capable people translate what others write and say, and the least capable people write about translation techniques.

If that's true, then I belong to the category of "less capable" because I translate for others. And, recently, I entered the category of "least capable," since I'm writing a thesis on translation skills.

While I was attending a training course for interpreters and translators, the institution didn't confer advanced degrees. So I didn't acquire a master's degree upon graduation in 1983. Now that my school confers graduate degrees, I've wasted no time in applying for a master's degree. A thesis is required, and I've been working on that for some time.

I began translating for Party and government leaders in late 1983. Now I'm able to enter a state of "conditional reflex" in which I forget for whom I'm interpreting. I concentrate only on listening to and interpreting what has been said, and hardly notice the people around me, now the flashing lights of cameras.

Because of my frequent appearances with leaders on television, many of my friends, including former classmates, think I'm fortunate. I told them that there's nothing about my work, which is very demanding and rigorous, that they should envy. I only play a tiny role in a round of talks between Chinese leaders and foreign dignitaries. Immediately after the meetings are over, I revert to being a nobody. People may envy me for those brief moments of glory, but I'm not sure I'd want my son, if I ever have one, to follow in my footsteps.

In a way, I'm only kidding. Despite the insignificance of my role, I love it and hope that I play it well. I think I've gained people's trust.

Though I've been an interpreter on numerous official and unofficial occasions, it's always a challenge doing a satisfactory job.

Some people might think it's easy to do translation. It isn't. Good translation requires a high proficiency in two languages. It also requires extensive knowledge. It's an art, in which training and proficiency are essential. Academic degrees don't help much.

Did you notice the woman translator at one of the press conferences held during the 13th Party Congress? That press conference was for China's educational personnel, and the woman translator is a Ph.D. from Qinghua University, just back from the United States. Her knowledge in her own field undoubtedly is thorough and extensive, but she obviously wasn't equipped to be an interpreter. When the speaker said four or five sentences, she'd translate only one or two. Later, she fell silent, and another person had to take over.

Despite my professional training and proficiency, I also meet challenges, which can crop up at any time and, of the five phases of translation, one can slip up at any time too. One of the biggest challenges I've ever encountered was at the second press conference of the 13th Party Congress. A journalist from Singapore asked two questions in English through a wireless microphone. Such a microphone must be spoken directly into for what's said to be heard distinctly. But he didn't do that. He held it in front of his chest. At first, I thought he was speaking Cantonese, which is Greek to me. I had to ask him to repeat his questions. This time, I understood he was speaking English. But I wasn't exactly sure what his question was. Did I dare ask him to repeat them again? Many people were looking at me and waiting for me to translate. Millions of TV viewers were also watching and waiting. My palms and forehead were sweaty. I tried hard to frame the question by intelligent guessing, which is a taboo in translation.

That was one of my most difficult experiences. So if something wrong occurs while listening, other phases are prone to errors. Many Chinese leaders speak with a regional accent. When I do translation for them, I listen very carefully so as to avoid errors. Their talks are too important to be misconstrued, and I dare not ask them to repeat. Luckily, I very seldom have had problems understanding them.

I won't say that my translation is the best, but I always try to do my best. I call my work "translation" instead of "interpretation," because I have to be very exact and accurate. I'm not in the position, and don't have the latitude, to make alterations in rendering official talks and documents into English. To do so could be an embarassment for the government.

Once, the Chinese government presented a note to the U.S. government, protesting its bombing of Libya. The translated version of the note contained this sentence: "Under the pretext of counterattacking international terrorism, the United States openly dispatched bombers to attack Libya."

Immediately, an official in the U.S. State Department went to the Chinese Embassy to the United States and lodged a protest with Ambassador Han Xu. He said it was common knowledge that Libya was involved in international terrorist activities. The protests of many other countries, including that of the Soviet Union, used the word "excuse." Why did the Chinese government use the word "pretext"? Han Xu felt obligated to make an apology, saying it was an error in translation. I didn't take part in the translation of that note of protest although I've translated many other diplomatic documents.

I feel that taking notes is one of my strong points. I can jot down everything in a conversation between two speakers. I use symbols that are convenient and recognizable to me. Sometimes they are Chinese characters, and sometimes English letters. After the session, I usually transcribe my notes into a full text in case they may be useful later. For instance, in my personal shorthand, "h" may represent "health" or "hegemonism." I must write these notes out immediately so that I won't forget what was meant.

I'm happy to say that I'm preparing for my wedding. My fiancée is a librarian at the Beijing Foreign Studies University. When I was a trainee there, I often went to check out books from her. Gradually we became close. She helped me select many good English books, three of which I've translated into Chinese and which have been published.

I've been told that other translators have often used their proximity to leaders to complain about their lack of housing, financial problems, or other difficulties. Certainly, I've had my own problems. My dormitory room was far from my office, and in order to remain close to where I work, I often slept in my office. People were surprised. Now, I'm lucky enough to have a three-room apartment, which is in Dongba in northeastern Beijing. Actually I only qualify for a two-room apartment because I'm young. I was supposed to share the three-room apartment with a colleague. The place was inconvenient for him, so he moved, and now I've the apartment all to myself. I just finished moving and feel very happy.

Since I became a translator at the Ministry of Foreign Affairs, I've traveled to many countries with leaders. Many of those places are beautiful. What I regret is that I have been too busy interpreting to do much sightseeing.

I love sightseeing. When I was a student at Suzhou University, I'd ride a bicycle to Shanghai all by myself on holidays. I enjoyed thoroughly the scenery along the way. One night, I slept in the People's Square in Shanghai. A policeman questioned me, but took no further action when I showed him my student identification card.

When I was a trainee in Beijing, I visited by bike the Badaling Great Wall and other scenic spots. My experience in Badaling was unforgettable. I wheeled my bicycle up the steep road to the top and then cycled down at a terrific speed. It was more fun coming down than going up.

My dream during student days was to make a trip around the world and see the things and places that interest me. Now that I've the opportunity to travel, I don't have the time to see all that I want to.

Soon, I'm going to work at the United Nations headquarters in New York. After that assignment, I'll return home.

I'm a professional translator and must adhere to certain rules that could be called a code of ethics.

A fundamental rule is never repeat what's said privately between leaders.

Part Five
Industry

Weaver: Meng Maying

Hard as the job is, I've never complained about it. After all, it's my own choice.

People tend to judge by appearance. In the case of textile workers, people generally think of them as neat, prettily dressed, nimble, and agile. But seldom do they think about the daily life and problems of these workers.

This story is about a forty-four-year-old weaver named Meng Maying. She has been working in the No.12 Textile Mill of Shanghai, one of the largest mills in China, for twenty-two years.

Meng lives with her husband and nineteen-year-old daughter, whom she desciribes as follows: "My husband's honest and hard-working. I want my daughter to have a better job than I have. I'd rather have her wait at home and support her than have her take up a tiring job as a weaver as I did."

I've been a textile worker for twenty-two years. Hard as the job is, I've never complained about it. After all, it's my own choice, right?

As you know, we textile workers rotate three different shifts—the morning (6:00 — 14:00), afternoon (14:00 — 22:00), and night (22:00 — 6:00) shifts.

I work night shift seven days, then afternoon shift six days, and then morning shift six days. Sometimes we work extra hours. We get two days off every eight days. Before, we used to have two days off every nine days.

The question is whether we now have more leisure time. We're more tired than before because the new machines demand faster manual operations. For the eight-hour shift, we're on our feet all the time walking up and down the rows of machines. We stop only for a meal and the w.c. We cannot sit for a moment for fear that there'll be broken ends somewhere. I've never tried to count how far I've walked in the workshop all these years. But I think I've walked a much longer distance than the Red Army's 12,500-kilometer Long March.

As a result, my feet are always swollen after a work shift. We all wear flat-soled cloth shoes in the workshop.

When I was young and loved to dress up, I used to squeeze my swollen feet into high-heeled leather shoes and walk home gritting my teeth to fight the terrible pain. Now that I'm old, I'd rather wear flat cloth shoes. Though ugly, they're more comfortable and convenient, too.

All the year round, we wear short-sleeved blouses in the workshop, where a constant temperature of about 26 degrees centigrade has to be maintained to keep a low breakage rate. For the first several winters I worked here, I'd often catch a cold when I came home from work no matter how much clothing I'd put on.

we always bring three things with us to work: scissors to cut off ends, a bag to collect waste yarn, and a cattail-leaf fan to keep cool. Since 1972, other workshops have been equipped with motor vehicles which have electric fans, bags, and small machines for doffing. A worker can sit in the vehicle and do the job more easily. Still, people complain that sitting like that for hours makes their legs numb and their backs sore. But I'd rather sit in the vehicle than work all day on my sore feet. Unfortunately, our workshop has no need for such vehicles.

We textile workers often complain about pains in the hands, feet, or back. Neurasthenia, stomachache, and spurs at the heels are other common ailments. Some workers have asked to quit but their requests were denied. The reason is simple: it's very difficult to recruit new workers in Shanghai. The young Shanghainese'd rather stay at home unemployed than put up with the aches and pains that a textile worker has on the job. So the mill has to recruit contract workers, often young girls from the countryside in Zhejiang Province. They come to the mill for the labor insurance the mill can provide.

Frankly speaking, I wouldn't let my only daughter follow in my footsteps. She can do whatever she likes except become a textile worker. Even if she's unemployed, I'd be willing to support her the best I can.

Even if I'd known earlier that the job was so demanding, I'd still have made it my career. I'd no other choice, you know.

I was nineteen years old when I graduated from junior high school. I wanted to go to senior high school, but I couldn't because things were very difficult economically for my family. I come from a large family of three brothers and three sisters. Mother was a housewife, so my father, an accountant, had to support the whole family alone. We were always short of money and father worried all the time about money matters. To reduce the burden on my father, I gave up the idea of going to high school and began to look for a job instead.

I chose the job of textile worker because it offered, relatively speaking, high pay. Besides, like many other girls then, I loved the outward appearance of a textile worker: clean and pretty in a white cap and a flowered cotton shirt. It wasn't long before I passed the entrance examination to the technical school set up by the mill to train new workers.

For the next three years, we went to the mill every other week to practice what we'd learned in the classroom. Those were the happiest days of my life. Everything seemed so full of promise and every classmate so carefree.

Later, I got pregnant. I felt terribly run down. Still I had to work a full eight-hour shift until the child was born. Today's young workers are luckier. Those who are seven-month pregnant can have a one-hour break each shift.

I got married at the age of twenty-six, considered rather late for marriage at that time. The funny thing is it had never occurred to me to make any decisions by myself about marriage. I simply left everything to my parents, believing them to be so knowledgeable and wise about such things. I also felt they'd know for certain if a man was reliable. I just didn't take the trouble myself to do a little thinking. I believed that if and when my parents decided "it was okay," the matter would be settled. I'd turned down several suitors before Lao Li, my husband, appeared. So when my parents came to the conclusion that he was honest and hard-working, Lao Li and I soon got married.

My parents were right: he really is an honest man.

Unlike most couples of our age, we've only one child. We didn't want to have more because my husband and I know from our own childhood experiences (my husband had six siblings) the handicaps of growing up in a large household where parental love and attention are divided up and money is always a problem. So we see to it that our only child gets all the love and care from us and enjoys the happy and carefree life that was denied us when we were their age.

Now nineteen years old, my daughter is studying in a vocational school. She wears nice, fashionable clothes and is pretty.

However, my daughter always tries to avoid her father. She seldom speaks to him no matter how hard he tries to communicate with her. She regards him as an intruder in a family of two: she and I. I think it's a result of his long separation from us. My husband worked in Guangzhou until 1986.

People say I'm fated to be a toiler, even at home. Perhaps they're right. I do all the household chores, you know, because I think no one can do them better than I. My husband and daughter sometimes try to share some of the chore, but I cannot keep from finding fault with the job they do. For instance, my husband washes clothes with a hard scrub brush, the sight of which I simply can't bear. So I'm busy all the time except for a few hours' of sleep every night.

It's been a dream of mine for years to travel to some scenic spots such as Hangzhou and Beijing. But money's the problem. I don't mean that we don't have any money. We're saving for our daughter, you know. We want to give her a decent dowry when she gets married.

Having gotten used to speaking loudly, sometimes even shouting to each other, above the noise made by the machines in the mill, it's hard to change that habit at home. So my neighbors are often puzzled by the noise we make. They think we're having a family squabble. With two of my sisters and one sister-in-law all working in the mill, it's a noisy scene whenever we've a family get-together.

The biggest problem I have, though, is housing. Only 7.98 square meters, the one-room place we live in is used as sitting room, bedroom, and kitchen. Every night, my husband has to wait outside the door while my daughter takes a bath. There's a single folding bed under the double bed. We've to pull it out every night and prop it up for my daughter to sleep in. Between the two beds we hung a long piece of cotton as a curtain. It's very inconvenient.

I've seldom invited colleagues home. There's simply no place for them to sit except on the bed. And if there're four or more people there, the room would be jammed.

Contract Laborer Abroad: Du Jiating

I went abroad to work to make money and to see the world. As it turned out, I did make a small fortune but didn't see much of the world.

Working abroad has helped his family financially. But he also paid a price—in suffering homesickness. Now that his family is financially quite "wealthy" by Chinese standards, he regrets his lack of skills and knowledge. Also, he knows that if he had done better in middle school, he could have been a manager and would not have had to go abroad to earn money.

Du Jiating, thirty, is an electrician at No.4 Jinan Construction Corporation. In October, 1983, he and 1,000 other construction workers from Jinan were selected to work in Kuwait, where they built fifty-four residence buildings in a two-year period.

He admires the work efficiency in this foreign country. But when he came back home, he found that his work unit had adopted the similar efficient system, which has made it possible for him to earn twice as much as he could have five years earlier.

Du is not sure whether he will work abroad again. If he does, he says money will be secondary to experience.

Du looks like an athlete. His wife is a worker in a stockings mill. Their home is well supplied with electrical appliances, but what is conspicuously absent in their modern-looking home is a touch of refinement.

I went abroad to work to make money and to see the world. As it turned out, I did bring back a small fortune but didn't see much of the world.

We were the first batch of contract laborers in our city to work abroad. Some in our group had worked abroad before, but they had only been part of foreign assistance programs in African countries.

It's different now working abroad. If you are healthy and are able to work independently, you are OK. Your family background and behavior are not examined and re-examined as was the case before. I find that nowadays our people are more conscious of economic factors. The government calls on us working abroad to promote friendship and win a good name for the country, but privately we tell ourselves that we are to earn foreign exchange for our country.

The state takes the biggest chunk, individuals get slices, and our company receives the remaining sum. Frankly, I don't think our work unit gained anything by sending us abroad, since building construction is now a profitable business in China. As a matter of fact, our company makes more money operating entirely at home than it does building projects abroad. So, our work unit won't continue to send the most skilled workers abroad in the future.

When they told me that I was chosen to work abroad, I thought probably I'd eventually bring back a color TV set and an ice box. As it turned out, I bought three color TV sets, three refrigerators, two motorcycles, a videocassette recorder, an electronic organ, watches, bicycles and jewelry. They're worth more than I can earn working a lifetime at home. I gave the extra TV sets and ice boxes to my four brothers and sisters and sold the two motorcycles. I'd wanted to keep one for myself, but I'd no garage to put it in. It was a bad bargain, for I'm told that imported motorcycles are selling at a much higher prices now.

You can make a fortune if you work hard abroad for some years. But you have to be prepared emotionally for homesickness. I was away for two years, which was too long. One year would have been all right.

The place I went to work is called *Ahertiya* in Kuwait. We were contracted to build two-story houses. There were a hundred of us in a team. The head of the team was an engineer from our province. Under him were section chiefs from our company. The supervisor, who looked like an Arab, didn't mix with us workers. We did our work, and he checked it. If there was anything that he thought wasn't up to standards, he'd tell the head of our unit. Then the head would call a meeting to inform those responsible to correct things. The supervisor was very strict about the quality of the project and examined everything we did. We didn't personally have any arguments with him. The only contact I had with him was to exchange greetings in his language.

I was a grade-four electrician at that time. My job was to install telephone sets, air conditioners, exhaust fans, and door bells. We were paid on a piece-work basis—the more we did, the more we got pay. We all worked very hard, especially at the beginning, because we all wanted to make money to buy big fancy articles to take home.

Our money was kept collectively. If you went to town on weekends, you'd draw your money from our own money keeper. As a matter of fact, we'd nothing special to buy, and our leaders encouraged us not to spend money foolishly. They told us to use the money to buy big things.

When we first arrived, we couldn't tell the east from the west. Nobody went to town the first half year. At the beginning we didn't have weekends off, because we all wanted to finish work early and go home. Later, when we were more accustomed, we had a day off every two weeks.

The place where we lived was quite near the work site. Our quarters looked like barracks, but it was comfortably arranged inside. Seven of us shared a room. We had in our room a carpet, an air conditioner and a refrigerator. Later, our leaders bought tape-recorders for each room. In the evenings we'd kill time by watching TV and video shows. We also had bathrooms, so it was possible to shower every day. At the beginning, we were self-disciplined and kept the room clean. Later, when we were tired, we'd be too lazy even to take off our shoes. We shuffled along on the carpet with muddy shoes and flung ourselves on the beds without taking off our dirty clothes.

Food was abundant. Our meals included beef, chicken, eggs, fish, shrimp and all sorts of vegetables and fruits. It was similar to what we've here. At first, we ate bread and pancakes bought at the market. But we couldn't stomach such exotic food, so we bought rice and flour to prepare our own food. We'd eat meat dumplings whenever we liked. We'd our own cooks. As a consequence, I gained a lot of weight. Some were too homesick to eat anything. Fortunately, I wasn't bothered that way.

One person was so homesick, he stopped working and pleaded with the leaders to be allowed to go home. That was impossible. The leaders tried to comfort him. Those who were married missed their wives and children. The single men missed their girl friends and parents. I didn't have a girl friend, and my mother had died many years ago. I had only my father to be concerned about.

Homesick or not, you'd go home only after you'd finished your contract. It was useless to entertain illusions of leaving before them.

You forgot to be homesick while busy working. When you were idle, you were bored. In free time, we played poker, chess and listened to music. On weekends we watched closed-circuit TV. The videotapes were mostly provided by the Chinese embassy and included Hong Kong *kongfu* thrillers and movies produced in China. The videotape on the New Year's Eve (lunar calendar) entertainment celebration in China arrived in a month's time.

The loneliest moment came during Spring Festival (Chinese lunar New Year). Although no one else celebrated this Chinese festival, but we couldn't stop thinking about home. People from the Chinese embassy would come to visit us. Once a delegation from our home province came specially to see us. We all felt they were so dear to us and bombarded them with questions about our hometowns.

The embassy often sent us the *People's Daily*. I'd never particularly cared about this newspaper at home, but in Kuwait I always tried to be the first to read it. I wanted to know what was happening at home.

Receiving letters from home was our happiest moments. Those who got letters were overjoyed and the object of envy. People who didn't hear from home became worried. Sometimes we shared letters so that those who didn't receive anything would be cheered up.

When I wrote home, I tried to be very positive. I never said I was tired, although I actually was. I wanted to tell my family that all was well so that they wouldn't be worried.

We were all very careful on the work site, because nobody wanted to get injured and worry their families. None of us had any serious injuries. The worst was when someone stepped on nails. We'd a doctor with us who gave us whatever medical attentions we needed. If someone was very ill, he'd be sent to a local hospital for treatment.

Kuwait is hotter than my hometown. A woolen sweater is sufficient for winter. But strangely, I never sweated a lot there, although it was hot. When the wind blew in from the sea, you felt unpleasantly damp.

The work site was a vast open ground. You saw very few local people. If we went shopping, it was necessary to take a taxi or a bus. Women, in that country, wear veils. I never dared to get familiar with them. Men there can have several wives, some of whom may be Westerners. Each family seems to have a large number of children. Isn't it strange that they don't practise birth control, yet don't have population problems?

Kuwait, in some ways, is too wealthy. It imports almost everything, even soil. None of its citizens do manual labor to make a living. The construction workers were from other Asian countries. Even the shop attendants at supermarkets were foreigners.

It seems that the country has no thieves. At noon, when shopkeepers go home for lunch, they merely covered their stalls with cloth, and left them unattended. They weren't afraid of being robbed. Their police use helicopters so they can see what's happening below.

I felt the biggest difference we have from them is that their tools are better than ours. They also have superior management, work efficiency, and quality. However, in the past two years I find that China is doing many things the way we learned to do them in Kuwait. We have adopted the contract system. We are paid on the basis of personal productivity. You get more if you work harder.

My monthly salary is seventy-two yuan. Actually I get 300 yuan, because I receive bonuses and income from other work. My wife doesn't receive a large bonus, so I don't expect a great contribution from her.

I got to know her through a relative. This was after I came back from Kuwait. My father thought it was time for me to get married. We were married in 1986. I found married life boring. You go home after work and cook meals. You hardly have time to chat with your buddies.

My wife is six months pregnant. It doesn't matter much to me whether it's a girl or a boy. A girl would be better. Be that as it may, I don't want the child to become a laborer. I have bought an electronic organ for our child. It isn't being used now because neither my wife nor I'm interested in music. I've deposited several thousand yuan in the bank. I want my child to have a college education. I didn't do well at school, but it's too late to do anything about that. If I'd had a better education, I wouldn't have gone abroad to work and make money. With a better education, I perhaps could have been a manager, and I'd have worked very enthusiastically in that position.

I might work abroad again. For one year. I wouldn't want it to be longer than that. Last year there was an opportunity. But the project was cancelled. However, it doesn't matter if I don't have another chance. I've got everything that I want right now. I've good things to watch, to listen to, and to play with. Money isn't so important now. What I want to do is to see the world. My family isn't happy when I leave. Last time my father was particularly unhappy. He was afraid that the plane I took might have an accident. When I came back from Kuwait last time, I didn't tell him the exact date of my arrival, so he wouldn't worry. It was a happy surprise for him when I arrived home and greeted him.

We stopped in Thailand on our way home from Kuwait. Our leaders told us not to wander around the street because they feared that some of us might go into brothels. As a matter of fact, even if I'd passed one, I wouldn't have risked going in. Home was almost in sight. Only fools would ask for that kind of trouble.

Part Six

Social Affairs

Blind Worker: Lai Xiaomao

Despite my blindness, I enjoy life. I have a good family. I love my wife, and she loves me and we have two bright, handsome children.

Pre-Liberation poverty and poor medical care have left China with a large number of disabled people. In Shanghai alone, half a million among the city's twelve million residents are blind, deafmutes or otherwise disabled.

Lai Xiaomao, forty-nine, is one of the unfortunate half a million.

He was orphaned when he was only a few months old. At the age of four, he came down with measles, and lost his eyesight because his widowed grandmother could not afford to give him proper medical care. He led a vagrant life until his sister found him a job in 1959 in a factory for the blind in Shanghai.

Since then, life has improved. After his reunion with his sister, a series of happy events occurred. He was cited as an "advanced worker." He married one of the prettiest girls in his factory, and they have two healthy children. He has had consistent pay raises, and has been allotted a new apartment.

Unlike many other people who complain about life, Lai Xiaomao is happy. Of course, his principal dissatisfaction is that he is blind.

I've a new two-room apartment with balcony, kitchen, and toilet. Although it isn't very spacious for the four of us, I'm quite satisfied. Many families in Shanghai have much more cramped quarters than we do. We were among the first batch of workers in our factory to get a new apartment. The housing problem in this city is serious. In some cases, three generations of a family of six share just one room. To save space, their beds have to be double-decked.

My wife also is blind. But she was one of the prettiest girls in our factory when she married me. And what is important, she is very considerate. In our twenty-three years of married life, we've never quarrelled. We have a son who is twenty-one and a daughter who is nineteen. They are intelligent and, fortunately, have normal eyesight. My son works as a bank clerk, and my daughter is a receptionist in a five-star hotel. With all four of us working, we have a comfortable life.

But my childhood was a nightmare. I was born in a poor farmer's family in Shandong Province.

My father and mother died when I was only a few months old. My sister and I were taken care of by our widowed grandmother. When I was four, I suffered an acute attack of measles and ran a high fever. Grandma was too poor to send me to a doctor. I survived but became blind. Since then I've been living in total darkness.

It seems to be true that misfortunes never come alone. When I was thirteen, my grandmother died. I think she must have died of exhaustion because it was extremely difficult for an old widow to bring up two grandchildren in the country.

In order to survive, my sister, who was five years

older than I was, married a rich crippled farmer twice her age. Naturally, my sister couldn't let me live with them, so I was left to my own resources.

An uncle of mine, who also was blind, came to my rescue. He was a little over thirty and sang local opera. He earned his living by singing opera in the streets. He took me along and taught me to play a three-stringed fiddle to accompany his singing.

He and I roamed from place to place, most of the time in neighboring Henan Province. My uncle's opera pieces were old-fashioned, telling stories of ancient heroes. But his voice wasn't great. So we played for a while and begged from the audience afterwards.

I did this for seven years until I got word from my sister that she was alive and in Shanghai and wished me to join her.

That was in 1959 when I was twenty years old. My sister had divorced her first husband and married a worker in Shanghai. She got me work in a factory for the blind.

There are more than 800 workers in our factory, about half of whom are blind. Those who aren't blind do maintenance work, operate the vital machines, and help the blind learn skills.

Our workshop produces copper pins for electrical plugs. There are railings between rows of machines, and all the cogwheels, belts and other moving parts are covered so that we blind workers can operate safely.

I was extremely happy to get a decent job and lead an independent life. So I worked very hard. I also learned Braille in the spare-time school run by my factory. I was elected a model worker in 1963.

One day shortly after that, the factory director

called me to his office. Sitting in his wheelchair (he is crippled), he said to me: "Lai Xiaomao, I don't want to talk to you about production, but about your personal affairs. I'd like to introduce Liu Qiaoyun to you. She is the prettiest girl in our factory."

I said: "Are you kidding, director? I know about Liu Qiaoyun. There are many handsome young men with normal eyesight who are attracted to her. I'm a blind man. I'm no match."

But the director insisted that I was intelligent and had a good heart. He was sure Liu Qiaoyun would like me. So Liu Qiaoyun and I became friends. Three years later we got married. Later my wife told me that she had originally intended to find herself a husband who had normal eyesight so that he'd take better care of her. But she was confident that I'd make a good husband.

Our society treats blind people well. My workmates in the factory are very helpful. Even the shop assistants at the food market are very helpful when I go shopping for meat and vegetables each morning. They always pick the best vegetables and meat for me. Some shoppers insist that I shouldn't have to stand in line.

So in response, I've always tried my best to pass on my production experience to others and never turned down anyone who came to me for help.

My wife and I earn 300 yuan each month. We also have a year-end bonus amounting to several hundred yuan. With this money, the four of us have a little surplus to put in the bank after buying food and clothing. We don't let our son and daughter contribute because we want them to save money for their future weddings.

I often say that my children have come to this world at the right time. My son acquired his bank job after graduating from senior high school. People say my daughter looks very much like her mother. She graduated from a vocational school where she learned English and French. Although they are at the beginning of their career, they earn almost as much as my wife and I do.

If people ask me whether I have any complaints in life, I'd say I've only one complaint, aside from my sightlessness. This city is too crowded. Some goods are always in short supply. That makes it necessary for the government to issue ration coupons for pork, cooking oil, soap, and eggs. Those coupons, which are all the same size and thickness, give us blind people many problems.

Prison Warder: Zhang Dakuan

I hope the prison will remember my name.

Zhang Dakuan, fifty-one, was born in Beijing, and lives with his wife in an apartment. As one of the cadres (equivalent to warders) in Beijing Prison, he assists the warden in the most difficult job in the prison: prisoner discipline. The 2,000 prisoners are divided into twelve teams. The chief of each team is in charge of production in the prison factory; the political instructor in each team has the job of reforming the prisoners, i.e., getting them to mend their ways and to abide by the law. Zhang Dakuan is the political instructor of the fifth team. He has worked in the Beijing Prison for sixteen years.

Although he is in his fifties and grey hairs have appeared, he still is full of vigor, with his sparkling sharp eyes. He has broad shoulders and holds himself erect. But, as the interview shows, his attitude both towards life and to the prisoners under his charge is full of contradictions.

Don't assume that I'm always as mild and amiable as I'm now. I'm different with prisoners. No sternness, no respect, I like to say. But cadres shouldn't always show an "iron face" to prisoners. Even tough cadres are those reforming and prisoners those being reformed, the former should let the latter feel that they're being taken care of and helped.

I often think it was a mistake for me to enter this field because originally I wasn't suited to the job. Before I started working as a warder, I worked in a factory. In 1962, the police force started recruiting workers for what they called "special tasks." The factory recommended me to apply for the examinations. My parents said it would be too dangerous for me. But my factory chief advised them I should do it because Party members should serve the country without hesitation. (I had joined the Communist Party in 1958.) As for me, I wanted a job that appealed to my imagination. I was one of the three selected out of 6,000 workers.

But, unfortunately, I wasn't sent to be trained or assigned to do the job I had been wanted. Instead, I was appointed to work in a reform-through-labor factory (for juvenile delinquents) near Beijing.

All the public security bodies, procuratorial offices and people's courts were disbanded during the Cultural Revolution. I and other cadres in the factory were sent for "reeducation" on a farm in the mountain area. I worked there for four years before I came to Beijing Prison in 1972. Since then, I've had my present job, which I don't like but have to do it well.

Prisoners are disgusting, especially habitual offenders. However, as cadres, we have to respect them and treat them as if we were their parents, doctors, or teachers. Doing it well isn't an easy thing. As a political instructor of the team, I've to take my responsibilities seriously.

To be strict with prisoners, cadres should first of all have strict team discipline. I've nine colleagues in my team, who supervise 140 prisoners. Cadres work as a collective: they cannot influence or reform prisoners if they themselves aren't united. I always say to other team members: "You can have a heated argument about work in the office, but not in front of the prisoners."

A cadre should be sure of what's wrong and what's right, what should be criticised and what should be praised. He'd be clear-headed. Generally speaking, I always try my best to help prisoners solve their problems, provided I can do within prison regulations. Keeping promises is the basis of trust.

Cadres should be observant. This is to prevent "accidents" happening that we'd have known about beforehand. Prisoners are like dry wood that can burst into fire with only a tiny spark. If a bloody accident happens, the instructor'll be given a disciplinary warning. One day, two prisoners in my team quarreled because one of them had broken the regulation about smoking in corridor. One threatened to have a "talk" with the other that evening. On hearing about their talk, I knew it was a dangerous situation, so I talked to them both. A fight was thus avoided.

But some prisoners are difficult to deal with. Most of this type are "repeat offenders" who are familiar with the prison system and have experience resisting the "reform" methods. On the "reform-through-labor" farm, they give the cadres lots of headaches. In prison, however, we've ways to deal with them. Last year, for example, eight young prisoners were sent to jail. Before they came here, we found out they were a gang of criminals. We divided them into different teams, thus preventing them from further contacts.

Of course, helping prisoners calls for patience and care. When a prisoner talks back to a cadre, the cadre should keep calm—maybe the prisoner acted as he did because he was fretting over something at the time. Dealing with such things at the height of someone's anger may only make things worse. As far as

I'm concerned, we've to be assertive without being cruel. If we criticise a prisoner wrongly once, the others will think we don't treat them with due respect.

My wife often says to me that I've gradually caught the "professional disease." She complains that I've got used to raising my voice and glowering at people as if to say: "You should listen to me." I don't think it's as serious as she says, but I have taken it as a warning.

Since I've been there in the Beijing Prison, there have been no disturbances nor escapes from my team, and no one has committed suicide. Last year, twenty-eight prisoners had their terms reduced, ranging from half a year to three years. Mitigation of sentences is based on reports submitted to the Beijing Reform Bureau by team chiefs. Because of this, prisoners are afraid of me and respect me.

The prisoners have had more freedom since 1980. In the past, they'd only do political study and labor. Now they can watch TV programs at least three nights a week and see movies in the yard in summer. On holidays, we sometimes allow prisoners, especially young married prisoners, to live at home for one or two days. The prison also provides prisoners with opportunities to study and work either in the plastics factory or in the classrooms. Skilled prisoners can become teachers.

The hardest working cadres are those who work in the teams, as opposed to those in offices. As for me, I get up at 5:30, do the roll call of prisoners, and then take the latter to work. During the daytime, I do an inspection tour in the corridors, talk to prisoners in their spare time, or have meetings with my colleagues. I go home at 10:00 p.m. I've spent so many Spring Festivals (Chinese lunar New Year) working that I've forgotten how many. I've become accustomed to my job. It's not boring.

My wife's retired. All three of my children have married and moved away from home. I don't have to worry about them anymore and can devote all my energies to work. However, my wife sometimes complains: "You shouldn't work in a jail. You go out early and come back late, leaving me alone at home. I've no one to talk to." Despite her complaints, she's never held me back.

Nevertheless, not everything's gone my way. Higher officials here are very strict and don't like cadres doing things on their own initiative. But I don't like working that way. I always do what I want and never acknowledge their seniority. Moreover, I like to speak frankly and shoot my mouth off which gives an impression that I look down upon them. Therefore, they think it's difficult for me to accept their leadership. In the annual appraisal of the "advanced worker" (which is a system commonly used in China to honor workers), I was always eliminated in the final rounds even though many people nominated me. I don't take it seriously. It doesn't matter me too much whether I get this honor or not. I'll be happy as long as I try my best to do my job well.

I've been an instructor for nearly fifteen years. During this time, I've never gotten a promotion. That's because I was born into a worker's family and didn't have formal secondary school education. Nowadays those promoted to leadership positions are young people. However, I haven't had my salary raised for twenty years: it's still 110 yuan a month

(US$30). You might think it would be a great disappointment for me. But compared to my exile in 1968, it's great. At that time, I worked on a farm a long way from Beijing, leaving my wife and one-year-old son at home. They were badly off. We weren't allowed to go back home then. Risking reprisals, I often used to bike more than 20 kilometers from the farm to home after work every day, and then back the next morning. Inevitably, I was publicly criticised by farm chiefs. Besides being physically exhausted much of the time, I was also under mental stress. We were then treated just as the "five sinister elements"—landlords, rich peasants, counter-revolutionaries, criminals, and rightists—as if we were prisoners. But this, I think, has been my only setback.

My philosophy is avoiding having mistakes happen, which is more important than stacking up a lot of achievements.

Sometimes I like to develop new ideas in work. For example, I once suggested a hundred-point system in the team in order to make it easier to restrain prisoners. Points were given according to prisoners' behavior at work, the quality of their products, and their daily routine tasks. This system produced good results. I submitted a report to the prison authorities asking for it to be widely implemented, but they neglected my report. Yet a prison in Zhejiang Province heard about it, implemented it, and was lauded by the Ministry of Justice. I felt, naturally, sorry that the authorities hadn't let me....

What makes me most happy? When I learn that a prisoner from my team who has left prison has made a contribution to society. Ma Bozhong, one of the former prisoners in my team, left prison in 1982. Now he's director of a boiler factory in Beijing, and has frequent business contacts with the prison factory.

My life now is leisurely and carefree. I've a small garden in jail looked after by a prisoner. In my spare time I play table-tennis and *go*. Several years ago I won third place in the table-tennis match held by Beijing Reform Bureau. I still have a few years before retiring, though I haven't yet planned what I'll do then. The only thing I wish now is to make no mistakes in my work during my remaining years at the prison. And what else? I hope the prison will remember my name.

Prisoner: Ma Zhixin

I don't care whether people have a good opinion of me or not. The most important thing's to "go straight" and make my own living.

In southwest Beijing there is a seventy-seven-year-old jail. It was rebuilt by the Japanese in World War II. It now is three tower buildings, which, from above, look like fans. There is a guard tower above the main central hall, on both sides of which are corridors where the prisoners live; each hall has many doors, but there is only one exit. It's easy to get in but difficult to get out.

The jail has nearly 2,000 prisoners, whose average prison term is ten years. Prisoners are divided into twelve teams in order to keep them under strict control. There is a plastics plant and a shoe-making plant where the prisoners work.

Ma Zhixin, thirty-one, was born in Beijing, and is one of 140 prisoners in the fifth team. He was sentenced to life imprisonment for a number of crimes, including attempted rape. For good remedied behavior, his sentence has been commuted three times, but he still has eight years left. He is dressed in a black jail uniform and wears a black cap. Thin as he is, his ruddy complexion makes him look quite healthy.

When I first came to the prison, cadres (equivalent to warders) asked me why I'd committed crimes. Even today, I'm afraid I cannot sum up the reasons easily.

I remembered that my parents divorced when I was six. After the divorce, my father took my younger brother, and I went with my mother to live with my grandmother. My mother changed my surname to Ma, after her family name, and my given name to Zhixin, meaning both that my future would be promising and that I'd be reunited with my brother.

Four years later, she married again. For a long time, I lived with grandma, who raised me. I was then fond of books, especially novels whether or not they were suitable for me, including *Love Pagoda*, the classic pornographic novel. Although grandma warned me not to read such kind of books, she was illiterate.

These books had a direct influence on me, and, I think, led me to breaking the law. I admired the lives of the bad characters in the novels and often thought to myself that it'd be wonderful if I'd live like that. I acquainted myself with bad sorts of boys outside school and started stealing articles from bicycles or machines. However, I still couldn't prove to my peers that I was able, on my own, to get money and buy cigarettes. So I began to steal wallets on buses.

I was caught red-handed committing a theft on bus at the age of fourteen. The police held me in custody for a day, then released me. My mother was very surprised and upset to hear the news. In her view, I'd acted against her will instead of bringing credit to her. The neighborhood committee didn't try to help me; instead, they criticised and denounced me at a public meeting. After that, the "*laotaitai*" (old ladies) of the committee frequently went to my home to check on me, using the pretext of examining hygiene in the flat. They kept watch on me as if I were the most troublesome boy in the street. My teachers regarded me with suspicion. Classmates mocked me.

I began to steal money again. I spent four years living like that until I was caught again in Qianmen in central Beijing. The police took me into custody for half a day before releasing me. Since my home had no telephone, the police called the neighborhood committee, who deliberately delayed delivering the message to my mother. As no one came to fetch me, the police station sent me to the head station, which checked my records. As a result, I was taken to the Daxing Farm near Beijing for "reeducation" (of juvenile delinquents through labor).

There I met the dregs of society, including lazy workers who always went out to restaurants after work. The farm wasn't closed off.

I envied their money and tried to get some for myself. I often left the farm to commit crimes in nearby villages, stealing farmers' things which I'd then sell, or attacking women. I wasn't discovered until one day I tried to rape a woman, who, however, successfully fought me off.

After questioning by the police, they found that I was responsible for several crimes. I was taken to Daxing County and tried in public. The farmers there were so enraged that they'd have beaten me to death if the police hadn't prevented them. I was sentenced to life imprisonment. I was then nineteen years old.

On receiving the court verdict, I was suddenly shocked at my own bad behavior. Having no clear idea of what overstepping the bounds of the law was, I'd never thought that this would happen. But, by then, it was too late. On arriving at prison, the first thing I did was to plead guilty (which the cadres required me to do). But like all the other prisoners, I complained that the court had sentenced me too harshly and that I intended to appeal. In prison, however, those who appeal are considered to be disobedient. So I came to accept the sentence and, at first, worked as a machine repairer in the prison's plastics factory.

My second year in prison, 1979, was at a time when the government in China was reversing unjust charges made against people during the Cultural Revolution. Prisoners lodged appeals one after another. I lodged appeals three times to the intermediate and higher people's courts, but it was always decided that my appeals were "unreasonable" which annoyed me, and I started working in a slapdash manner and was always intentionally absent-minded. I was responsible for causing three work accidents in succession due to my carelessness. The products I made were worse than any others. I was then considered the most slipshod and unsafe worker.

Even then, the cadres didn't punish me severely. They knew that I was short-tempered and impetuous. They offered me a choice of three other jobs. Their leniency touched me a lot. Believing that it might be useful in future, I chose benchwork.

For a long time after I went to prison, I didn't have any contacts with my mother, not even by letter. I was too ashamed to face her. The cadres found me sitting alone during the once monthly "visiting time." They persuaded my mother to have more faith in me. Later, my mother and father occasionally came to visit me.

After I'd done the new job for six months, I was

made group chief in the workshop. One of the cadres said that this was a good opportunity for me to reform since I was still young and since my sentence was long. At the same time, the Beijing Reform Bureau reexamined my case and agreed to commute the sentence to eighteen years.

This gave me more hope about eventually leaving the prison and I began to make preparations for my future. One day, I read in a newspaper that in Beijing there was a new self-study course at university. I registered in the name of my brother fearing that I wouldn't be accepted. The university, of course, sent all the materials to my home, but my mother passed them on to me.

Then the prison started supporting my studies. The university, too, gave me special consideration. I took the examination in prison, passed all the exams, and got a diploma. This, unfortunately, wasn't worth anything since the university wasn't approved by the Beijing Educational Commission.

But I persevered. Since 1986, the State Education Commission has allowed anyone to take part in examinations to get a higher degree through self-study. The prison set up a special class for prisoners, and teachers from colleges came to give lessons. So far, I've passed logic, Chinese history, and Communist Party history. I plan to pass all ten exams.

My behavior has been much better since I changed jobs. But some relapses have been unavoidable. For example, one day, I happened to meet a prisoner who'd been on the farm at Daxing. We exchanged a few words in the corridor. A cadre discovered us talking and he warned me not to do it again because prison regulations stipulate that prisoners in different "teams" aren't allowed to talk to each other. (This is because prisoners are divided into teams to prevent past criminal associations continuing.)

"A man should have feelings wherever he is. Why was I wrong?" I asked. The cadre and I started to argue and nearly ended up fighting. As a result, I was handcuffed and made to do "self-examination" for a whole day.

Of course, not every prisoner abides by the regulations and behave himself. Some enjoy trying to build themselves up by talking to the cadres about others behind their backs. But such prisoners are finding less and less support, especially since the cadres are aware of these tactics.

For prisoners, we've our own organization: the reform activists' committee. Members of the committee are all prisoners elected once a year by fellow prisoners and approved by the cadres. The committee's four groups, which assist cadres in arranging prisoners' daily lives, study, and work. I'm one of the group chiefs in charge of reading.

We work eight hours a day. We also have two nights for political study and three nights for cultural study every week. We're allowed recreation on Wednesday and Saturday evenings and on Sundays. On some holidays, like the Spring Festival (Chinese lunar New Year), prisoners' families are invited to join tea parties, or to come and make dumplings together.

Being a chief of two groups, I find it difficult to find time to study except on Sundays and for one hour each night after supper. Of course, it's not glorious to be imprisoned. But it has done me a good turn. I've learnt some skills here. In September 1986,

I took part in examinations set by the plastics factory. I got the fourth grade, the initial step towards becoming a "qualified prisoner." This entitles me to three yuan pocket money each month. On top of that I average seven yuan bonus from the factory. My mother sometimes gives me money to buy books.

Since 1981, when my sentence was commuted to eighteen years, my sentence has twice again been reduced—that's to say I still have eight years in prison. Cadres say that we can leave prison sooner, "depending on us." As for me, it's not too late to reform and become a good citizen. There've been great changes in the country. It's hard for me to predict what'll happen in the future. But, anyhow, knowledge and professional skills are what are most in demand and, hence, are what I'm striving for.

I was told that some prisoners find it difficult to get work after they leave, because they're discriminated against. I don't think that'll be a problem for me. Perhaps I've experienced too much. I don't care whether people have a good opinion of me or not. The most important thing is to "go straight" and make my own living. I've plans to set up a private plant when I go out, doing what I'm doing now. My mother is often downhearted about me, but she still has hopes for me. She's prepared everything for my future workshop at home. For her sake at least, I'd like to do well.

It's true. I've had nothing to be proud of in the last twenty years. The only thing worth calling to mind was primary school and when I was then admitted to Beijing Foreign Languages School, which closed down during the Cultural Revolution—just at the time when they accepted me. Maybe, if the turmoil of the 1960s hadn't happened and I'd gone to that school, I wouldn't now be in prison.

Part Seven

On the Run

Seaman: Xie Zhansan

Our ships often get cheated in dealing with foreign clients.

Xie Zhansan, fifty-two, is one of the very few old-timers still running on international ocean-liners. He has been a seaman at the China Ocean Shipping Company almost since the beginning of the company's existence, twenty-seven years ago. The state-owned company employs 38,000 seamen who work on thirty-seven international routes.

Xie, a college graduate, is an honest and hard-working man, who thinks and does things differently from the young generation of seamen. His wife is a high school teacher. They have two sons.

I'm a chief-engineer. People of my age are rarely employed on ships these days, but I'm an exception. Fortunately, my health is good, and I'm accustomed to working aboard ships. Physically demanding? No problem. See these muscles, I'm strong as a horse. Some people don't think I look my age. They say I'm in my early forties at most.

Some people may think life at sea is boring. I've no time to be bored. I wear a boiler suit twenty-four hours a day. I wear it even in bed.

Why? We work with machines, oil pipes, and are filthy all the time. Four hours a shift, twelve hours a day is standard for engineers. I'm not on any standard shift, since I'm in charge. Say there's a problem, I'm the one to respond. Young people today call on you for help even if it's only a very small problem. If you don't handle it for them, nothing will get fixed.

Our engine room is towards the bottom of the ship. You can't see where we work from the outside because there are decks above us. We've two main engines. One propels the ship and the other generates electricity. It gets very hot where we work. The temperature gets up to 40 to 50 degrees centigrade and sometimes even to 60 degrees centigrade. I remember once I had no strength to continue to climb up to my cabin after I climbed to an upper deck. I just lay there for hours before next shift began.

Today conditions have improved a great deal compared with the old days. Most of the ships have automatic devices that save a lot of manual labor. All you have to do is press the buttons. In the past, the furnace burned coal instead of oil. We shoveled the coal with spades.

I went to the Ocean Shipping Company in 1962 after six years of college. At that time the company had been in business for about a year. We'd several very antiquated ships then. Those old ships, as well as my old friends, are no longer around. All my old friends have retired.

I've served on all types of ships: passenger ships, oil tankers, cargo ships and containers. It's hard to count the number of places I've been to. Except for Canada, Australia, South Africa, and Taiwan, there are few countries or places in the world whose ports I haven't visited.

I remember the first time I went to sea. It was out in the South China Sea, and I was so sick I couldn't eat for three days. But, of course, you had to work. Finally, I overcame my seasickness—the first, and most pressing problem for seamen. I always tell the young men that the first voyage is the most important. Once you overcome your first bout of seasickness, you won't come down so badly with it again.

See, I've never been sick since the first time. It's all a matter of will power. Young guys don't believe me. One of my friends ate and drank nothing for seven days and survived. No kidding.

Almost everyone suffers from seasickness at the beginning. Once it happens, you are sick as a dog after eating. Not eating is even worse. You vomit bile and blood. The young people envy us oil-timers because we've got a good appetite no matter how high the waves are. Sometimes no one prepares food because the cooks themselves are sick. Then we open tins, and drink beer. The heavier the wind, the more we eat. Many suffer from chronic stomachache and insomnia, but fortunately I've never suffered from these things.

I'm preoccupied by work. We've been married for more than two decades, but I've never been home for more than three months a year. Others rest at home for at least that long after being at sea for less than ten months. I often stay aboard ships for one or two years straight. Then a one-month ashore and I'm off to sea again as soon as I receive a telegram. So for many years, I seldom, if ever, spent a holiday with my family.

Once I got a telegram on the second day of the Spring Festival (Chinese lunar New Year). I left immediately. Guess what they said when I got there? They said: "We knew you'd come. We contacted three people before we called you. They all refused, but we knew you'd come."

Let's put it this way. If there isn't an emergency, the leader won't ask me to come.

I can write reports in English and commerce in English with foreigners. Maybe that's the reason why they put me aboard ships with young captains who don't know their business well. I often act as an interpreter and the captains consult me on everything, including where to anchor.

It does no harm if you do more work than others. If I don't do the work, somebody else will have to. Looking back on the past, I've been quite lucky. I studied ship engineering in college and have worked in this profession all my life, even during the ten-year turmoil of the Cultural Revolution. We, and the army, were exempted from participation in the class struggle. I did manual labor for only two years and that was when I was in college. One year I harvested Chinese cabbage, and the other year I spent in an iron-and-steel mill. Heard about the nationwide Great Leap Forward in 1958? So, for only two years I did do something not connected with my profession. One of my friends became a cook although his major was ship engineering. Many people were forced to change their profession or ordered to do manual labor on reform farms during the Cultural Revolution. Compared with them, I've no complaints.

I was transferred to work at the headquarters for a time, but then I asked to return to the ship because

I couldn't fit in there. I didn't know how to interact with others. I've always been used to the quiet life at sea. Sitting in the office, lighting a cigarette, having a cup of tea, and reading a newspaper to kill time make me uneasy.

The heads of the company all know me. They've worked with me or under me. But I don't know my immediate boss. I don't have *guanxi* (connections). I never have sent them any gifts. So I have to go to old ships now. There's one advantage. All those on board are people like me, in that they have no *guanxi*, but have real skills. We get along quite well.

There's a saying, "Young men, new ship; old men, old ship." It isn't strange that many seamen want to change their jobs. People are practical nowadays. Once I saw a young man arriving at the port with his luggage. At sight of an old ship, he turned and left without a word.

We are really underpaid for our work. A foreign chief-engineer makes around $1,500 a month, generally speaking. A foreign captain makes more than our ship's entire crew put together. They don't spend a lifetime at sea either. They sign contracts with their company. Once they've earned enough money, they leave. I hear in Britain, if you are at sea for more than six months, you aren't responsible for any losses you cause at sea. Ours is a lifetime employment. Once you are assigned to a company, you cannot leave. That's why many people delay, or refuse, going to sea.

They stay at home, work at a second job, and earn big money. Many who go to sea want to work on foreign ships because they can earn higher wages. However, after about three months, they leave, either being fired by angry foreign bosses or realizing that they couldn't bear the life. Work on our ships is much easier than on foreign ones. On foreign ships, they work eight hours a day. On our ships, not more than two hours. I worked on an American ship for sixteen months, the longest in our company. Foreign bosses know how to make money. Although the American ship I worked on was an old one, the boss didn't send it to be repaired for three years. Each year he would allocate 250,000 dollars for maintenance and leave the rest to his crew, not like us who check and repair our ships every time we dock, spending 500,000 to one million *yuan* each time.

In the end, the Americans asked me to sell the ship for them and wanted to renew my contract, saying that the others could go but not me. They wanted me to train a group of Filipinos. My wife didn't want me to do that, as it was more than a year since I was home.

People say seamen are better off than others. But I'm not. We still live in a one-and-a-half-room flat. I'm the eldest of six brothers and sisters. I had to support my younger sisters and brothers when they were young. And my wife and I have parents to look after. Life in the past was really hard for us. I've bought only a watch, a camera, and a tape-recorder for my family. Not even a TV set. Our oldest son is studying at college to become a seaman. He wanted to follow in my footsteps.

I rarely spend money. I don't smoke and occasionally drink. I give all the money to my wife. I think the more money you get, the more you want. There's no limit. As long as we've enough money to live on, it's all right.

Our ships often get cheated in dealing with foreign clients. This is because some captains don't understand business and have a poor command of English and so have no idea when they are being cheated. I'm not afraid of settling disputes with clients in court because I know I'd win. Otherwise, I wouldn't go to court. I won the last time, although nobody said anything at the time. If I had lost, I'd have been criticised throughout the company. "You asked for it," they'd have said.

Retirement? We're supposed to retire at fifty-five, but I find people older than that still working and I've seen no document at the company. I'm healthy, so, I will continue working and see what happens.

Captain on the Yangtze River: *Chen Kexiong*

The river's changed my character. Even the most restless person would become more tranquil after sailing so many years on the Yangtze River.

He was eating fish that was mostly bone when we met in his tiny cabin on Jiangyu No.2. Clad in a cotton-padded jacket with several holes still unpatched, he does not look at all like the captain of a ship sailing on the Yangtze River, China's longest river. But his big, bright eyes sparkle with self-confidence and convince you that he can, indeed, name all of the major spots on the course of the 6,300-kilometer-long river.

Forty-seven-year-old Chen Kexiong has sailed on the Yangtze, the third longest river in the world, since he was seventeen. This 3,500-ton ship, capable of carrying over 1,000 passengers, is one of the largest liners of the Chongqing Shipping Company. The company is one of a dozen state-run shipping enterprises transporting passengers and cargo along the Yangtze in and out of Sichuan Province.

His ship sails between Chongqing, in the interior, and Shanghai, at the mouth of the river, a distance of 2,399 kilometers. A round trip takes twelve days, five days downstream, and seven days up. More than 400 ships of various tonnage sail on the river.

I grew up in a small village by the Jialing River, a tributary of the Yangtze. When I was a child, I loved to play by the river. I'd sit there, gazing at the vast expanse of water that flows eastward. As my eyes would follow the seagulls gliding over the water and the boats navigating up and down the river, I often wondered where the water came from and where it flowed to, why seagulls always flew behind the boats, and why the ship sometimes sounded one whistle and sometimes two, and what these whistles meant.

These questions made a sailing career seem fascinating to me, then the son of a farmer, and they had been answered over the years. Seagulls trail a ship because they're hungry and are looking for food. The ship blows one whistle to signal that it's going to pass another ship on its starboard, and two whistles to show that it's going to pass its port.

The Yangtze River has three sections. Each has its own characteristics. In the lower reaches, the river bed is full of dirt and sand, and the river is wide. In the middle reaches, the river also is wide, but there're quite a number of shoals, and the water level is only several meters in some places. It's so shallow that sometimes the bottom of the ship almost touches the river bed. In the upper reaches, the river course is narrow and tortuous, and full of rocks and abrupt turns.

The most dangerous part is the upper reaches, especially the section known as Chuanjiang. The section begins at Yibin, a city down from Chongqing in Sichuan Province, and ends at Yichang in Hubei. It's more than 1,100 kilometers long, and is noted for a world-famous attraction, the Three Gorges.

Each year, thousands of people come here from China and abroad, especially in the summer, to take a boat trip through the Three Gorges. For them, the gorges are a scenic wonder, while for us boatmen, however, the place is hell.

The Chuanjiang section has many high, steep mountain gorges and is full of twists and turns, some of them so abrupt that you almost have to turn the ship 90 degrees. The river's very narrow, with the narrowest point being no more than 40 meters in width. It would be impossible for another ship as large as ours to pass. The current is rapid during the flood season, three meters a second. Also, there're about 2,000 rocks and reefs in the section between Chongqing and Yichang, which could prove to be quite dangerous.

The Three Gorges used to be the worst part of this section. No one has counted how many lives have been lost in this hell. Because it was so difficult to navigate boats on this part of the river, in the past the boats had to be towed by boat-trackers, who worked like coolies. They walked on the bank and towed the boats using ropes. It was a misery for these people.

That was in the past. You don't see boat-trackers now since the government has transformed the course of the river and blasted away many of the big rocks that used to block the way. But the water level remained shallow for many years. However, after the Gezhouba Dam was built in 1981 near Yichang, the water level in the Three Gorges rose by about 20 meters. Sailing down the gorges is no longer as dangerous as it used to be.

Still sailing on the Chuanjiang and the gorges is often a battle. You must always be on the alert. A small mistake can turn into disaster. And accidents, such as hitting a reef, or colliding with another boat, do occur from time to time.

Not long ago, we collided with a private cargo

boat that was ferrying goods across the river.

The owner of that ship was in such a hurry to get the job done that he had his men move before we'd cleared. Their boat hit on us on the stern. We suffered no damage, since our ship was made of steel, but the cargo boat was severely damaged. They asked us to pay damages. Since it wasn't our fault, we refused. But they threatened not to let us pass until we had given them money. Blocking our way, they refused to budge. In the end we paid them 1,000 *yuan* just to get going. Nowadays, there're more and more such boats sailing on the Yangtze. They're small in size, pay little attention to regulations, and cause us a lot of trouble. Each year our company chalks up anywhere from 300,000 to 400,000 *yuan* in losses on account of accidents of this sort.

There's another type of incident that's very distressing. Some people try to kill themselves on the trip. Last year, a young lady at midnight jumped over the side of the ship. When I learned of this, I ordered the ship to stop immediately, and we started a search. We searched up and down the river for several hours, but couldn't find the woman. Those who attempt to commit suicide always seem to choose to do so at midnight, probably because they don't want to be seen and saved.

On board here you see many things, such as quarreling, fighting, and stealing. In this sense, life on a passenger ship is no different from that on land. There're a few policemen on our ship as a security measure, and we've a special department that mediates conflicts among passengers, all of which save me a lot of trouble.

I graduated from a navigation school. I was a

sailor, helmsman, third mate, second mate, and first mate. I worked on a cargo vessel for ten years, then was transferred to a passenger ship. I've been on four ships, one cargo, and three carrying passengers. I became a captain in 1985, after studying a year at a navigation management school in Chongqing.

My greatest ambition when I was young was to become a captain, which was the most prestigious position on the river. I had a quick temper before. But the river has changed me. I think even the most restless person can become patient after sailing so many years on the Yangtze. But we aren't like those seamen whose horizons are broader. We sail a narrow course and we must be very prudent and cautious.

We've a TV room on the ship. To offer more entertainment to our passengers we recently opened a ballroom. But what's most important to the passengers is safety. That's why my cabin is by the bridge. Although I've three associates—first mate, second mate, and third mate—and although we could, in principle, rotates shifts, I always am on duty when we're sailing through the Three Gorges, passing the Gezhouba Dam, going under bridges, or approaching a port. There're four bridges across the river, and a dozen ports. We seldom assign the third mate to be on duty when we're sailing at night, or in the upper reaches, because he's young and less experienced. There're at least three people on duty on the ship's bridge each shift: a helmsman, a signal man, and an officer in charge. Each shift lasts four hours and each of them works two shifts a day.

My sailing experience has enabled me to see a lot of things that I'd never seen before, hear a lot of things that I'd never heard about, know a lot of interesting people, and learn a lot of worthwhile things. For instance, I'm now able to forecast changes in climate in advance just like a weather man, since our sailing is greatly influenced by weather. Sometimes we've to anchor for days because of unfavorable weather.

But there're problems, too, with this kind of life, for example, a sailor doesn't get much good food or leisure time. Moreover, he's to be so devoted to his work that he's little time to spend with his family. A married sailor spends more time with his colleagues than with his wife and children. And his folks have to pay if they want to take a boat trip. His family gets no special privileges. That's why so many young sailors have difficulty in finding a marriage partner. There're also more divorces among the sailors than there used to be.

I'm lucky. I've been married for more than twenty years, when being a sailor was a much more admired occupation. My wife is a saleswoman and we get along very well. Only I often feel guilty that I haven't taken good care of her and our children. I couldn't be with her even when she was ill. Every year I've been at home for only a total of three months. I've decided that after I retire, I'll stay at home and be with my wife. I owe her so much.

One complaint I have is that our government is investing too little in harnessing the Yangtze. The problems of silt and pollution are terrible. I know in the United States they've spent a lot of money to tame the Mississippi River. The Yangtze is as important to China as the Mississippi is to the States, or maybe even more so. I hope the government will pay more attention to the Yangtze.

I'm a heavy smoker. Everyday I consume about two packs of cigarettes. Each month I spend nearly thirty *yuan* on smoking. My monthly salary is 190 *yuan*.

I've two children, a daughter and a son. My son works as a helmsman on my ship. When he decided to become a sailor after graduation from high school, my wife was against it. But I supported him. Although a sailor's life is hard, someone has to do the work.

Fisherman: Lin Muwang

The sea is the courtyard of the Dragon King. If you know what the weather's going to be, you won't get caught in his maze.

Lin Muwang, sixty-three, started his fishing career as a teenager. He now has worked on a sea-side farm for two years, cultivating aquatic animals and plants. The farm is part of the production brigade of Jiantin Village where Lin lives. It has a population of 1,504, and is located in the northeast suburbs of Fuzhou on eastern coastal China. Some 317 members of the brigade, the majority of the village's labor force, fish for a living. The farm is cultivated mostly by women and retired fishermen.

As the government has encouraged rural people to find ways to get rich, some fishermen have dropped out of the brigade collective to operate their own businesses. Lin's son is one of them. Talking about this, you can see disappointment on his weather-beaten face.

You see the shining brick house over there on the hillside? My son built it last year. He asked us to move in, but I was ashamed to do so. My son and I used to be on the same ship. When I was transferred to work on the farm, he dropped out of the brigade. Sometimes he was away from home for several months, but didn't tell me where he'd been. His wife also didn't tell me. His mother said he was out making money. I tried to persuade him to stay in the brigade, but he wouldn't listen.

Then one day he came back with an old twenty-ton ship. Some guys helped him paint the ship in dark green. And then they sailed away. Two months later, they returned. My son was said to have earned 20,000 yuan. Some people began to follow their example.

I began working for a shipowner when I was twelve. Now you see new shipowners. One of the leading ones is my own son. I hate to think that my son is getting rich by being a shipowner.

I was born in a houseboat. My grandparents, parents, brother, sister, and I lived in a 10-square-meter space which was the kitchen as well as the bedroom. I was named Lin Muwang (meaning luxuriant wood), in the hope we'd have wood to build a bigger boat. Never did we dream of having a house on shore. Fishermen were among the poorest people then. People called us "water ducks," because our legs were banded due to balancing on the decks.

The houseboat could only go out so far from the edge of the sea. The family sailed out in the early hours of the morning. The men cast nets and placed fishhooks, while the women did cooking and washing, and the children played. In the evening, we used to return with four or five kilograms of fish or shrimp. Father sold them to fish merchants and with this money bought food which he brought back with him the next day.

As we grew up, the boat seemed to get smaller. We couldn't afford to buy another boat, so my brother and I went to work for a shipowner. The ship which I worked on for nine years weighed 20 tons. We sailed up and down the coastline and the shipowner sold the fish we caught in those places.

My parents helped my brother set up his own family in a new houseboat and they'd almost nothing left for me. I married a young widow whose former husband had left her a houseboat. We were floating on the water and also floating towards the new society.

The year was 1955. A group of five came to our mooring place. They inspected one boat after another. Two of them were said to be government officials. They spoke Mandarin. The others who interpreted for them came from the neighboring village. They said that their villagers had formed a cooperative and that they were going to have big ships owned by all the fishermen. With their help, we formed our own cooperative in five months.

Within a year and a half we had sixty-ton ships. We went farther out to sea than we had ever gone before. The communally owned ship sailed all night. When we looked at the water the next morning, everyone was astonished. For the first time we saw the real color of the sea. It was blue.

We moved into houses on land in 1960. Men went to sea, while their wives stayed home caring for children and making nets.

The state-run aquatic company invested in building the ships and we sold our fish to the company's purchasing station. The government bought us ships to fish with, and bought us houses to live in on land. I'm grateful to the government. The government has also set up a wireless communication center to give advice to us fishermen. We reported to the center when we had come across large schools of fish, or rushed to another fishing zone when they told us of large quantities of fish in such-and-such an area. The center also transmitted weather information to us.

In the past few years, the government has lifted the fixed price on sea food. You can sell one picul (50 kilograms) for the price you used to get for three piculs.

Merchants with different accents come to our village. The prices they pay are higher than the purchasing station. But they can only buy a small part of our fish, and they spend a lot of time bargaining. We "water ducks" aren't good at that. So most of the fish we catch still goes to the purchasing station. They've huge freezing facilities to contain what they buy.

Most of us prefer to stay in the brigade rather than drop out. We don't want to take the risk.

People like my son make money easier and faster in their own way. They go out and catch whatever they can. Sometimes I see them bring back tiny mummy hairtails. They've no sense. The sea is going to take revenge. I remember in the early 1970s our brigade had a record harvest. But the next year, a ship sank in a thunderstorm in which two died. People talked about that for several years, but now they must have forgotten.

It's a good idea to send large fry back to the sea. The Municipal Aquatic Research Center uses our farm as one of its bases to do these experiments. They also help us to plant kelp and raise prawns.

We work eight hours a day, have weekends off, and are paid five yuan a day by the brigade. It's like being a worker in the city. My two daughters are married. My wife is now a nurse in the village's kindergarten. With both our salaries, we're pretty well-off. My wife handles the money at home. She's just bought a color TV set. I hope it wasn't bought with my son's money.

I don't watch TV much. I can't understand Mandarin very well. Sitting there till 8:00 in the evening, I start to doze off. I wake up early at five in the morning. After smoking a pipe, a news broadcast comes on the radio. I've an old habit of listening to the morning weather forecast at the end of the news broadcast. To catch the forecast, I've to listen to all the news, or I won't get the forecast. The sea is the courtyard of the Dragon King. If you know what the weather is going to be, you won't be caught in his maze.

At 7:00, I set off for the farm. It's fifteen-minute walk from my home, but it takes me almost an hour to get there. You always find things to look at and people to talk with. On my way to work the other day, my brigade leader told me that our brigade was planning to build a steel vessel. It'll be big enough to travel far out to sea. He said he'd let me go then.

Part Eight

Traffic

Bus Ticket Seller: Zhang Baoqing

The bus is a microcosm of society where I interact with different types of people every day.

In the sprawling Chinese capital of Beijing, commuters are served by 169 bus routes. Working on the 4,000 buses are 19,196 conductors, of which 14,076, or nearly three quarters, are women. Forty-year-old Zhang Baoqing is one of them.

The mother of a ten-year-old son, Zhang has been working for twenty years selling tickets on Bus No.43 which runs a distance of 13.25 kilometers, with sixteen stops.

For her efficient, friendly service, Zhang has been cited as a "model worker" every year for the past twenty years, with only one exception in 1978, when she was on maternity leave.

She can't figure out why many of her colleagues dislike their work. She explains why "I'll stay here until I retire."

The bus is a microcosm of society where one sees different types of people every day. A conductor has more to do than merely sell tickets. I have to talk all the time. I have to ask commuters to buy tickets, as well as look for seats for the sick, disabled, elderly, and children. I also have to tell commuters how to change buses.

There are often bad-tempered commuters on the bus. Yet you have to be patient. Some are unhappy when you ask them to show their monthly passes. Some youngsters are very rude. Sometimes they shove tickets in your face while they ask you several times, "Seeing it?" Once a girl conductor asked a youngster to show his ticket, the boy slowly took out his ticket, saying in a sarcastic tone of voice, "Look to your heart's content if you like."

The other day I asked an old farmer if he'd bought a ticket. He flew into a rage, saying, "Why did you only ask me and not anyone else?" As he was having trouble stepping off the bus, I tried to support him. But the old man brushed away my hand and said, "Don't look down upon country folks and old people." Our good intentions aren't always recognized by others.

I have to work hard to fulfill my daily ticket quota. A problem is that some people don't want to pay. So I have to make them buy tickets by constantly asking them if they have tickets or not. In most cases I can see from the expression on their faces whether they have bought tickets or not. I still remember the day when a youngster told me, "We intended to get off without paying, but your work attitude was so good that we felt embarrassed to leave without buying tickets."

It's really tough to spend hours on a crowded bus in the heat of summer. I have to get up at four o'clock in the morning to get ready to go to work.

Our bus is a model bus. So I have to do everything right. The roar of the bus really makes you sleepy. But

I have to keep myself alert. A minibox of cooling ointment is my best remedy against sleep.

In winter the lowest temperature may drop to 20 degrees below zero centigrade. Yet, you have to take off your gloves and sell tickets, and be fast at it. Every day my face and hands are covered with dust. After returning home the blood in my feet is still pulsating as if my feet were still on the bus. However, I can stand that, thanks to good health.

My work is really tiring, but I receive wide public support and understanding. My riders also appreciate my work. A doctor at Chaoyang Hospital has told me that if I fall ill, he will do his best to give me whatever medical attention he can give. One day as I was queuing for vegetables, a stranger came up to me and said, "Let me take them home for you." I felt confused about this until he told me he was a regular rider on my bus.

I regard every bus rider as my friend. Our bus covers a long distance, from Tuanjie Lake in Northeast Beijing to Liujiayao in Southern Beijing. Since the bus goes past residential areas and a hospital, I have to take special care of riders.

Once when an old woman couldn't find a seat on a crowded bus, I asked her to take mine. Some passengers looked on incredulously. After she got off the bus, someone asked me if the old woman was my mother. "She always treats old people this way," another rider interjected.

On buses in Beijing, seats often are offered to the sick, weak, elderly, and women carrying babies. But not always. Once a man with only one leg got on. I asked everyone on the bus who would be kind enough to offer a seat to this man. There was no response. I turned to several young people for help but they didn't move. So I offered my seat to him while I stood. I've got many regular commuters. Some even remember the number of our bus (54701). Some know my work number is 5088. A little girl calls me "Aunt 88" whenever she sees me. Some blind people also know me well and recognize me by my voice.

Some deaf-mutes "speak" to me in sign language. Putting one fist upon another means "work." Rubbing the left shoulder means "rest."

The disabled deserve our sympathy and shouldn't be looked down upon. I treat foreigners the same way as I treat everyone else. But it's difficult to judge the age of foreigners because some young foreigners have white hair. You can only tell by their complexion and by the wrinkles on their faces.

There's a school for the mentally retarded on my bus route. I take special care of a child who cannot speak or walk normally. One day, a boy stood at the bus stop, waiting for my bus. He held in his hand a newspaper carrying an article about me. As soon as he saw me, he pointed to the paper and then to his heart, meaning the paper expressed what he couldn't say directly to me.

Bus No.43 belongs to the Fifth Yard of the Beijing Public Bus Company which has 169 bus routes. Generally it takes us forty-three minutes to do an entire run from the starting point to the terminus. When traffic jams occur, it will be over an hour before we get to the end of the run. Each day we travel back and forth three and a half times. Our bus has forty-four seats, with a total passenger capacity of 185. But at peak hours, more than 200 are squeezed into the bus. Although each square meter of the bus floor can hold no more than nine people, there sometimes are thirteen people jammed into one square meter.

To relieve traffic jams, the authorities have taken measures such as adding more bus routes. Some new bus routes are expected to be added this year, too. An experiment is being carried out along a few routes for which monthly passes no longer can be used. Still, traffic jams remain one of the biggest headaches for Beijing commuters, who always complain about bus service.

According to regulations, a bus ticket seller has to fulfill a daily quota of eight *yuan* in ticket sales. If you surpass the quota, you can get bonuses. However, the more passengers on the bus, the less tickets you can sell. Most bus riders have monthly passes. The public bus is a non-profit-making business. A monthly bus pass that costs five *yuan* requires a 1.95 *yuan* subsidy from the state. Yet, we have to make it work. Since the salaries of bus ticket sellers are quite small, many want to change jobs. But the authorities, while prohibiting such transfer, have begun to introduce a contract system since last October. Under this system, conductors can get "distance fees." That means, the longer the bus routes, the more you earn provided no accident occurs.

I graduated from Beijing's No.55 High School. I became a bus ticket seller at eighteen. But I had never expected to become one because I was always a quiet girl and had never taken a bus before. After I took up the job, I found it hard to even think about finding other work. Now I've a ten-year-old son. Unfortunately, I cannot care for him as other mothers care for their children. He once burned his new jacket while playing with fireworks. If I'd been with him, it wouldn't have happened. It grieves me whenever I think of it.

I earn a salary of 150 *yuan*, including bonuses and subsidies. My husband earns 100. He's a worker at the Fifth Yard too. We live a fairly good life. But we are packed into a 7.2-square-meter room. In fact, the room doesn't really belong to me. I took it over from my sister, who works elsewhere. As the apartment building doesn't belong to our unit, I've been often urged to move out. But where can I move? Though our unit has built a new apartment building, I'm at the bottom of the list for an apartment there. At present, my greatest hope is to live in a better place of my own. I don't plan to leave my work unit until I retire. Our bus is a model bus. I'll continue to strive hard to contribute my bit to make it a model bus of the city level.

Air Stewardess: Wang Lianying

My job looks simple, but actually it isn't.

Thirty-two-year-old Wang Lianying has been an airline stewardess with the Civil Aviation Administration of China for thirteen years. She has flown on all major domestic and international routes and has been to more than twenty countries.

Wang speaks fluent French and knows English. She likes French literature, especially the works of Alexandre Dumas. Of all the big cities in the world, she likes Paris the best.

She was married at thirty, and has a two-year-old daughter. Her husband, a college graduate, is in charge of quality control at the Beijing Smeltery. They live in Beijing with her parents-in-law who are in their seventies.

Both Wang and her husband are amateur photographers. At home she likes to play badminton or stroll with her husband in a nearby park. She also likes visiting her daughter who lives with Wang's parents in Tianjin, about 100 kilometers away from Beijing.

When I was in high school, I had made up my mind to become an attendant some day. My classmates said I had made the right choice because I was good-tempered, liked to talk, smile, and do exercise.

When I finished junior high school, the Shanghai Aviation Bureau under CAAC recruited employees from my school. I was so excited that my blood pressure shot up so high that I didn't pass the physical examination. Upon graduation from senior high school, I applied to the Beijing Aviation Bureau once again. This time I didn't get so excited, and my blood pressure was normal. My dream came true.

After ten months' training, I began to fly in a plane so small that it tossed about a great deal. All thirty-odd new stewardesses except me were air-sick. They fainted and threw up.

Later I was recommended to study French in Xi'an Foreign Languages Institute for three years. I had studied English in high school and usually got good marks on tests. So I acquired two foreign languages which are extremely useful in my work as stewardess on international routes.

I began to fly on the international routes in 1980 and have been to more than twenty countries. I've been to San Francisco and New York in the U.S., Paris in France, Frankfurt in the Federal Republic of Germany, Zurich in Switzerland, and Moscow in the Soviet Union, and other places where CAAC goes. I love visiting the Kremlin, Pushkin Art Meseum, Versailles, and the Louvre. Of all the foreign cities I've visited, I like Paris the best. I'm impressed by its beautiful classic architecture and the women's clothing.

We've a couple of days, sometimes a week off when we go to another country. We use the time to go sightseeing, learn local customs and language. When we go to a country where the weather is pleasant we like to lie on the lawn and enjoy the beauty of nature, and indulge in reverie. Sometimes we jump, run, and play.

My salary isn't high compared to that of a foreign stewardess. But it's quite high for Chinese. My basic salary is eighty-eight *yuan* plus a nine-*yuan* floating sum. That's as much as a college lecturer makes. In addition, I've subsidies. If I fly on a domestic route, I get 0.8 *yuan* for an hour's work; if I fly on an international route, I get 0.8 in foreign exchange certificates. The food subsidy is 240 *yuan*, enough to feed an ordinary worker's family of four. So my life is very good.

Since stewardesses enjoy favorable treatment and are considered to be good-looking, we are much sought after in marriage. But our suitors will be disillusioned if they only saw the "sweet side," and failed to see the "bitter" side of our lives.

Take me for example. My husband's parents had been apprehensive before our marriage thinking my work too dangerous. I gave them some figures to convince them that working on planes was less dangerous than working on trains or buses. They gradually changed their minds.

My husband and I didn't want to have a child in the first two years of our marriage for fear it would affect my work. My superiors have treated me very well, and I would be unhappy if I couldn't fly because I was pregnant. Later when we finally decided to have a child, I didn't get pregnant because I was away from home more than two-thirds of the year. It wasn't until I was thirty that we had a baby-girl.

Because of my work, I'm unable to take care of her, and my husband isn't in good health. So she lives with my mother in Tianjin. My parents both have jobs, so my daughter goes to a day-care center.

I was chosen as a deputy political instructor in charge of ideological work among stewardesses in 1985. That meant more responsibilities. Sometimes when I miss my daughter badly, I would get a train ticket and go to see her. But something urgent always props up to upset my plan. I go to Tianjin five or six times a year staying a couple of days each time. My daughter mistook me for a stranger at first. She is very close to her grandparents. My husband says jokingly that I'm neither a good wife, nor a kind mother. I guess I can't deny it. If a person marries a stewardess and wants her to be both a good wife and kind mother, and be with him every day, then he's made a mistake. Actually, some stewardesses have gotten divorced because they didn't live up to their husbands' expectations.

My job looks simple but actually it isn't. On the surface, we serve people drinks and food and that's all. But it's not that simple if you do the work well. You must know foreign languages, be knowledgeable, and understand passengers. The passengers vary from state leaders to ordinary people in different professions and trades and from different countries.

When I first worked as a stewardess, I encountered a foreign passenger who spoke to me for a long time in English. But I only caught the word "pillow." Even though I found a pillow for him, he still shook his head. So I asked an interpreter for help. What the passenger was saying was that he had left his keys and wallet under a pillow at his hotel and was asking us to help him get them back. I realized that if I didn't know foreign languages, I couldn't communicate with my passengers and do my job well.

In dealing with people, you must not only be polite, but also know how to be tactful. There is much to learn. Once when I was serving drinks, a passenger took a cup of orange juice and after one sip of it complained that it had a bitter taste. He pointed to the ice cubes on the serving vehicle and said he wanted some crystal sugar. If I had told him that it was ice, not sugar, I was afraid I'd embarrass him. So I smiled and said: "You see, the juice is squeezed from a whole orange, including the rind. It's nutritious and relieves internal heat. I'll put some more ice cubes in it. You'll find it cool and nice." And the passenger nodded his head.

To serve the passengers well, you must both be hospitable and ready to help no matter how tiring it is. A few years ago, a Chinese man in his seventies traveled on my plane on his way to see his son in the United States. We arranged for him to sit near the lavatory. He was in poor health. Also, he was so nervous that he kept slobbering. So I had to clean the sides of his mouth every now and then. The man was grateful, telling me that I was like a daughter-in-law.

I think more than ninety percent of us stewardesses or stewards love our work and treat our passengers well. Some of those recently hired aren't considerate to passengers, but we old hands try our best to help them.

CAAC is improving its performance. I'm always happy when we get praises from the passengers. But CAAC consists of different sections. If one section isn't working well, CAAC's reputation will be affected. It's often that those of us in forefront get the worst part of it and our efforts are useless if people in other departments don't do their jobs well. The passengers tend to pour all their grievances about ground service to us and say unpleasant things too. In such a situation, I used to try to put myself in their shoes. And I'll do my best to protect our reputation which I think is my obligation.

I'm over thirty now. According to regulations, we can no longer work as stewardesses after forty. We must then work in CAAC ground services. Usually the period from marriage to child-birth is the most chancy period. If you don't handle the situation well, you'll have to quit.

I plan to compile an air service handbook in foreign languages after I'm retired. The textbook we used at college is too formal; in fact; it's quite a bit different from what the way foreigners actually speak. They use shorter sentences, and simpler words. We old-timers should pave the way for the newcomers so that they can serve passengers better.

Train Conductor: Chen Shaowen

A train conductor's many opportunities to earn more money if he chooses to violate rules.

He works on the 119/120 express between Beijing and the scenic city of Hangzhou. He is among the 120,000 conductors serving in the green, Soviet-style passenger carriages moving along the "arteries of transportation," as railways are called in this vast and populous developing country. In a tiny cabin compartment on the train, he talks as mildly and steadily as he would in the small room of his home in Hangzhou. He has spent ten years in both.

As a train conductor, whether one's tall or short, one's to put the center of gravity on two legs instead of on one. And one doesn't have to worry about balance. How can one fall down in such a crowded carriage? But I still have to watch where I step. If I don't, the passengers may complain. And it'd be dangerous when I'm carrying a pot of hot water.

I've served on this train for almost ten years, ever since the line was opened on August 1, 1978. I'm thirty-three and considered old to be a conductor on an express train. Most of my colleagues in the other carriages're younger than I'm. Older conductors're usually assigned to slower trains and shorter lines, where the work's easier. My superiors keep me here. Perhaps they don't want to leave everything to the youngsters.

We've to listen to our leaders. The railway's known for its semi-military administration. We're supposed to obey commands. I was once a soldier, so I always accept what the leaders say we must do.

I've traveled many many miles on trains. The distance between Hangzhou and Beijing's 1,651 kilometers. A round trip's 3,302 kilometers. In a year's time a round trip every week will mean that I've traveled a distance equivalent to four trips around the world. In ten years, therefore, I've traveled the equivalent of forty round-the-world trips.

An air stewardess may travel more miles than we do. Yet unlike on an airplane, on a train you've a vivid impression of the trees and cities that pass all the time. Conductors have to look out of the window often to know where they're, and then have to make decisions.

I took a plane once, several years ago, when we were sent to Changchun (in Northeast China, the location of the country's biggest railway carriage manufacturer) to bring back our new carriages. They were, of course, more comfortable.

It takes us twenty-eight hours and twenty-seven minutes to go from Beijing to Hangzhou, and twenty-seven hours going back. There're two conductors in every carriage. We alternate shifts. Each of us works twelve hours. In the few hours after the run begins, and when the train approaches its destination, we work together.

This train's the only one between Hangzhou and Beijing. It's one of the most crowded in China. With 1,452 seats and berths, the average passenger load's 2,600 passengers. Sometimes you can't walk even down the corridor of the carriage; at such times we have to, when the train stops, deliver hot water through windows to passengers. As some of my colleagues joke: "Walking on such a train for ten years would make you a ballerina!"

Well, it's a bit better here than out in the hard-seat carriage. But not much. This's too small to be called the "conductor's office." It's wide enough only to sit with your legs folded. And we aren't allowed to close the door and stay here all the time.

The train wasn't so crowded ten years ago. At that time, most passengers were employees of state-owned institutions and enterprises and they were either on business trips or on home leaves with the expenses covered by their employers. People seldom traveled at their own expense.

But now you can see all kinds of people in this tightly-limited space. Every spring, many northerners go south; and every autumn, many southerners go northwards on honeymoons or for sightseeing. Every summer and winter, the carriages would be heated by the noisy college students on their way home or to school. After the Spring Festival (Chinese lunar New Year), laborers from the small counties of Zhejiang Province would go up north to fluff cotton, repair shoes, work on construction sites, or work as pedlars. Most of them go homewards before the New Year. You can see from their dirty clothes and cautious faces that they've made some money.

The real ones with money are the self-employed businessmen from Wenzhou, a coastal city in East Zhejiang. They dress expensively and gaudily, smoke foreign cigarettes, order extravagant dishes in the dining carriage, and always complain about the accommodations on the train. You meet all kinds of people—even beggars and thieves.

At home, my room's rather cramped. My son prefers to play in the courtyard with our neighbors' children. I love this room, though. I'm home for only four days a week. It feels particularly comfortable the first night I come back. I've just mopped the floor. I enjoy doing housework. Why shouldn't I be industrious in my own home, since I've served so many strangers on the train?

Each time the train sets off, the conductor must provide hot water for the passengers and put it into their cups or glasses. Then more water should be made available on the hour. Sometimes ten pots of water are needed in making a single round. Besides, he needs to clean the tables and floor constantly, help passengers at the door at each stop, find seats for the aged, sick, crippled or pregnant women, make sure the passengers do not smoke, and warn them about inflammable and combustible materials. A conductor must be as busy and considerate as a housewife. Perhaps that's one of the reasons why a number of my colleagues have moved to other professions.

However, being a conductor was considered a "good" job when I joined the railway in 1978. I was born in a village of Anji County, a small place in Zhejiang Province. After graduation from junior high school, I worked for four years in the country and then joined the Army. I was discharged in 1978, just when applications for employment on the railway were being made. A conductor's job was in demand. Conductors then could travel a lot, compared with ordinary people. His monthly salary was seven *yuan* higher than that of a worker or a clerk. That was a considerable sum since there were no bonuses then. Well, these no longer seem to be great privileges now, although my home villagers still envy me and in particular my smart uniform.

However, now the job's becoming popular again. Despite its hardships and low pay, lower than that of many factory jobs, a lot of young persons applied for jobs during a recent recruitment. It's thought that a conductor can get acquainted with many people and thus acquire more "back doors" (a Chinese saying for connections) than an ordinary worker.

We've twenty-six stops on our way from Beijing to Hangzhou, and twenty-seven stops on the way back. It's hard to tell how many passengers get on our train on a single trip.

My monthly income's about 100 *yuan* (US$ 27 or so). With my wife's pay, we make together about 250 (US$ 66).

A train conductor's many opportunities to earn more money if he wants to violate rules. For instance, during a recent trip to Beijing, a merchant asked me to get him a berth in a sleeping car. The money he offered me was double the ticket price. I turned him down. If he'd been an old man, or ill, I'd have helped him. Without charge. Another man, a pedlar, stuffed several packages of foreign cigarettes into my pockets while asking me to let him go with excess luggage—seven bags of fish. I gave him the cigarettes back and collected the fine. Things like this occur quite often.

Some conductors've been punished or even discharged for breaking the rules, so it's not worth taking chances.

We're rewarded for good work. The amount's

decided, to a considerable extent, by passengers' letters of thanks. I've seldom been criticized, at least in letters. Yet sometimes passengers'll praise you for something trivial. For example, when we stopped in Shanghai recently, three old tourists made their way over the platform. They were on their way back to Beijing. I helped them to board, an incident that I'd almost completely forgotten a couple of weeks later when a letter of thanks was sent to the Hangzhou rail station. It was on a large piece of red paper. Those letters're all kept by my leaders.

I've even carried down to the platform the bodies of two passengers who'd suddenly died on the train.

You come across all kinds of things on a train. No wonder it's often called a "small society."

And this may be the biggest benefit of my job. Since I was a small country boy, I'd dreamed of seeing the world.

Now, on the first sight of a person, I can tell quite accurately his age, profession, and personality.

To me, a great disadvantage of this job's that I've put too heavy a burden on my wife. She's a worker in the Hangzhou Xiongwei Silk Factory. Also very busy, she does most of the housework. She visited Beijing last year. It was the farthest trip from home she'd ever made in her life.

A great pity's that she probably will have to bear a heavier burden in future years. I said that to maintain your balance on the train, you'd put the center of gravity on two legs instead of on one. But I'm afraid I can do nothing but work on the railway. It's too late for me to change jobs. I've never gone to college. And I've no special skills. But I've grown accustomed to the work of being a conductor.

Private Taxi Driver: Li Duofu

I guess I belong to the lost generation in China.

Li Duofu is a *Getihu*, a phrase in China meaning someone engaged in private businesses. But when it was first used ten years ago, people, who had just emerged from the chaos of the Cultural Revolution, could hardly believe such occupations would re-emerge in socialist China.

But now they know that they will. The bold economic reforms and the open-door policy that Chinese leader Deng Xiaoping introduced in the late 1970s has made it possible for private business, once prohibited, to exist.

Li, twenty-nine, is one of the 2,060 private taxi drivers in Shanghai. Today there is a total of 10,458 taxis in the largest city in China, twenty times the figure ten years ago. Li could have had an "iron rice bowl," another popular expression in china meaning ensured life-long employment, in his original work unit, a pharmaceutical marketing-supply station in Shanghai. He was a porter there, a job that involved much hard labor for little money and brought him endless troubles.

As a result, he left that job in the summer of 1986 and decided to get into the lucrative private taxi business.

Of medium build, the slim Li doesn't appear to be a typical businessman. He speaks slowly, sometimes with long pauses. His manner of speaking betrays both his frankness and introversion.

He lights a cigarette and begins recounting his personal story, never told before in such detail.

Some acquaintances and neighbors have asked

me: "Why did you want to be a *Getihu*? For money's sake?" They can hardly believe I would resign a job from a state-owned enterprise. I gave them a somewhat forced smile. I thought to myself: "They don't really understand me. They aren't too wrong to believe that I'm doing it for money. But that's not the whole reason. What I want to do isn't only earn money, but also to make my life meaningful and independent."

That may sound too idealistic. To put it bluntly, I want to buy high-quality hi-fi stereo equipment because I'm a music fan, and also a new house and pieces of furniture for my marriage. More importantly, I want to make up for the time lost which should have been spent getting an education. There have to be colleges where one can enroll at one's own expense.

It's true that there're people who start private businesses merely to lead a decent life and nothing else. Few of them have a future career clearly in mind. With bulging wallets, many private businessmen go to dance halls and coffee bars at night. But they disregard a basic fact of life. Without knowledge, a man can achieve nothing and is useless to society.

I think if a man loses his career goal, he loses the meaning of his existence. Maybe I'm going too far when I say this, but at least I set such demands on myself.

I think a man has to be independent. I made up my mind to resign from my previous job in the summer of 1986 and to become a private taxi driver. My unit agreed to my resignation immediately. The problem was that the letter of resignation had to be signed by my father who, at first, didn't agree with my decision. He's a very stubborn person. He thought, and still thinks, that a private businessman in China is low on the social ladder. He felt he'd lose face if his son became one.

Finally, my persistence won. I told him either to give me 3,000 yuan for my marriage or his signature on my letter of resignation. Since he was reluctant to give me the money, he made a concession, adding that he wouldn't help me out financially even in the event of an emergency later on.

This is typical of my father. He's a radio engineer in a factory in Shanghai. He's been married four times. My mother and he were divorced when I was only three years old. I've a sister. After the divorce, I lived with father, while my sister went to live with my mother. As a child, I didn't get as much fatherly love as I needed.

He seldom cared for me. I spent my childhood in a very acrimonious family environment. Father, and later my step-mother, often quarreled violently, and this resulted in divorce.

In 1976, I graduated from high school. I'd have been sent to the countryside for re-education, since at the time leftist influences were still strong. It was mother who went to the schoolmaster and asked for his assistance.

She said I was too weak physically to do heavy manual labor in the countryside. The schoolmaster listened to mother. As a result, I was assigned a job at a pharmaceutical marketing-supply station under the municipal bureau of commerce in October of 1976.

Meanwhile, father was preparing for another marriage and he decided that he and I shouldn't live together. I moved to a shabby matchbox of a room, just large enough for a bed and a table. I was happy not to be with a surly father and a belligerent family. Having a room of my own was good. I used the quiet environment to read, study, and listen to music. And I was free to do whatever I wanted without his interference.

I guess I belong to the lost generation in China. During my primary and high school days, I received little education. Schools were closed from time to time for frequent political campaigns. Most of our time was spent waving banners on the streets and shouting slogans eulogizing the Cultural Revolution.

While working as a porter during the day, I took high school-level courses at night school in 1977 at my own expense. This schooling lasted for about three years. I did quite well, passing all the examinations and receiving a diploma in 1980.

However, it seemed that I still wasn't qualified to enter a college. I failed three times on college entrance examinations between 1981 and 1983. But I haven't given up my ambitions, feeling confident that I'll succeed some day.

During that period I nearly used up all my savings to pay for tuition and books. I felt life was quite empty at the time. I no longer wanted to stay at the unit, where I received a monthly wage of about 100 *yuan*, including subsidies and bonus, just barely enough to make ends meet.

When I decided to get into private business, I first thought of doing work that would require specialized skills. So I chose to drive a taxi, because drivers are always needed in this city. If I failed, I always could find a job in a state-owned enterprise as a contract worker. The principal problem was how to get enough money to buy a car. The cheapest car available for private business in Shanghai is the Polish-assembled Fiat four-seat mini-car, which costs 11,000 yuan.

My sister, learning of my decision, helped me. She gave me 3,000 yuan. The rest was contributed by friends and relatives.

Before obtaining a driver's licence, I had to spend four months at a training center in a suburb of Shanghai. I paid more than 3,000 yuan in tuition fees. Again, my sister came and lent me a helping hand.

When I finally succeeded in obtaining the licence, I was extremely happy. It was a turning point in my life.

Unlike workers in factories, people engaged in private business have no days off. Usually, I drive more than 100 kilometers or about ten hours a day.

There are times when I'm so busy that I can't even take ten minutes out during the workday. One time, I drove two passengers to the railway station. If I had driven slowly, they would have missed the train. On the way, I suddenly felt that I needed to go to the bathroom. I looked at my watch and realized that their train would leave in ten minutes. And I was still about five or six minutes away from the station. When we arrived, they just barely made the train. When I finally found the rest room. I already had wet my pants. What a day!

Late at night, as I drag myself home, I feel exhausted. Many a time lying in bed, I stare at the ceiling and think of many things, even of giving up. Then I seem to hear a voice from high above: "Where is the perseverence that you had, young man, when you decided to take up this occupation?"

Most people often associate us private businessmen with *wanyuanhu* (an expression in China referring to people with a wealth of 10,000 yuan). Yes, we can earn such amounts. On the average, I net about 1,200 yuan a month or even as high as 1,800 yuan in peak seasons. But people should also know how much and what kind of work that represents. I think I deserve what I'm paid. My only complaint is that many unreasonable taxes are imposed upon us, such as civil construction taxes, education taxes, social welfare taxes, to name only a few.

My gasoline allotment per season is 600 liters. My car consumes at least 900 liters. I have to buy the extra petrol coupons on the black market at a much higher price than I pay for the gasoline allotted to me.

I think my service is good. I treat passengers fairly. I'm more willing to provide service to northerners because they're very straightforward and seldom try to strike a hard bargain with you. The people I like the least to take are young Shanghainese.

Last year, I drove three young people, two men and one woman, to a dance hall located in an alley. The alley is blocked off to vehicle traffic. But these people insisted that I drive them to the entrance of the hall, or they wouldn't pay the fare. I told them I couldn't violate the traffic law and, furthermore, politely asked them to get out, free of charge. As soon as I opened the door, I was hit on the head from the behind. as I turned around, another blow, heavier than the first, hit me in the face. My nose started to bleed. I restrained my intense rage and just let them go. If I fought with them, I felt they might damage my car, and my means of making a livelihood would, thus, be destroyed.

I have to work all day long despite whatever frustrations and misfortunes I meet.

The state gives us a lot of help. For example, my car and I are insured. Every year I pay about 300 yuan for insurance. So far, I've had two accidents, which caused slight damage to my car. I paid only 20 percent of the repair fees. The rest was covered by the insurance company.

Reading and listening to music are two of the leisure activities I enjoy the most. I was exposed to music when I was in primary school. Later I learned to play the piano. In high school, I learned to play the violin. But I never performed publicly.

A friend recognized my musical talent and wanted to help me apply to a music conservatory in Shanghai. I had to reject his kindness. I couldn't afford to buy a violin at that time as father never gave me any pocket money.

I like Beethoven and Mozart. Now I also like the rhythm of rock 'n 'roll music.

The magazine that I'm most interested in is *Reader's Digest*, which is compiled and published by a Chinese publishing house. From it, I learn a lot about the realities of life. I also like to read novels and detective fictions. I consider my reading a kind of preparation for entering a college.

I rarely go out after work. Though I earn a lot, compared with ordinary workers, I never spend the money in a lavish manner. In addition, I have to pay back the money I borrowed to buy the car. Life, at least it seems to me now, is hard. If I remained in business for a relatively long time, say, five years, I think my situation would be better.

In early 1988, an epidemic of hepatitis A hit

Shanghai. Unfortunately, I was one of the victims. I asked a friend who has a driver's licence to continue the business for me. I gave him 500 yuan a month.

Without the care of my present girl friend, I would have been hospitalized. I recovered in a month.

My first love? When I was a porter, I had a girl friend who was a university student. I was kind to her, and treated her like my own sister. For some time, she seldom accepted my invitation to go to parks and concerts. Though she didn't say it, I sensed that the reason she wasn't interested was that we came from two different socio-economic backgrounds. For the first time, my self-esteem was badly hurt.

My present girl friend is a friend of a good friend. I once took her out shopping. I don't know exactly why she likes me. Perhaps, I hope, my good intentions won her heart. She's a worker in an electrical fan factory. At present, I can't say if I'll marry her in the near future. I still have many things to do.

Another reason that I don't want to get married soon is that I'm going to study in Japan in August 1988. My brother-in-law is a Tokyo-stationed correspondent of the Shanghai-based *World Economic Herald*. He'll provide financial aid for my studies and accomodations there. Still, I'm going to have to find a job. I told my brother-in-law that I'll reward his faith in me by studying and working hard.

I think a man's pursuit of life should be many-sided. One should try by every possible means to lead a better and more meaningful life. It's this belief that has made me decide to go abroad.

I'll sell my car to one of my friends before going

to Japan.

Some friends think I won't come back if I do well in Japan. But I told them I will. Though my motherland is still poor and underdeveloped, I'm after all Chinese and should contribute all I can to the place where I was born.

Pedicab Driver: Wang Fugen

I'm still pedaling a pedicab after thirty-eight years because I don't want to stop. Otherwise, I'll lose my good health.

Ten years ago, people in China were talking about sending the last pedicab into the museum of history. But this old form of transportation has endured, because bus and taxi service has always been inadequate. Also, now, the new policy encourages people to run private businesses, including private taxis and pedicabs.

But still, in China's metropolis of Shanghai, where urban public transportation is fairly developed, the pedicab is part of the past. From 80,000 at the ultimate in the 1950s, the number of pedicabs in this city has dwindled to a hundred, according to the municipal pedicab management office. All the drivers are men in their sixties and seventies who don't want to retire.

Wang Fugen is one who can't accept retirement, although he and his wife have a pension of a hundred yuan each. His son, a college graduate, works in a research institute. His daughter-in-law works in the laboratory of the institute.

I'm seventy-one. Many of my acquaintances wonder I'm still working. They don't realize how dull it'd be for me to be idle with nothing to do after thirty-eight years of pedaling my pedicab. Also, I'm proud of my knowledge of the city. I know the three thousand streets and lanes in this city as well as the lines of my palm. Sometimes at the railway station, I notice taxi drivers who're at a total loss when a customer gives the name of a very small back lane. I can often seize the opportunity and say to the customer: "I know the place. Come on, and I'll take you there." I'm happy that because of my experience, I've been able to best even the young drivers, no matter how new their taxis are.

When I first arrived in the city from the countryside, I knew nothing about Shanghai. Fortunately I'd a sturdy build, a pair of big feet, and powerful legs. A merchant hired me to be his private pedicab driver.

At that time, the socialist transformation of the economy (1953-1956) hadn't yet started, and there were private businessmen everywhere. My boss was rich. He'd a wife and a concubine, six children, a cook, and a housemaid. My job was to take my boss to his office in the morning and then per his instructions to deliver goods. That'd keep me busy the whole day. At the end of the day, I pedaled the boss home. But that was by no means my entire work. When my boss's wives went shopping, visited friends, or went to the theater or cinema, it also was my job to take them there.

I did my best to do a good job. I drove my pedicab carefully and I kept it spick and span. And I never missed an appointment, which my boss appreciated. He not only raised my salary but agreed to let his housemaid marry me. After our marriage, we continued to work for him.

Then came the socialist transformation in 1956. In that campaign, my boss's confectionery was turned into a jointly state-private owned enterprise. One afternoon my boss called me and my wife, Ahxiang, to his sitting room. He told us: "Fugen and Ahxiang, haven't you heard the beating of drums and gongs and the setting off of firecrackers everywhere in Shanghai these days? They're in celebration of Shanghai's entering socialism. And socialism disapproves of exploitation. I'm a capitalist. I must become a man living off my own labor. So I can no longer afford to hire you two. You'd leave, but you can keep my pedicab as a present from me. It's no use to me anyway."

So I and Ahxiang left. Since I was an illiterate and could do nothing else, I continued to drive my pedicab—this time on my own.

Then came the so-called Great Leap Forward, a drive aimed at wiping out all traces of capitalism. Private ownership of a pedicab was also considered a sign of capitalist ownership. So the municipal government took over the operation of pedicab service. The State bought our pedicabs, and we became pedicab workers, on a fixed monthly wage.

Under the new management, we pedicab workers had to give every patron a ticket and, at the end of every day's work, hand in every coin we'd received. Everybody received the same pay regardless of how much one turned in that month. There was no incentive, and nobody cared about getting more fares.

But things've been different in recent years, thanks to the reforms. I understand pedicab drivers're allowed to operate privately in other cities.

Here in Shanghai, we've dropped the fixed wage system among pedicab drivers. We now can keep sixty percent of our daily income; the remaining forty percent goes to the pedicab management office. The office uses that money to pay for pensions, maintenance of our cabs, and taxes.

Under this new system, I need only to get one or two fares a day and make a gross monthly income of 400 yuan. After handing in forty percent to management, I still have 240 yuan. With this money, plus Ahxiang's and my pensions, we don't have to be too careful about how we spend money.

People say the pedicab's a backward form of transportation, because it requires muscle power only, and that it'll be abandoned for good some day. Although I agree with them, I also believe the pedicab has its advantage. What's more, a pedicab can enter a narrow lane which'd be inaccessible to a taxi.

Because the pedicab can go into narrow lanes and pick up a customer at his or her door, people prefer to call a pedicab when they need to rush a patient or pregnant woman to a hospital. For this reason, I don't believe the pedicab'll disappear very soon in China.

The other day when I was walking in the street, a young lady pushing a pram greeted me warmly. Before I'd recall who she was, she said to me: "Don't you remember, old uncle, the night that you saved my life and the life of this baby?"

She was right. One evening, when my wife and I were returning home from the cinema, we saw a young pregnant lady who was groaning beside a lamp post. I guessed she was about to give birth. I asked my wife to stay with her, and I rushed home to get my pedicab. When we reached the nearest hospital, the woman already had fainted, leaving a patch of blood on the seat of my cab. Later, the doctors said that if we hadn't arrived when we had, both the mother's and baby's lives would have been endangered.

I've made it a rule never to overcharge a customer. I always use my cab as a means to help people. Although money's important, I value people's appreciation of my work more.

Airforce Pilot: Xue Wenshu

In spite of all the hardships, I never have regretted becoming a pilot.... A great regret in my life is that I cannot wear my beautiful hair long.

China's air force does not have many super-grade women pilots. Xue Wenshu is one of them.

Solidly built and suntanned, the fifty-two-year-old pilot has chalked up over 3,000 flying hours without an accident since she graduated from the Beijing Aeronautics Institute in 1958. She has flown the equivalent of twenty trips around the earth.

Being one of 142 women pilots of the second group trained after 1949, Xue has thirty years of flying experience. She has piloted six types of air freighters. She is known in the air force for her courage and exceptional aviation skills.

"I don't think I have anything to say except that I'm a lucky dog and always feel good," she says in the euphonious Beijing dialect. "Perhaps I feel lucky because I'm often up in the air and can get away from earthly cares."

Is it really the case? With three medals for her military exploits, she surely has more to tell.

To tell you the truth, I never dreamed that one day I'd be a pilot and stay with it. Even now, thinking about it seems rather strange. What I really meant to be was a scientist or an artist or something like that.

I was perhaps out of my mind to choose flying as a career. But at that time, pilots were greatly respected and besides, I was so impressed by the military uniforms. That was when I was nineteen.

As a high school graduate, I had many plans for the future. But in the end I decided to enter a university since I was fortunate to be one of the best students in my school. However, when I learned that the air force was recruiting women pilots, I changed my mind.

As I've said, a pilot got a lot more respect than college students. To become enrolled in an aeronautics institute, you had to go through not only many physical tests, but also unbelievably elaborate political ones even regarding distant relatives—to see if you had a proper family background. Only those who enjoyed good health and had a correct family background could pass the tests.

So you see, it was really a challenge to everybody, especially to me, who had always been trying to be the best. I couldn't suppress the impulse to apply.

The tests to determine your physical condition were quite exciting, and demanding, too. Many applicants failed. I still remember the swivel chair. We were required to sit in it and were spinned fifteen revolutions. Five with your eyes closed, five with your head lowered. I was asked to do it with another girl. In the tenth round, with her head tilted, the girl suddenly fainted. All the people on the spot, including the officers in charge of the tests, ran to assist her. I was left there, forgot. Later, unfortunately, I was asked to do it again—another fifteen rounds. Still, I passed easily.

I was certainly proud of myself. It was said only thirteen girls were chosen out of the thousands of applicants. And I was one of them.

Two years in preparatory school, and then the

aeronautics institute, meant hard work. Have you ever seen a hanging ladder of a rolling exerciser? Every time we practised on it, we did at least 150 rounds. Two thirds of the trainees were eliminated. But I stayed. To me, the training wasn't as difficult as some of my comrades said it was. Oh God, I'm not modest, am I?

Fear? I think it'd be impossible for anyone not to have fear flying the real bird for the first time. In my case, I was almost paralysed with fear while waiting to take off. My heart seemed ready to jump out. But as soon as I was up in the sky, I felt better.

There were some prejudice against women pilots. The critics said we are slow in responding, not tough enough, and easily affected by small things, and so on. I don't think these opinions are valid. Flying a plane isn't play. It takes real guts and skills. A highly skilled pilot is greatly respected by all regardless of sex.

I still remember the time when the first atomic bomb of our country exploded. Our unit was to collect samples in order to measure the extent of radiation. It certainly was a dangerous job, but a challenge, too, for it required both skill and courage. Some pilots stepped back, but not me. I went straight to our commander and asked for the assignment. Gazing at me for a moment, he said, "I know you are one of the best and are quite experienced, but this time, are you sure you can do it?" I said: "Yes." "Good," he said. Then, I was appointed the captain of an all-man crew.

We took off from the northeastern part of the country and flew southward. The temperature went up accordingly, from ten degrees below zero centigrade, to over thirty above zero. At first we were in cotton coats, but later even shirts were too warm. The cockpit was so hot that we'd hardly stand it. To make matters worse, the air currents were so strong that day that the plane bounced up and down. Everyone was sick to their stomach. When at last we landed, some of the crew had to be helped down from the plane, although I walked down by myself. Everyone on the spot stared at me as if they hadn't known me before.

When you have ability and use it, you'll win respect from your colleagues.

To tell you a secret, not only did I win my colleagues' respect, but also the heart of my husband, an ace pilot who had never hidden his contempt for women pilots.

He was quite handsome. I fell in love with him at first sight. However, I dared not let him know my feelings for fear of rejection. The chance came during a training program when we were to do hedgehopping. No one volunteered to try first except me. I did a good job, and when I came down from the plane, I saw surprise and admiration in my husband's eyes.

That was the beginning of our love affair. Since school leaders at the aeronautical institute declared that no one could marry during the six years of training, our relationship had to be kept secret. We exchanged messages through a friend at dinner time. And we dated in a place unfrequented by other people. It was just like, say, a guerilla war.

Our love was hard but exciting. No. I don't mean sex, really. Now, young people can walk hand-in-hand on the street and few people make a fuss about it. You can even kiss in public. But at that time, we dared not. We'd shy away the minute we touched accidentally, feeling the two of us owned the whole world.

Narrow escapes? Yes. Once the two of us were walking on a street when we caught sight of our unit leader coming in our direction. We were scared to death. We turned the street corner and, for a moment, couldn't move.

Fortunately, he was near-sighted and didn't see us. We stopped seeing each other for a whole month.

I was twenty-six and Old Li thirty when we finally got married. We'd our first child four years later.

My children weren't a burden, as my mother looked after them for me. We sent her money every month. Old Li and I tend to spoil our children. Only once did my husband slap his son, who had been naughty. But that very evening, he told me just how much he regretted doing so.

The family was unable to get together every day. Old Li and I came home once a week, usually on Sundays. But whenever we'd a family reunion, we try to enjoy it fully. I like outdoor activities, and Old Li loves to eat. The children love both. So we go to a picnic frequently.

Money? No, money isn't a problem. Pilots earn a bit more than other army officers. Besides, we don't spend much on clothing—since we wear uniforms throughout the year except on informal social occasions such as calling on a friend. Several suits of civilian clothes are enough. That's to say, we spend much of our money on food. Old Li, the food-lover in the family, gets up early everyday and runs about three kilometers to keep fit and be in good shape.

Old Li and I used to work in two cities and meet only in the annual one-month vacation. I missed him very much, of course. He didn't write many letters and sometimes I wondered if he was still alive.

For all its hardships, I never have regretted becoming a pilot. Flying, I've a broad view and an easy mind that cannot be obtained on earth. If you were a pilot, I'm sure you'd feel the same way.

I've passed the fixed retirement age of fifty for women pilots, but I still want to fly a few years longer. When the day comes when I can't fly, I'll ask to be a teacher at an aeronautics institute. The thought of staying at home for the rest of my life is nightmarish. I'd be bored to death staying at home doing nothing.

As for the household chores, Old Li and I each shoulder a share. But when both of us are lazy, we play a finger-guessing game. The loser does all the chores. But I don't know why I'm always the loser. Anyhow, Old Li is always ready to play it.

Unfortunately, neither of our children wants to be a pilot like their parents. My daughter told me she even wouldn't marry a pilot though, she said, pilots are strong, handsome, and charming. She said when she was a child, she'd ask her grandmother where I was. Grandmother would always point to the sky saying her mother was busy there. From then on, my daughter developed a hatred of the sky. She said it was too high for her to reach me. Now she's studying at Beijing Agriculture College.

When I was in high school, everybody admired

my long, thick pigtails. But after joining the air force, I had to have them cut short according to regulations. One of the great regret of my life is that I cannot wear my beautiful hair long.

Part Nine
Teaching

Kindergarten Teacher: Zhang Jing

I like to be with kids. I love them.

The kindergarten is located deep in an alley, typical in the city of Changzhou, where there are more alleys than streets.

The kindergarten is a bungalow with a small playground. It has forty-five children between two and five years old enrolled and ten teachers.

It's the hour for the children's outdoor exercise. Some are going down the slide, others are playing on the seesaw, and still others are riding on the rocking wooden horses.

Standing beside the children is a slim, tall, smiling girl. She is their teacher Zhang Jing. She is only twenty-two, but she has already worked here for four years.

Everyone has his or her own dream. My childhood dream was to become a university teacher. But instead of being a university teacher, I became a kindergarten teacher.

I became a kindergarten teacher in 1984. Before that, I studied at Wuxi Teachers' School for Preschool Education for two years. I entered that school after I graduated from junior high school.

My original plan was to go on to a senior high

school and then to a university. But mother was opposed to it. She wanted me to apply to a vocational school, for she thought that by doing so, I not only could continue my education and receive a diploma, but also could save the family some money.

Our family is a big one. When grandmother was still alive (she died four years ago), we'd seven persons in our family. At that time, my two elder brothers were in college.

Each month, my parents spent a lot of money on our education. My father is an army officer, and my mother a cadre. Both of them make fairly good salaries. But because they had such a large family to support, they always seemed to be in want of money. I remember when most of our neighbors had color TV sets, we still were watching a black-and-white one.

I understood how mother felt vis-a-vis money, so I finally agreed with her. I'm the only one of the four children who hasn't received a higher education. My younger brother is now a university student, too. Mother often says that I'm the person who's made the most contributions to our family. I know she was sorry that I didn't have an opportunity to enter college like my brothers.

My two years' study in Wuxi, a nearby city, were the happiest days of my life. There were twenty students in our class, all girls of my age. At that time, I was sixteen, and it was the first time I'd been away from home. There, I'd almost do anything I liked. I didn't have to listen to my mother nagging me, or asking me to do this or to do that. There, I not only learned how to care for babies, but also learned music, dance, painting, and many other new things. I found that being a kindergarten teacher wasn't as bad as I thought it was.

Compared with many other kindergarten teachers, I'm lucky, since I work in the daycare section and my kids are five-year-olds, the oldest in the kindergarten. I don't have to give them milk bottles, as the teachers in the babies' section have to, nor do I have to change their diapers, or stay up at night while they're sleeping. But this isn't to say that I don't have difficulties. I remember when I first changed the trousers that had been stained with a child's excrement, I didn't eat for the rest of the day.

There are fifteen children in my class. I start work at 8 o'clock in the morning, but usually I get to the school a bit earlier. Every morning, at about 8 o'clock, parents bring their children to the kindergarten. Breakfast is at 8:30. We begin our first lessons at 9:00. Usually we'll have two lessons in the morning, each lasting about half an hour. After lunch, the children take a nap. The afternoon's lesson begins at 3 o'clock. The supper hour is at 4:00. At about 5:00, parents arrive to pick up their children. I'm not able to leave until all the children have left.

Being a kindergarten teacher isn't easy. In order to teach a half-hour lesson, I often put in two or three hours of preparation, sometimes longer.

As a kindergarten teacher, you have to be good at many things. You'd be able to teach the children not only language, but also arithmetic, music, dance, and painting. You even should be good at paper-cutting and building blocks. Usually we kindergarten teachers use stories to illustrate for the children the difference between right and wrong, between beautiful and ugly, and between good and evil.

I used to have difficulty telling stories. At first, the stories that I told didn't interest the children. I did a lot of reading and have practised hard to become a better story-teller. I've read Andersen, Green, Aesop, and many Chinese and foreign fairy tales and fables. I've told many stories to the children of our neighbors. Now, I not only feel very comfortable in telling stories, but I can compose some of my own. Some of the children will follow me all day, begging me to tell them a story.

Today, nearly every child is the only child in the family. They're spoilt and willful. At home, each of them is a "little emperor." A child like this seldom shows concern for others and doesn't like to do things they're able to. Understanding this situation, we encourage them to become involved in group activities. We also require all the children here to dress themselves and make their beds. Watching the children dress sometimes can be amusing. Some of them are so eager that they mistake jackets for their trousers, and trousers for their jackets. Once, a boy proudly told me that he was the first to get dressed. I was surprised for he used to be the slowest at dressing. As I looked down, I found out the reason for his success. He had put both of his legs into one trouser leg.

Children are fond of play, and restless, by nature. Sometimes, however, they may go too far and can be very irritating. Some will run out of the classroom chasing a cricket when you are teaching a lesson; others may keep scratching here and there while you are talking to them. What can you do when these things happen? Try to change them? It would be in vain. I often let kids play as much as they want. When they have played enough, they'll want something different. That's when you teach them a song or dance or tell them a story. Children remember things that you tell them at this point. I think play itself is a kind of education. Education isn't something that's confined to the classroom. It's everywhere. I often take the children to the zoo or movie theater.

Kids are very curious. Wherever they go, whatever they see, they'll ask questions. Some of these can prove embarrassing. Once a child asked me why the eyes of a chicken are on the side of its head? How can they see the things in front of them? I didn't have the answer. A teacher isn't someone who knows everything. When you cannot answer a question raised by a child, you'd tell him or her honestly that you don't know. You should never deceive them, for children take your words as truth. One of the most popular sayings among kids is that "my teacher told me so."

Kids understand physical things better than abstract things, so the language you use must be simple and vivid. Generally speaking, their understanding is in a developmental stage, and it takes some time for them to respond. A kindergarten teacher shouldn't get impatient when they've failed to answer a question correctly or immediately. Patience is what a kindergarten teacher needs most. You'd never shout at kids. I used to have a quick temper, but over the past four years, I've changed a great deal. I find that the more you shout at a kid, the louder he or she cries. But that doesn't mean you shouldn't criticize them when they do something wrong. When you criticize them, you must control yourself enough that you don't frighten them.

I like to be with kids. I love them. My salary isn't high. My basic monthly income is less than fifty yuan, yet I often buy gifts for the children on their birthdays. Each year I buy a gift for each of the children in my class. Whenever a child is hospitalized, I'll go to see them, and take some fruit. I've a good rapport with the children. They like me. Last year, the children in my class were going to leave to enter primary school, so we had a party. Some of the children's parents also attended. Many children cried. Some of them grabbed the corner of my clothes, and didn't want to leave. On such occasions, I feel very sad, because I've lost something.

I've many hobbies. I like dancing, singing, and playing the accordian. I'm also very fond of traveling. Each summer vacation, I go sightseeing. Over the years, I've developed a keen interest in toys. I've collected a lot of toys, such as dolls, small flower baskets, teddy-bears, pandas, kittens, puppies, rabbits, trains and planes. I often invite the children to my room to show them these toys.

I think reading is my favorite pastime. Besides all the books that are related to my work, I also like to read novels, especially love stories.

I used to have a boyfriend. He was good, but he had a bad temper. He could get angry at anything at any time. I couldn't stand it, so we parted. Mother doesn't want me to make friends with boys on my own. She's afraid that I might be hurt. She still treats me as a child, and that often annoys me.

Rural Primary School Teacher:
Xiao Wenxin

I'm proud of being a teacher, a profession I dreamed of when I was a little girl. But sometimes I wish I weren't a teacher. I guess I really have mixed feelings about it.

She became a teacher since 1970, when she was graduated from a local high school at nineteen. She is now teaching Chinese to a fifth-grade class in a rural primary school in Dingxian County, Hebei Province, North China. She works hard and is repeatedly awarded titles such as "model teacher," or "advanced worker." Her diligent work has paid off. Her students almost always win first-class prizes at school contests and are among the best ones in the local township—Zhidong—where twelve primary schools are located.

But she seems a bit depressed when talking about her salary, no more than 70 *yuan* a month plus subsidies and bonuses, for the simple reason that she comes from the countryside and does not possess the status of urban residence. She is a locally-employed teacher. But most of her colleagues are state-employed teachers and earn one-third more than she does because they come from urban areas. She complains a lot about the "birthplace discrimination." However, she is optimistic about her future and places hopes on the current reform in the educational field.

I'm an ordinary elementary school teacher. I teach Chinese to a fifth-grade class. I also teach music to five classes of students that range from the third to sixth grade.

I started teaching when I finished high school at Dingxian County High School in 1970. I was very excited when I was told that I would have a job as a teacher at the primary school in my native village school. In my hometown, a poverty-stricken area, it wasn't an easy thing to get a job like a teacher, a decent job respected by everyone. I'm still proud of being a teacher, a job which I've admired ever since the first day I walked into an elementary school at six years old and saw my widely respected teacher dressed neatly. Even adults respected her as if she were their parent. Teachers are "high-class" people, I thought at that time.

The school I work in now is called the West Zhidong Primary School, named after the village where I was born and still live. The school is, I'm not joking, a group of "sheds" each serving as a classroom, rather than a formal school that should have at least a classroom building. The classrooms are shabby adobe houses, the desks and chairs squeak and wobble when you use them, and the blackboards are plastered walls painted black. No thief would want such worthless things. Perhaps that's why there's no doorkeeper at the school and all the employees are teachers, including the headmaster who also teaches mathematics to a sixth-grade class.

In addition to my regular teaching work, I'm fond of singing. So I'm always the organizer of after-school activities and theatrical performance contests at our school. I can play the organ which, though worth something, is of no use to a thief since the thief won't be able to sell it easily. I also like dancing. But to be frank, I don't like disco. We rural people don't like such "hip-swinging" dance. Disco movements aren't graceful, in my opinion. They are ugly. However, if children dance disco, it seems cute.

Although my school is poorly equipped, it's still a "formal" school. All the students have to study those subjects stipulated in regulations set by the Ministry of Education. I'm a "locally-employed" teacher. That means I'm not wholly state-employed and earn less than state-recruited teachers. They earn about one-third more than I, because they come from urban areas, although we all work hard. But I don't need to buy food because my family has a piece of land, about one-third of a hectare, contracted from the village committee, the lowest rural governing body.

My daily life is routine; changes seldom take place. I arrive at school before 8 o'clock. Four classes in the morning. Go home after 12 o'clock. Three classes in the afternoon. Go home again at 5 o'clock. Then back to the school at 6:30 and coach the students to review or correct homework, or prepare lessons for tomorrow.

I'm very busy. I've two children, a boy and a girl. The boy, nine years old, is a fourth-grade student and the girl, seven, a first-year pupil. They are studetns at my school. They are good kids and sensible. I don't spend much time on them. The boy is my helper. He looks after his younger sister. I also raise two pigs and more than twenty chickens and till the farmland. I've a lot of work to do everyday: get up at 5 a.m., then prepare meals, feed the pigs and chickens, and collect eggs. At 7 a.m., I call the kids out of bed and have them eat breakfast. After that, I've to rush them with me to school. Sometimes I go out to the field to do farm work.

My students help me a lot. They help me sow seeds and harvest crops. One very interesting thing is that the students who don't study well and whom I don't like seem more helpful than those who study well and whom I like most.

I love the kids not only because they help me, but also because they work harder than those in urban areas. When I was a high school student in the county seat, I found many of my classmates didn't work hard. They were lazy and didn't even wash their own clothes. You know, studying in a classroom is more comfortable than tilling the field.

My husband cannot help me. He works in Beijing, some 180 kilometers north of my hometown. A man should do "big work," not household chores and the like. He's really something. He's the head of a construction team of more than 100 workers in Beijing. The team he led has constructed many high-rise buildings in Beijing, Shijiazhuang (the capital of Hebei Province), Baoding and some other cities. He earns much money. Much much much more than me. (Silence. Then her face shows a bit of dissatisfaction and she heaves a deep sigh.) As a locally-employed teacher, I earn a monthly salary of thirty-seven *yuan*. With all subsidies, allowances and bonus, I can earn no more than seventy *yuan* a month, much lower than what a state-employed teacher makes. To be a teacher like me isn't an ideal money-making job. One earns little but works hard. You know, I'm a locally-employed teacher; if the school is going to fire a teacher, I'm always the first choice.

Sometimes I really don't want to be a teacher. My hometown is well-known as the nation's "Home of

Wushu" (martial arts). It produces swords used by the nation's sword players. The actors and actresses in many Chinese *kungfu* films including some Hong Kong ones use the "Blue Dragon" swords made here. The "Blue Dragon" brand swords are a well-known brand which are exported to Hong Kong, Macao and some southeast Asian countries. If I stamped the trademark "*Qinglongjian*" (Blue Dragon Sword) on the swords I'd earn much more money than I earn now. It's an easy job, a job you don't need to spend much time to do well. If you are healthy and strong you can stamp 100 swords a day. That means ten yuan a day. Our school lacks qualified teachers. The local Party organization sent me to receive further education at the Dingxian County Teachers' School between 1971 and 1975. I went because I didn't want to let the Party officials down. I'd devote all my life to the Party's educational undertakings. Also I love the profession and the students.

To improve my work, I read and study a lot of books in areas such as children's psychology and educational psychology. My efforts have paid off. Three students of mine are now college students including one at Qinghua University, China's M.I.T. Last year, Yuan Xuguang, one of my favorite fifth-grade students, defeated all his rivals from twelve local primary schools at the Zhidong Township Students' Calligraphy Contest and won first-prize. Three of my students have won third prize among the 80-plus students in a recent township composition contest. I'm proud to say my students are among the best ones at this school. Our school has seventeen classes ranging from first grade to sixth grade.

I'm an optimist. But sometimes I feel that it's

unfair that because I'm from the countryside, I'm still considered only a locally recruited teacher. I've been in the teaching profession for eighteen years and I'm a model teacher. How I wish I were a formal teacher earning the same pay as those from urban areas!

I also feel lonely sometimes when I go to bed late at night after a hard day. My husband doesn't come back until the Spring Festival (Chinese lunar New Year) for a month or more. Anyway I understand. He's to go out to make "big" money. We've built a new brick house. Now I'm living in this new house, while there are still those who live in poorly built, adobe houses. So I suppose I shouldn't complain.

I'm still young. After another eighteen years of working as a teacher, I'm sure, I'll join the regular ranks of teachers.

University Professor: Jin Kaicheng

China's educational system has long neglected the application of knowledge and the nurturing of creative minds.

Jin Kaicheng and his family of four live in a three-room apartment at Beijing University in northwest suburban Beijing. A full professor and a tutor for doctoral candidates, Jin, fifty-six, is in the forefront of applying theories of psychology to the study of Chinese art and literature. He is the author of seven books.

He is of medium height and wears a pair of black-rimmed glasses. He is eloquent and outspoken. His lectures are welcomed by the students in Beijing University, one of the most prestigious universities in China.

At the Seventh National Congress of Chinese People's Political Consultative Conference, which ended in mid-April, 1988, Professor Jin was elected a member of the Standing Committee. As a leading figure of the Jiusan Society, a democratic party in China, Jin plays an active role in political and social life, offering his opinions and suggestions.

In my opinion, to give a lecture is to provide a service. I believe that the ultimate purpose in lecturing is to establish communication with the students. You talk in the hope that others will listen, and understand, just like when you write. When my students nod their heads in agreement, I'm greatly pleased.

When I lecture in class, I always try to broaden the horizons of my students. I try not to repeat what's unnecessary. I also am careful in the way I express myself.

A university professor should point the way to students, rather than lead them by the hand. The present generation has a strong sense of self-identity. They dislike compulsary education.

Intellectuals in China aren't as respected as they'd be. Many people have expressed themselves on this point, but little has been done.

Most intellectuals in China are underpaid. They live in crowded houses and aren't in good health. Everything is going up in price. No wonder many of the students and young teachers in our university say: "Knowledge is useless." Some of my students want to go into business to make money, while others want to go abroad for the experience.

For me, reading, writing, and lecturing have become second nature. I find pleasure in my work and what I do isn't routine, but spiritual sustenance.

As a professor, my salary is 160 yuan a month, roughly 40 U.S. dollars. My wife, who's an associate professor in the Chinese department, has a monthly income of 140 yuan. We obviously aren't very rich. Materially, we're above the average.

We've one daughter, who's married and still lives with us. She's a teacher at the Beijing Television College. My son-in-law is a copy editor of a magazine at our university. The magazine specializes in the study of ancient archives. They each receive a salary of about 100 yuan a month for their work. So, by comparison with others, my family is well off.

I moved to this apartment two years ago. The rent

is fifteen yuan. This is only a small part in my family's total income of 500 yuan. We have to spend much on food and clothing, because prices for these things are going up. Buying books accounts for a large part of our expenditures, too.

To be frank, we don't seem to know how to entertain or enjoy ourselves. Life in a university can be a rather hollow one. we have to find pleasure of our own in this environment. My life may seem to be dull to some. I sit at a table, reading, and writing all day. Or I go to the classroom and give a lecture. Once you get accustomed to it, you have to find pleasure in it.

I have quite a few hobbies. In my sprare time, I practise calligraphy, paint pictures, or engrave seals on stones. My favorite pasttime is watching films. The pity is I can only go to the cinema once or twice a year. There is a cinema on the campus. There are over 10,000 students and 4,000 staff members at the university, and tickets are usually hard to get. I'm not strong enough to jostle in a queue to buy a ticket. The Political Consultative Conference sometimes sponsors the showing of films downtown, but I cannot see them, since transportation is difficult.

Anyhow, in my limited spare time, I can listen to the radio or watch TV. I liked to listen to Peking Opera when I was young. Now I particularly like *pingtan*, a kind of storytelling and ballad singing in the Suzhou dialect. *Pingtan* is a very popular form of performance in my native town. I cultivated a love for it early in my childhood.

I'm a member of the Jiusan Society instead of the Communist Party. I tried to join the Communist Party, but I wasn't accepted. When the Jiusan Society, an independent party mainly composed of intellectuals, asked for my opinions in 1981, I became interested. Since I joined the Society, I have been promoted quickly. I'm now in charge of the propaganda work for the Society's central committee.

Leaders of the Jiusan Society meet twice a week. To engage in the social activities occupies some of my time, but I'm interested in taking part in political life. As a scholar, you just pay attention to research. However, as a person responsible for a group, you have to take care of others, and think of the problems confronting intellectuals. I feel this work has broadened my mind and expanded my horizons. I now have a greater understanding than I did before.

At present, people are talking about China's process of democratization and I think an important thing is that we must have a more open press. I recognized the importance of the press in the recently concluded Political Consultative Conference. We need greater openness in our politics, and the press can give us a better understanding of what's happening.

To digress a bit, a poll has shown that the life expectancy of China's intellectuals is fifty-eight years, which is ten years less than the average life expectancy among the population at large. In my department few teachers are in good health. They aren't given regular medical check-ups and it's very difficult for them to see a doctor.

Up to now, I've published seven books on various subjects, including one on the study of classical Chinese literature, and three on the psychology in the arts and literature. I also have published seventy full-length papers. For me, writing an article is a creative effort rather than merely an accumulation of knowledge.

Some scholars say: "One should concentrate on reading books when one is young and begin writing articles when one is fifty." I don't think this is right. You cannot separate creativity from learning.

One acquires knowledge just like one buys meat or vegetables. One writes an article just like one cooks a dish. Different cooks make different dishes. And one must cook the meat or vegetables before he can enjoy them.

Knowledge is strength. But it's strength only when it's used. china's education has long neglected the application of knowledge as well as the nurturing of creative thinking.

In the past twenty years, I've engaged in many fields including literary theory, aesthetics, modern literature, classics, news writing, the study of ancient books, studies on calligraphy, and psychology in art and literature. Some people call me an "all-rounder" and ask me why I carry on so much research work. I tell them that I was forced to do this or that.

My experience in life hasn't been smooth. In 1957, because I openly expressed my views on social conditions in China, I was labeled a "rightist" and ousted from my teaching post. At that time, I was an assistant to Professor Wang Yao who was teaching modern literature. When that happened, I had to collect data for others in the reference room.

At that time, I was very lonely. No one talked to me, and I suffered a great deal mentally.

In 1959, I returned to my teaching post. From that year till 1965, I was assistant to Professor You Guo'en in teaching classics. In 1971, I was assigned to teach news writing, and in 1980, I began to lecture on psychology in Chinese art and literature. My feeling is that if you do things well, you'll come to like what you're doing.

My character has been influenced by my parents and my education. I was born in the city of Wuxi in Jiangsu Province in East China. My father was a shop assistant. My mother was a practitioner of Chinese medicine. She wrote a good hand, and had a good understanding of ancient Chinese culture, teaching me many things when I was young.

I received my primary and high school education in my native hometown. I was at the top of my class at Furen High School, and wasn't charged tuition there. English was an important part of the high school curriculum there. We could write simple articles in English when we graduated from that high school. However, I've forgotten much of the language.

I was admitted into Beijing University shortly after I graduated from my high school in 1951. Four years later, I graduated and became employed by my university.

Long years of education and competition have become a way of life for me. I want to continue to do my best.

Part Ten
Learning

Vocational School Student: Yuan Jun

Where there's a will, there's a way. I'm sure I've a will, but I'm afraid I haven't found the way yet. Maybe I'll find it in the Year of Dragon.

Junior high school graduates in China used to regard the senior high school as their only way out, because senior high school was the only passage to a college diploma that would secure a job for life. Back in 1980, the ratio of those enrolled in senior high schools to those enrolled in vocational schools was 3.68:1.

Although most of the teenagers still aim at entrance into highly competitive and selective institutions of higher learning, their interests are more diversified as they have more alternatives. More and more general senior high schools have become institutes of vocational training. By the end of 1986, the ratio of total student enrollments in high school versus the corresponding enrollment in vocational schools changed to 1.25:1, which the total number of vocational schools increased to 11,969, 2.5 times the 1986 figure.

Yuan Jun, nineteen, is one of the 3.5 million vocational students throughout China. She is a third-year cooking student at Beijing No.103 Vocational Senior High School, located at Xiannongtan down from bustling Qianmen Street.

Growing up in an "open-minded" family, as she puts it,

she gives an impression of confidence when she talks about herself and other things. With a chubby face, she takes after her fifty-year-old mother, who retired from the Beijing Electronic Tube Factory. Her father, fifty, used to be a serviceman in the Chinese Air Force and now is a manager of a small hotel in Beijing's Xuanwu District.

She is the second of three children in the family. Her elder sister is a kindergarten teacher and graduate of a vocational school. Her younger brother is studying food processing at a vocational school. The three children all have been vocationally involved, as the father said.

It's true that I'm eager to make my own living and can't wait to start a real life; but at the thought of the rigorous life ahead of me, my heart pounds. I wonder if other teens have the same feeling.

When sitting in the classroom, I often looked out the windows and don't concentrate enough on the books before me. But when I'm out in the "real" life, I imagine I'd prefer to be a student forever. This is what often troubles me. My mind is just like a swaying pendulum.

Three years ago, when I finished my studies at a junior high school, I went to Beijing No.103 Vocational Senior High School to learn cooking skills. "Vocational" doesn't sound attractive to many high school students. I also had dreamed of being a university student. But I found my grades in junior high school were just average. I said to my parents that it might be a waste of time for me to study further in a high school in preparation for a college education, and I realized it would be wise to be a vocational school student.

My parents didn't object to my decision. Daddy said, "Your mother and I won't force you to accept our ideas. However, you must be convinced about your decision, since it's you that have made it." I understood what they meant. I told myself that I must work hard and bring credit to them.

After all, it was the first important decision I'd ever made for myself. I was only sixteen years old at the time. I felt grateful to my parents, because they were supporting me instead of trying to interfere. I'll be much more grateful to them if I succeed. And I believe that I'll succeed.

Many of my former classmates were surprised at my decision to be a chef. They said the job wasn't respectable, especially for a girl. Some advised me to go with them to a training school for Beijing hotel and restaurant attendants. I knew it is easier for a girl to be a waitress, but I still wanted to be a chef, because when I grew old, I can still be a chef while a wrinkled old woman could no longer work as a waitress. Anyway each one has her own ideas about life.

Frankly, will-power is needed for girls aspiring to be involved in the cooking trade. In our country, chefs are often called in a derogatory way *chuzi*. But I don't care what I'm called. Someone has to do the work. I'd do it even if no one else would.

Some of the girls in my class are embarrassed to tell their friends that they are being trained as chefs, not because they are afraid of not finding boyfriends. They will have no difficulty if that is what they want. Rather, they are embarrassed to be considered inferior to other people.

Not many girls are being trained to be chefs. Only thirteen out of the seventy students in our class are girls. In Beijing there are few qualified women chefs, the trade having long been dominated by men. I don't know exactly why, but I'm proud of myself and that I think of my job as a challenge in a man-dominated vocation.

It's often said that people become dissatisfied with their jobs as time passes. It's strange, but I haven't. After nearly three years of learning, I find it satisfying to be able to produce an artful hors d'oeuvre. I'm delighted to see that I can cut vegetables and meat into different shapes and arrange them into exquisite designs. And I'm very proud when diners are pleased with what I've done for them.

In June 1986, when I was a first-year student, I was chosen to take part in a cuisine competition in which twelve Beijing vocational schools took part. I was chosen just a week before the competition started and I was very nervous. My teachers and classmates encouraged and supported me. What could I do but say to myself, "Go ahead, you silly girl!"

In the competition I was to prepare cucumber, eggs, Beijing duck breast, and other ingredients into a design of two parrots. I forgot practically everything as soon as the start signal went off. In the first few minutes, I felt my heart go bang, bang, bang, as if it was bursting, and my hands trembled. I tried hard in vain to calm myself. I was really angry with myself. "What are you nervous about?" I asked myself. Strange enough, that question seemed to have composed me. I looked around at the other competitors. They seemed to be in the same state too. "No better than me," I thought and my hands began working dexterously.

It took me one hour and fourteen minutes to complete the dish, sixteen minutes ahead of schedule, but not the quickest. My heart pounded again as the judges came up to examine the pair of parrots I'd made. I went to a corner and sat down with anxiety. There were seven students, including me, competing for the first prize. "It'll be okay even if I don't get a place," I said to my classmates sitting beside me.

Suddenly I heard someone congratulating me. It was our schoolmaster. I jumped up and ran over to him. "You've won first prize," he said excitedly, as if it were he who had taken part in the competition. Someone told me later he had been pacing up and down in the hall and looking at his watch frequently. He's a kindly elderly man.

The honor was much appreciated, but something else made me even happier. I was unaware that a top-class woman chef, Wu Jinhua, from the Beijing Cuisine Association, had been watching the competition. When the competition was over, I was introduced to her. Mrs. Wu looked at me for a while and said, "Please be my apprentice."

I couldn't believe my ears. It was unheard of that a top-class chef would offer to take a cooking student on as an apprentice. This was what many young students dreamed of. To be her apprentice would be a great honor to me.

But I wasn't in a position to do so, for I already had been contracted to the Beijing Steel and Iron Works, which had paid 4,500 yuan to the school. If I left and became an apprentice to Mrs. Wu, I'd have to pay the school back. And where could I get the money? But I made up my mind that some day I'd be a top-class chef like her.

Chinese cuisine requires a lot of training, and it's not easy to become a master of it. I'm now learning to do assorted cold dishes, which call for great skills in cutting, cooking, and arranging ingredients together. The more I study, the more I see what's meant by the saying "Knowledge is infinite."

A few months ago, the school leadership asked me if I'd like to stay as a teacher after graduation. The school would pay 4,500 yuan to the Works if I agreed. I talked with my parents, and they said it was up to me. Well, I had to make another decision.

My elder sister graduated from a vocational school and is now a teacher in a kindergarten. From what I saw and heard, I knew that a school teacher doesn't earn as big a salary as a chef. Who wouldn't want to earn more money? My parents aren't rich: their monthly income is only about 250 yuan. In recent years, they've spent much of their earnings on my studies. Besides, my younger brother also needs financial support for his studies at a vocational school. I knew my parents would prefer that I work for the International Service Center run by the Works. I also knew that they've sacrificed a lot all these years for their children. All parents in the world would like their children to be better off than they are.

So I hesitated for a few days. I talked to my close friends, but none of them could give me advice. Finally I decided to stay at the school. I know I won't earn much, but I'll have time to do some research on Chinese cuisine while teaching. Frankly, what also made me stay was the school's promise to send me to a cooking college for further studies this year.

Now I'm apprenticed to Li Gang, a first class chef. He is also a teacher in our school. Mr. Li is well known in Beijing's cuisine circles for his outstanding skill in cutting and preparing artistic dishes. I'm pleased that he took me on as an apprentice, and am grateful that he passed on all his cooking skills to me without preserve.

Students at vocational schools study many subjects besides their vocation. Our curriculum includes Chinese, English, math, physics, and music. There are as many subjects as in an ordinary high school, although our school emphasizes on cuisine.

My teachers are very kind to me. They not only have taught me general knowledge, but also ways to deal with life. I hope they'll remain as helpful when I'm no longer a student. At school, I'm often told that life is complicated and that dealing with people is far more difficult than learning a skill. I really can't understand why people can't treat each other with respect.

In my spare time I like to listen to music and hum pop songs as many teens do. Sometimes I paint. Last year I went twice a week to learn painting at an art school. The painting class began at seven p.m. and ended at nine in the evening. I had to hurry, for our school had opened a dining hall and I had to work there until six p.m. Many times I arrived at the art school out of breath. I paid my own tuition, of course, but I cared little how much money I spent on my studies.

I remember my mother once gave me some money to buy a watch. But I wanted to spend the money on a camera. When she objected, I explained I'd manage without a watch, but not without a camera. I'd use it to take pictures of artful cold dishes done by well-known chefs. Dad said he wouldn't say no, and Mother gave in in the end.

I like to browse in bookstores on whatever is

related to cuisine, including Chinese food health care. I'm aware that my knowledge is very limited. I think time is best spent on what will add to my talent. I hate wasting my time on something like window shopping or gossiping.

Sometimes I read magazines, especially the Chinese *Readers' Digest*. I found it interesting and philosophical. I seldom read popular novels. My classmates do. When they talk about what they've read, I find myself ignorant of the subject and stand aside, listening silently.

As a vocational school student, I must have practical experience in cooking before I'm qualified for a job. Recently, I haven't been able to find the time to do things I'd like to do. Since I agreed to stay on as a teacher, I'm no longer treated as a student. The school has assigned several students under my charge, and sent me to work as a chef in a new school-run restaurant. The practical work is good for my training, but bad for my sparetime hobbies. Since I do not finish in the restaurant before 7:30 in the evening, I have to stop going to my painting class. I'm tired when I get home and am in no mood to read.

I'm the class monitor and am popular with my classmates. They, especially girls, often tell me their troubles; I also like to confide in them.

We talk about anything that interests us. Sometimes about boyfriends. It isn't shameful to talk about it, is it? But we have to talk about it behind our teachers' back because the school fordids students to have anything to do with the opposite sex. I think such a rule is necessary. It protects students from the harm of teenage love. But I have heard some students say that many celebrated people have had early romantic relationship which had been beneficial to their work.

Some say early love is nothing but promiscuous friendship. I don't think it's fair to say so. Although some students don't have a serious attitude towards friendship, not all of them are frivolous and empty-headed about love. Besides, early love doesn't mean early marriage, does it?

I find some older persons don't understand us teenagers. They often look on us as little children and expect us to follow their ways as they have followed that of their predecessors. I say there really is a lack of understanding between generations. We need communication, don't we?

You might think from what I say that I've a boyfriend. To tell the truth, so far I haven't found an ideal person to be my boyfriend. Also, I think it's a little early for me to direct my attention to the matter. Once I talked about it with my mother. She advised: "If you make a choice in a hurry, what will you do when there's someone better than him?" I think I'm well advised to wait until I find the person who will be my "Mr. Right."

Once I had a chat with a boy classmate. He asked me what kind of man I'd look for as a life companion. I didn't answer him at once, but asked him what he expected of a girl. He said he'd prefer a non-career-oriented woman. I replied that I'd look for a man who is career-oriented.

"See, girl? You still have a long way to go," I thought to myself. When I told my parents about it, they encouraged me by telling me that "where there is a will, there is a way." I'm sure I've a will, but I'm afraid I haven't found the way yet. Maybe I'll find it in the Year of Dragon, which is believed to help those who help themselves.

University Student: Cheng Ming

I'm worried about my future.

Twenty-two-year-old Cheng Ming is one of the nearly two million college students in China. What makes him different from many Chinese students is the fact that he is among the few in China who have tried two or more disciplines in four years and that he is studying at one of the country's best universities.

Beijing University, or *Beida* as it is usually referred in Chinese, was the standard bearer of several large-scale students' movements that shook Old China. The "May Fourth" movement of 1919 was the progenitor of modern-day Chinese political movements. Its slogan was "Down With Feudalism, Down With Imperialist Aggression!" The "December 9th" movement in 1935 reflected the Chinese people's wrath in the face of the Japanese invasion. In both of these and other movements, *Beida* students played a leading role.

Cheng Ming, who is now a senior, started as a freshman in the mathematics department. Finding the curricula of the mathematics department too structured and rigid, he switched to the department of Chinese language and literature.

Cheng shares a room with six other students in the students' dorm. As there are four bunk beds in the room, there is one vacant bed left for the students to stack their trunks and other belongings on. There are only four small desks, making it necessary for some of them to find classrooms to study in the evening.

Tuition and lodging are free. But Cheng spends about 100 yuan on food and books and other expenses a month. Fifty yuan comes from his father, who is a farmer, twenty from the university and forty yuan he earns working as a waiter in the students' cafeteria each Saturday night.

I was born the son of a farmer in Jiangning County, Jiangsu Province. I'm the first college student for generations in my family. When I passed the college entrance examination and was admitted to Beijing University, my mother was so overjoyed that she cried.

When I graduated from the high school, father and mother had an argument over whether I'd continue my education. Father wanted me to stay at home because I was the eldest child in the family and because my sister and brother were still too young to offer him much help. What was more, he said, providing me with a college education would be too much of a financial burden on the family.

Mother however insisted that I'd go since I'd done well in high school, saying that I'd have a better future if I became a learned man. Any farming family'd gladly send their son to a college if they thought he'd "make the grade," she pointed out.

Although neither of my parents has had much education, both of them have great respect for scholars. They hold many different views, such as on the question of my education.

So when I left home for Beijing, I swore to myself that I'd work hard to live up to my mother's expectations.

In my high school days I was good at mathematics and aspired to become a great mathematician. So I chose mathematics as my major.

I was amazed to find there were so many extracurricular activities on the campus—lectures, speech and poetry competitions, clubs, snackshops, dances, and athletic events. Yet, I couldn't participate in many of these activities because the curriculum was so demanding in the mathematics department that I worked like a robot and had little time left to my own disposal. There's a color TV set on each floor of our dorms. I enjoyed watching ball games, but I couldn't because I'd too much homework to do in the evening.

After the first year, I decided to switch to the department of Chinese language and literature. I applied and took another examination. Thanks to my deep interest in Chinese literature, I passed.

The Chinese language and literature department was much easier and more interesting. I don't have as much homework and I've far fewer classes to attend. We've about four courses each semester and this semester we've only one. All I need to do is read, read, and read.

I also like modern Western writers. James Joyce is one of my favorite writers and I can recite whole passages from T.S. Eliot's *The Wasterland*. The only regret is that I read all these works in Chinese translation. I'd like to read them in the original. That's why I'm working hard on my English. The school provides English lessons only the first two years. Nonetheless, I'm studying it on my own now.

Beida provides many elective courses. Since I transferred to the present department, I've taken about ten elective courses, among them Western philosophy. The young associate professor from the philosophy department is well-read and very eloquent. His lectures're very good. Whenever he gives a lecture, there're people standing outside the classroom windows listening to it.

Western philosophy is much in vogue among *Beida* students nowadays. Some time ago there was a Freud cult. Then there was a time many studied Sartre. And now Neitzsche is a hot topic of conversation in the students' dorms.

As a literature student, I read extensively and indiscriminately. I even think conversation and traveling are forms of learning for a student of literature. One of the best periods of the day is when all seven of us in the same room lie in bed talking freely after the lights are turned off at night, letting our conversations drift from one subject to another.

Some time ago one of our school-mates was killed by some hooligans from a nearby village. Students in *Beida* took part in protests and demonstrations. I think the protests were justified. Not long after the culprits were brought to court and the murderer was sentenced to death and executed.

I didn't take part in the demonstration, because I've my graduation to think of. Now some departments're very choosy in employing college graduates. They have to, because many are already overstaffed. We college graduates are also choosy. I was an idealist when I first entered this university. After four years of study, I've become very practical. I'm not a mature writer. I don't want to be a high school teacher, a job very easy to find, because a high school teacher's pay is low and the workload is heavy. I hope I can find a job in a Chinese-foreign joint venture, but it won't be easy, I know. So I'm worried about my future.

Nowadays both the government and educational experts are talking about educational reforms, which, in my opinion, are urgently needed. The curriculum should be more flexible. The contents of teaching materials should be constantly updated. If the state stops assigning jobs for college graduates, conditions should be created for all graduates to compete on an equal footing so that people without "connections" like me won't be losers.

The state has been issuing three types of monthly allowances—20, 15, and 10 yuan—to students from low-income families. Now a scholarship system is going to gradually replace the allowance system to give greater incentive to academic achievement. Now even those with state allowances feel pinched, with prices going up so fast. So the authorities are encouraging students to work their way through college. In addition to the cafe where I work on Saturday nights, there're students running a laundry and working in stores selling food, clothes, and stationery. Some students earn money by tutoring high school students.

I've a girl friend who's working as a tax collector in Jiangsu Province. She was my high school classmate. She's pretty. At first her parents were opposed to our relationship because they felt that I was too short and dark. But she loves me. Now I'm thinking about how to get her to live with me in Beijing if I get a job in the capital. Or is it maybe better for me to go work where she is? I haven't decided yet.

Part Eleven

To Search and Research

Geologist: Chang Chengfa

If I'd another lifetime, I guess I'd choose to study geology again.

Chang Chengfa looks like a typical Chinese intellectual: thin, greying, uncombed hair and a pair of narrow eyes staring through gold-rimmed glasses.

Now fifty-nine, he was one of the first college students trained in New China. He is associated with the Chinese Academy of Sciences and is among the 1,570 specialists who have been involved in eight major comprehensive, multi-disciplinary surveys of the Qinghai-Tibet Plateau conducted by the Academy since 1951.

Although he doesn't remember exactly how many expeditions he has made to Tibet, he says he has been there at least a dozen times. But his scientific explanation of the formation and evolution of the world's highest, largest, and youngest plateau is well-known and widely accepted in geological circles. Professor Augusto Gansser, a Swiss expert on the Himalayas, has called him the man who "knows Tibet better than any other scientist alive."

We met in his office in a five-storey building in the northern suburbs of Beijing. Crammed in the matchbox-like building are five institutes, including the Geological Institute where he works. He shares the 30-square-meter room with four other colleagues. Ink and pens seem to be all the "office equipment" these scientists possess.

Today, it's much easier to get to Tibet—it's barely a day by plane. When I first went there in 1960, things were quite different. The train terminated at Lanzhou, the capital of Gansu Province. From there, we began a truck ride that was to last a fortnight. I wasn't sitting in the cab. We rode in the wagon, which was temporarily covered over with canvas.

I felt sick because of the altitude—which in Tibet averages 4,000 meters above sea level. My head swam. I vomitted many times, and had no appetite. As there was no medicine for altitude sickness, I'd only suffer in silence. A person seems to become better after the suffering gets beyond a certain point. That was my case. Strange to say, the times I went to Tibet when I was young, I became very sick; but as I grew older, I felt better. Possibly, growing older dulls certain physiological reactions.

Lhasa has always impressed me as a beautiful city, one surrounded by hills, from which granite was quarried to build the many edifices in this city which were unique in their use of this material. In 1960, Tibet was a rather bleak and desolate area. Nowadays, we ride jeeps to do field work, while in those days we'd only hire horses for our trips.

The saddles were uncomfortable and it was easy to fall out of them. I fell down frequently. There were many burrows on the ground, which often made the horses stumble and gave the rider quite a jolt. Sometimes, it wasn't possible to find a way for the horse, and then it was necessary to walk on foot. We spent the night in a local folk's house or in our own tent.

The most scary thing on the plateau? I'd say it was crossing a river. There were no bridges, and our ferry-boat was nothing but an ox-hide raft, with a capacity of no more than three persons. The river was full of rapids, and the water icy, since its source was melted snow from the mountains. A fall into the river could be fatal. The frequent thunder in the summer was also quite frightening.

Wild animals? I never saw any of the legendary "snowmen" or "lake monsters." I don't believe they exist. I definitely have never seen one.

During the first few trips, we carried our own food, which included *zanba* (a kind of roasted *qingke* barley flour, the staple food of Tibetans) and butter. Although they smelled bad, I could stand the taste. Later, we had a jeep, in which we'd carry cooking utensils. And still later, we were able to cook rice. But of course we couldn't do without the pressure cooker. Green vegetables were a rarity. You can't eat canned food all the time, can you?

The tools we geologists use are rather simple. My special interest is tectonics, or geological structural features. I observe the types of rocks that I see on my expenditions, hammer off interesting samples, and then bring them back and analyze them in the lab.

As a scientist, I'm not easily enthused. But once you spot something unusual, something you'd long expected, but never seen, you can get excited—such as a certain kind of basalt. This dark-colored rock of volcanic origin with its willow-like pattern is normally found at the bottom of the ocean. I was delighted to find examples of it along the Yarlung Zangbo River. This part of Tibet was a sea bed before it rose as the result of the collision of continental plates three million years ago.

Information about the plateau was scarce when we first went to Tibet. Before our expedition, only one person of our institute had been to the area, such as Professor Li Pu who went to Tibet in 1951 with the People's Liberation Army. He'd done basic research on the age of the strata, the distribution of rocks, and the areas having mineral deposits. His records still remain valuable. But his research had been limited to the eastern and central portion of Tibet. He never got to where he went later. As for foreign scholars, they'd done some work mainly in the western corner, near Xinjiang.

Chinese geologists have done the most research on the Qinghai-Tibet Plateau, which has been the most extensive. It's benefited not only China, but the whole international geoscientific community as well.

I didn't choose Tibet as a place to study. It was assigned to me. But my interest grew as the research progressed, and I became more intrigued.

I enrolled in the Geological Department of Beijing University in 1950. Upon graduation in 1953, I was asked to remain for a three-year graduate course, given by Russians. My final paper, I remember, was about the petroleum structure of the Sichuan Basin.

In 1956, I joined the Geological Institute. My first assignment was to go to Qaidam Basin in Qinghai Province to study the petroleum structure. The following year I went to the Altun Mountains, which extend from Qinghai to Xinjiang. I also edited China's first tectonic chart.

Now that I'd been almost to the border of Tibet, my curiosity about the place multiplied. The Qinghai-Tibet Plateau is vast, covering an area of 2.2 million square kilometers, or one fifth of our land territory. And it contained answers to many urgent questions. I wanted to know, for instance, how and when such an immense land, at such an altitude, was formed, what its features were, and the impact of such a formation on the surrounding environment.

And in 1960, my curiosity was rewarded when the institute asked me to join the Academy's expedition to the plateau. Since then, I've made a trip to Tibet nearly every year.

Usually we go to Tibet early in May, and return home in September. We've no Sundays off while working in the fields. And you don't have time to miss home when you're buried in work. I used to write to my family once a month, but it took at least a month and sometimes even two, for the letter to reach them.

I was married in 1963, when I was thirty-five. Many people of my generation tended to marry later. My wife, Guo Bozhi, studied agro-sciences. We'd known each other since childhood. She's had to shoulder most of the family burden, since I'm frequently away from home. I didn't even know when my boy was born. And for nearly twenty years since we were married, we've been apart, since she didn't work in Beijing. She brought up our son and daughter single-handedly. And the children got used to my coming and going.

The Cultural Revolution? Of course it influenced our research to some extent. We'd planned to stay through the year in Tibet in 1966. But the political conditions interrupted it halfway through. Back at the institute, we'd nothing to do but have meetings and study sessions. We grouped into "companies" and "platoons" and some cab drivers became our "commanders." The dominating idea in those days was "the workers must supervise everything," you know.

However, the scientific survey on the Tibetan Plateau remained a major program of the Academy. There was always somebody in the Academy in charge of the work even in those years. We made yearly trips to Tibet in 1967, 1968, and 1969. Even the Gang of Four (the four leftist leaders who actually dominated the political scene in China during the Cultural Revolution) needed our achievements for propagandistic purposes. Once what we were doing was a page one story in the *People's Daily*.

I went to cadre school in 1977, when the Cultural Revolution was just over. We were among the last group. The "ultra-leftists" insisted that everyone partake of that "experience." Since I'd missed the "lesson," I had to make it up. I didn't care. I wasn't afraid of physical labor. I'd worked in the fields when I was a child. In the cadre school I planted rice. And I was a pace-setter at it. But I didn't stay long. A few months later, I was recalled to meet with some visiting foreign colleagues.

I was born in a poor village in Shanxi Province in North China. My father died when I was a baby. We were a poor rural family, but I loved to read. I was attending primary school when the Japanese invaded China. I fled from the invaders with my uncles, who were small businessmen. We walked all the way from Shanxi to Henan, and later to Shaanxi in the Northwest. I kept reading on the way. Finally we settled in Hanzhong.

On that hard journey I was fascinated by the shapes of the mountains I saw on the way. I dearly wanted to know how they'd been formed. It was probably then that I became intrigued, without realizing it, by geology.

After many years of research, I think we've got a rather good understanding of the Qinghai-Tibet Plateau. Our project has won a special national award for research in the natural sciences. It's involved scientists of many disciplines, such as those in geography, botany, biology, zoology, physiology, and others.

Money for the award? They said we'd get some money, but it never happened. Perhaps it would have been impossible to divide the money among so many participants. My principal concern is whether the theories I've expounded in papers are challenged or widely accepted. I think my achievements are reflected in my papers.

My hair turned grey at an early age. And my teeth aren't good. Several of them have broken off at the gum. Some of my colleagues have lost all their teeth. People say it's a result of working so long in Tibet.

Ours is basic research, and our achievements are not totally understood by many. I became the first Chinese member of the French Society of Geology and of the European Federation of Geosciences. But few seem to know me here in China. It's hard to tell why. Basic research doesn't yield the immediate economic results that applied research does, and you can't get rich by publishing papers. But for me, it's all right, as long as the work gets done. From a long-term point of view, however, basic research is the foundation of our work. Without a solid base, applied research is useless.

The trouble now is that you need money for whatever you do. Even in your own institute, you have to pay for xeroxing, lab analysis, and so on.

If I had another lifetime? I guess I'd choose to

study geology again. Now that the research on the Qinghai-Tibet Plateau is almost completed, I'm studying the Hengduan Mountains, which are an extension of the plateau. I hope afterwards to have time to study the areas in Southern China, to obtain an overall view of China's geological structure. I also expect to publish a book on the plateau in English.

I don't have much time for hobbies. I enjoy watching ball games and traditional Chinese operas when I'm not doing field work. But I've managed to keep fit. I live on the twelfth floor of an apartment building, but I never use the elevator unless I'm in a hurry, like keeping an urgent appointment. I prefer to climb up and down the stairs, step by step, and I never feel tired.

First Tibetan Ph.D in China: Gaile

I'm interested in trying to explain the behavior, attitudes, and beliefs of Tibetan communities in China today.

He is the only Tibetan with a doctoral degree among the 3,870,000 Tibetans in China. Born into a serf's family in 1948, Gaile lived up to his mother's expectations of him to become a lama. He did so for two reasons: his dedication to Tibetan studies and his Tibetan origin. He now is working at the Beijing Research Center of Tibetan Studies after having graduated from Zhongshan University with a doctoral degree in culture anthropology two years ago.

Gaile has worked out the most comprehensive and systematic analysis of the origins of the Tibetan people, as well as their historical and cultural relationships with other nationalities, either inside or outside China. Now leading a four-member group of the center who are devoted to a five-year research program starting in 1987, Gaile has been shuttling between Beijing and Tibet, hoping to gather enough information for the study of the feudal serf system that existed in pre-1956 Tibet.

Gaile married his classmate in 1971. They have a daughter and a son. His family lives in a two-room apartment on the first floor of a three-storey building belonging to the center.

I don't know my birthday, as is the case with most of the Tibetans. I think this is a result of the primitiveness of the nationality. I haven't seen my father since he left us to work for another serf-owner (after I was born). My mother was a devout Lamaist believer. She couldn't read or write, but she thought it would be great if I'd learn to read and write and become a lama. As the only son of the family, she placed all her hopes on me. And I think she also regarded it as a matter of pride for the family.

When I was seven, I went to study elementary Tibetan language with a monk in a serf-owner's private temple. I started by murmuring Buddhist chants day after day though I didn't understand a single word or sound. I learned to write by practicing the Tibetan alphabet on a home-made blackboard that was coated with yak butter and ash. There were no pencils or paper, and I had to practice writing with a piece of wood. It was like writing on sand. I was terribly afraid of entering my teacher's dark room. It was full of portraits of gods and ghosts, whose shadows seemed to be moving in the dim, flickering light of a butter lamp. I kept running away from the "school" because the teacher beat me a great deal, but each time my mother sent me back. She was quite determined that I'd become a lama.

Things changed a great deal in 1956 during the period of democratic reforms. New public schools were set up by the new government in the town. I was the first in my village to study at the new school. Other people were hesitant to send their children to the school and took a wait-and-see attitude toward the new government. But my mother was sure of one thing: nothing was more important for me than to go and study in a school with free room and board. I never realized that my early education was, in fact, made possible by my dear mother.

And I still feel sad about her death because I wasn't at her bedside when she was dying. I got her letter asking me to come back. I knew she expected to see me before she died. That was in 1967 when I was on my way home. But I was stranded for two months because the trains stopped running due to constant outbreaks of fighting between various "revolutionary" factions during the Cultural Revolution. You can easily imagine how desperate I was.

My career would be absolutely different if I hadn't attended a three-year special Tibetan-Chinese translation class at the Southwest China Institute for Nationalities in Chengdu in 1964 when I was just sixteen. This also was prompted by my mother. Other people had suggested that I work as a secretary in my hometown.

I got very interested in reading, especially books on history and literature. I read a history book written by a well-known scholar on the history of my hometown. Feeling that this book was quite mediocre, I said to myself: if something as mediocre as this could get published, then I certainly could, too. I've always been inquisitive and enjoyed reading. And I always have wanted to write something myself.

After I graduated from the translation class, I was assigned to work at a broadcasting station in Seda County which is next to my home county of Garze. I was there for ten years and got to know lots of stories about the area from the local people. I also had a chance to chat with former feudal landowners and tribal chiefs, who told me stories about the past. This will be a big boon, I think, for my future researches into Tibetan society.

Going to college was quite entraordinary in Seda

County. Usually, a person with a high-school diploma was considered well-educated. Many of my high-school classmates got a job after they graduated and became officials several years later. You can always become a "boss" after some time. I was then the secretary of the Communist Youth League Committee of the county. When I told some of my classmates that I was going to study at a college, they were excited and encouraged me. "Just let us have the jobs with power, and you can go on with your studies to become a scholar," they told me.

I passed the college entrance exam in 1977, which had been restored after a ten-year suspension, and was again admitted into the Southwest China Institute for Nationalities. I stayed there to study Chinese literature, but only for half a year, since the professors thought further study at the institute wouldn't be challenging enough for me and urged me to further my studies at a higher level. Again I passed the exam to enter the Chinese Academy of Social Sciences to study ethnology.

While preparing for the exam, I tried to find a book on Tibetan history and went to the Chengdu Municipal Library. Quite unexpectedly, there I found a terrific stock of valuable books on Tibet, all published before the founding of the People's Republic. I was elated and thought it would be far better to sit there and read, rather than cram for the upcoming exam. I skimmed all the books within two months. This was the first time I'd been able to read so many books on Tibet. Anyhow, I took the exam. The biggest benefit of this two-month reading program was that I began to look into historical issues critically, and with lots of questions.

My M.A. paper is, in fact, a historical record of Seda County. And almost half of the material was drawn from the notes I took during that period. While working on the thesis, I finished writing another book on the history of my hometown, Garze Autonomous Region, located in western Sichuan Province. It's mainly inhabited by Tibetans.

I feel that no matter what nationality you're, you can achieve something. Your ethnic origin doesn't matter very much as long as you work hard enough. When I was doing post-graduate work, all my classmates seemed to be better than I was. I had to learn classic Chinese and English from the beginning. It was really an all-work-no-play experience. I spent a lot of time on English, although it wasn't compulsory. I just felt that I'd be as competent as the others, despite the fact that I was a Tibetan and had a good command of the Tibetan language which, actually could have been considered a foreign language, too.

Let me tell you a college anecdote. A teacher at Zhongshan University suspected I'd been admitted just because I was a Tibetan and therefore was patronizing to me. He came to listen to my talk about my visit to Japan, because he wanted to listen to a Tibetan speaking Mandarin, and possibly to sneer. He didn't know that he'd be impressed by my talk. This experience again convinced me that I shouldn't lower my standards academically by using the excuse that I was a Tibetan.

I do enjoy scholastic life. To spend a whole day reading, thinking, and writing is most pleasant for me. And I always feel that I'm doing something of cultural value. I used to have a decent office in the Great Hall of the People when I was working for the

Nationalities Committee affiliated with the People's Congress. I then had a master's degree. But I soon found it wasn't the right place for me and decided to leave. The only way out then was to pursue further studies. I made a bargain with my boss there. I'd remain working there for the rest of my life if I failed the qualification exam. There was a large element of chance. But I won.

I prefer writing to speaking. I turned down an offer to stay and teach at Zhongshan University. And I seldom offer to give a lecture. I'm very nervous when speaking in public. I once stood about two hours on the platform, forgetting to sit on the chair beside me. And I forgot to smoke as well. This is remarkable since I'm a chain smoker. Listeners said my lectures were informative and interesting and I was flattered.

When engaged in writing, I want to be totally free of all interruptions. I shut myself in a room in Sichuan for over half a year to work on my doctoral dissertation. Only my friend had the key to my room and he brought me food every day.

Tibetan studies has always been the focus of my research efforts, and my personal interest is in explanations of the behavior, attitudes, and beliefs of the Tibetan communities in China today.

I don't agree with the belief that Tibet's becoming more and more influenced by Han Chinese culture, since no culture can develop, either economically or culturally, in isolation from other cultures. This is the case with Tibet. The assimilation process is inevitable. For example, Tibetans tend to wear jackets rather than the traditional long robes, because it's more casual and convenient to do so, while at the same time, remaining 100 percent Tibetan. For me, a Tibetan living among Hans feels no culture shock, but I can't deny that I really feel more at home when I get back to my native county and associate with those I knew before. They've an honesty, understanding, and mentality found nowhere else. I think that Tibetans are proud of their origin, but this doesn't mean they'd isolate themselves from the outside world. And the key to the modernization of Tibet is the introduction of education which will bring with it new ideas, new ways of thinking, and better ways of living.

Religion and freedom of belief have long been a controversial issue. Religion in Tibet is mainly concerned with Lamaism, which I think more or less hinders, rather than helps, the development of Tibet.

A survey conducted by the Secretariat of the Party showed that belief in religion's increasing. Children usually follow the examples set by their parents. However, the more education these children receive, the less likely they're to believe in Lamaism. I myself was brought up in a religious environment. I listened to my mother tell stories about gods and ghosts that had been brought down through the generations. Later, after I'd been exposed to books and other things, my interest in religion began to wane. Everyone must have some sort of spiritual dependence, and religion's one of these. The Tibetan people's practice of going to lamaseries and engaging in religious activities is comparable to urban residents going to movies, parks, and parties.

I don't believe that Tibetans are inferior to any other nationality in any way. Tibet itself is indeed a living saga and full of mysteries. People there are unique in many respects. I attended an international seminar on Tibet Studies in Hungary and visited the Soviet Union on the way. I was truly surprised to find that so many foreigners were learning the Tibetan language and studying Tibetan history and culture. It's a pity that most of them have never been able to visit Tibet even once. Many of the foreign scholars of Tibetan Studies have met few real Tibetans, and they're drawing conclusions out of the written material available to them. At the same time, I find that European scholars of Tibetan Studies are more research-oriented, while those in the United States seem to be more opinionated. I think the latter is a result of the Dalai Lama's propaganda efforts in American newspapers and other media. I think that Chinese scholars of Tibetan Studies should be more active in their study of Tibet and listen to more opinions and disagreements.

Tibetans enjoy a great deal of cultural, and historical heritage, and this heritage is second only to the Han nationality in China. In the study of this rich heritage, I don't want to follow anyone. Those historical records will keep me busy the rest of my life doing original research.

Prospector: Zhou Genfeng

It's a pity we devoted too much time to physical labor and political movements. If we hadn't, I'd be a better geologist today.

Twenty-five years ago, Zhou Genfeng left her home province in Southeast China, a renowned "land of fish and rice," for the oilfields in the desolate areas of the Northeast and then the Central South and Northwest.

Today, neither the sun-burnt face, nor the strong arms of this fifty-one-year-old woman, nor anything else about her except her still graceful bearing resembles that of the slim, delicate girl in a photograph treasured by her husband.

She gave birth to two children while in the oilfield and suffered a miscarriage because of overwork.

she works in the Zhejiang Provincial Petrogeological Brigade, one of the institutions jointly owned by each of the twenty-nine provinces, municipalities and ethnic autonomous regions on China's mainland.

My kids're crazy about this New Year's cake made of rice and preserved fruit. I made it myself. Since we've a family reunion only around the Spring Festival (Chinese lunar New Year), I do as much cooking then as possible. Their father's a terrible cook. He also is a geologist.

I've worked at five oilfields:

From August 1963 to September 1969 at the Daqing Oilfield in the Northeast, the biggest in China;

From September 1969 to November 1985 at the Jianghan Oilfield in Hubei Province in South Central China;

From the end of 1976 to mid-1977 at the Nanyang Oilfield in Henan Province in Central China;

From May 1986 to May 1987 at the Shengli Oilfield in Shandong Province in East China;

And from May 1987 up to now at the Xinjiang Oilfield in the Northwest.

The development of any oilfield in China involves personnel from throughout the country. I came to this present brigade in 1986. Members're constantly on the move, for no oil's been found in this province.

Most geological institutions are more or less "melting pots" since members come from different places. Due to the nature of our work, we go to all parts of the country and live and work in rather isolated communities. We're familiar with, and are accustomed to, remote areas. Once an oilfield's developed, it's time to leave for another.

Even our offices and apartments are located in the far suburbs of Hangzhou (capital of Zhejiang Province). Before the Spring Festival, I went downtown to do some shopping. I felt somewhat of a stranger in the hustle and bustle, although the streets haven't changed that much since the time I was in college and would go there quite often.

In many families living in these apartments, the husbands and wives work in the same brigade. Sometimes the wife may be living in the country.

Few people would marry a geologist, which is understandable. No one likes to get married and be alone most of the year. And a geologist has so little chance to mingle with others that he usually either marries a girl in his own community or a country girl from his home village, if he comes from the countryside. In the latter case, it all depends on the man's luck whether he can transfer his wife's *hukou* (household registration) from the rural area to the city, since China strictly limits its urban population.

My husband and I were classmates in the mathematics department of Zhejiang University. We were married in 1963, right after graduation. At that time, the state called on youngsters to take part in economic construction in remote areas. Many young people were eager to go. In fact, I was excited about it, believing that the further I went, the happier I'd be. Life in the Gobi Desert, beyond the horizon, despite its hardships, would be romantic, I thought. My husband agreed to go with me, inspired by his own ambitions rather than by romanticism.

But Old Li, my husband, wouldn't admit that it was ambition: he said he was going there out of a sense of responsibility, as a husband, towards me.

Three years older than I'm, Old Li is now director of the geological institute under the brigade.

Two weeks after our wedding celebrations in my hometown, Lanxi, and his, Shaoxing—both in Zhejiang Province—we started out for the Daqing Oilfield in Heilongjiang, the northernmost province. It took us six days.

My husband says that we didn't know it was an oilfield until we reached there because it was referred to as No.14 State-Run Farm for security reasons. The real name was officially revealed two years later, when large-scale production increased China's petrol output significantly.

Well, I was prepared for hardships. But I didn't have any specific expectations. The only image of it that I had was a vast grassland. It was there that I learned how hard it's to start from scratch.

I studied mathematics in college. Assigned to the geological department, I changed to fluid mechanics, which was more useful to the oilfields. The transition, which only took a year or so, wasn't very difficult. What I found more difficult was getting used to life out in the fields.

Southerners eat a lot of rice. At Daqing, we'd nothing but *gaoliang* (Chinese sorghum) and potatoes. It began to snow early in October. So vegetables were rare, not to mention meat and fish. We lived in earth-packed dormitories with each room shared by ten persons.

Since there were just a few married couples among the young people, on weekends, our leaders would "expel" the bachelors to the offices to give us some privacy. Our eldest daughter resulted from this.

A month before delivery, I went back to my hometown accompanied by my husband. He returned to the oilfield two nights later. A month after the child's birth, I left her in my mother's care and set off northwards.

Work in the oilfields was extremely busy. My job was to survey and determine the exact positions of drilling water-flooding wells. It required a lot of fieldwork, as well as office analysis. It was usually very busy and we didn't have time to think of home until we were too tired to continue.

We got a real home—a 7-square-meter earth-packed house—in 1965 when my mother brought my one-year-old daughter to Daqing. The oilfield provided the house for us. The only furniture was an earth-rammed bed and a box in which we kept our bowls and chopsticks. Our simple clothes were put under the pillows. Shocked at the conditions, my mother wept the first night of her arrival seeing the four members of our family crowded on a single bed. She looked after the child for about eight months, and then, no longer being able to stand the life, took her granddaughter back to Zhejiang.

Old Li and I didn't mind the hardships though. During the political movements in those years, the educated were always told to "remold their mind" through labor and learn from the workers and farmers. So, out in the fields, I often helped the workers load and unload the core barrels from the trucks and do odd jobs. To this day, I still prefer to be called "Master Zhou." I now have the rank of geological engineer. Also, before we were often required to do manual labor such as digging ditches for oil pipes, planting vegetables, and raising pigs. We never thought and never dared to think of it as hard toil.

I gave birth to my second daughter in 1968 in an oilfield area. Conditions were gradually getting better.

In 1969, we were transferred to Hubei Province, in South Central China, to develop another oilfield.

The Cultural Revolution (1966-1976) had us busy going through "mind-remolding" and taking part in political movements. In 1972, I'd a miscarriage.

At that time, I was seven months pregnant. One day some colleagues and I were bent over gathering soybeans, as we'd been for the past two days. I suddenly squatted down and put my hands over my stomach. We'd been hoping to have a son, for we already had two daughters. The lost baby was a boy.

We almost lost our fourth child, a son, a year later. Positioning a few water-flooding wells then, I insisted on surveying the fields by myself, although others'd offered to go instead. As I couldn't ride a bicycle, I walked in the fields. The sun was fierce that day, and when I arrived home that evening, I fainted from over-exhaustion.

I feel deeply sorry for my children. They've gone through too many hardships. We brought our oldest daughter to live with us in the late 1970s, after my mother died. Despite our large house, now a two-room apartment, she and her younger sister couldn't go to the kind of schools children in big cities go to. And very often, they'd to cook meals for themselves, because I was often away.

Of course, this has done them some good. They're more independent than ordinary children. Both of my daughters are now studying in college in Hubei. They can take care of themselves quite well. And my son is a top student in a junior high school an hour's bus ride from home in the western outskirts of Hangzhou.

We moved back to our home province in 1986 because of my age. At first, I meant to relax a bit, to enjoy a stable life after so many years of moving about. The leaders of my brigade approved my request and gave me permission to do computer work in the office. But soon I knew that I belonged to the oilfields. I thought: with so much experience working at some of China's biggest oilfields, it was about time to bring my career to a climax.

So I applied to go out. There was plenty of opportunity. As I've mentioned, members of this brigade move a lot. I did this not exactly out of a sense of responsibility as a Communist Party member—I joined the Party in 1985—but, more importantly, out of a professional dedication. Now I've added two more oilfields, Shengli Oilfield and Xinjiang Oilfield, to my experience. Yes, still much field work to do. Still too many hardships, especially for an old woman. I'd to go alone, because Old Li has been fully occupied with his work at his institute. However, I really feel good when I make more successful designs and write better reports.

I don't regret becoming a geologist, although I didn't chose this profession. It's raised, and tested my capabilities. Possibly I haven't achieved much, but I've tried my best. As Old Li says, our children like the profession as well. Both of our daughters major in petrol engineering and our son wants to become a journalist when he grows up—so he can write about those who work in the remote areas.

It's a pity that we devoted so much time to manual labor and political movements before, and, during the Cultural Revolution. Without them, I'd have been a better geologist.

My husband says that it's a pity that most of the time the five members of our family eat in five different places: me in the oilfields, our daughters in their colleges, our son at his school and him at home.

Agronomist: Ding Jian

The problem we face aren't unique. They reflect problems in grain production in this whole area.

One of the world's questions is just how full the bread baskets of China's more than one billion people are. Many people find it amazing that China has been able to feed one forth of the world's population with only seven percent of the world's arable land.

Despite this impressive achievement, the country's current output is still far from enough. Industrial consumption has to be controlled. Annually, large amounts of grain have to be imported to supplement domestic production. In fact, some experts are saying that the shortage may become even more severe. The momentum provided by the land contract system has peaked and is unlikely to bring about further increases in production.

The solution lies in the widespread use of new techniques. In the years to come, agronomists such as Ding Jian are destined to become more important.

Ding is fifty-two years old. He is short and thin. His face is dark and weather-beaten, with wrinkles on his forehead, around his eyes, and around the corners of his mouth.

He's been an agronomist for more than three decades. Now, he's manager of Dalian Seeds Company. (Dalian is a coastal city in Northeast China.)

His company is located in a nondescript, gray, three-storey brick building. Inside, the corridor is dark. Rooms line both sides of the hallway. His office is furnished with nothing more than an old sofa, two desks, with peeling paint, and two chairs.

"Look at my office and you know why young people don't want to be agronomists," he said, smiling thinly.

I've been an agronomist for over three decades. Now, although I head this company, I continue to conduct research. I came to this profession because I had no other choice. I was born in a farmer's family in a small village in Xinmin County, about a two to three hours train ride from Dalian.

My parents worked in the fields year around and barely managed to feed the family. When I was about to graduate from primary school, they were sorry they couldn't afford to let me continue my education. My older brother was in junior high school then. They simply couldn't have afforded it if I'd gone to junior high school also.

But I already had made up my mind not to be a farmer. Being a rural child, I'd seen and felt too much. I knew what life was for a farmer. You were restricted to your native village most of your life. You knew little about what was going on outside. Day in and day out, you sweated under the scorching sun, shivered in the piercing cold, or got drenched when it rained. But what for? Nothing except a hand-to-mouth existence.

Even the thought of such a life was enough of a chill to send shivers up my spine. So I applied to a local vocational agronomy school, although I'd no special interest in agriculture. At that time, in order to attract more students into careers as agronomists, these schools not only charged no fees, but also gave students some small allowances. For students like me, such "rebates" were appealing.

I studied for five years there. In 1957 I graduated and was assigned to a neighboring county's agricultural bureau. When I left school, I thought it would be the end of my education.

Yet I was lucky a year later when I was sent to Shenyang College of Agriculture to continue my studies. I still think it was a windfall. The four years on campus there was the best period of my life, and certainly the most carefree and tranquil. Yet time passed quickly, and once again it was time to graduate.

This time, with a bachelor's degree in agronomy, I was assigned to a state-run farm in Jinxian County, a short distance from the county where my home village was located. By that time I had developed a genuine interest in agriculture partly due to the fact that I was becoming an expert in it. I stayed there about eight years. Then I was promoted to an office under the Agricultural Bureau of the Dalian municipal government.

Since 1979, I've been here at this company.

It's not easy to be an agronomist. Whatever you discover in the laboratory, good as it may be for higher yields, is of no use if farmers can't use it. And, there are always practical problems to be solved on the spot. So I go to the countryside frequently.

Nowadays, many rural towns have guesthouses serving visitors. There were few when I first went to the countryside. Usually I arranged to live with a local family. I had to eat whatever food was offered. The chance to have a good rest after a day's hard work was rare.

The work was exhausting. Once two colleagues and I were conducting a study of rice disease. In one afternoon we walked more than thirty kilometers through rice paddies. There were no cars. Even if there had been, it would have been of little use. The winding footpath was just wide enough for three persons to walk abreast.

But things like this were relatively easy. Getting farmers to adopt new techniques was a bigger challenge. They were very skeptical of new things. Their suspicion was the strongest when a new method was different from what they had been familiar with.

So first you had to persuade them into trying it, usually on a small scale. To them, research results and data were neither intelligible or reliable. If they did get higher per-unit output at harvest time, the new method would be accepted and used on a much larger scale the next year. So first results were extremely important. You had to be patient with them, and make sure that the right procedure was followed and that no step was skipped.

Once I went to a village to help introduce a new technique that would increase rice production. Under this new method, the land had to be plowed in autumn and harrowed before first rain came. Seedlings had to be transplanted earlier and raised under plastic sheets. I stayed in the village and worked closely with the farmers using the new technique. Finally it came time to transplant seedlings.

It was done by hand and one had to stand barefoot in water. It was early April and the water was still very cold. By the time the work was finished, I had gotten arthritis. My knees still ache whenever it's cloudy.

An agronomist can't find the time to spend with his or her family. Once, a sudden attack of plant disease broke out and we were asked to get it under control. I had to leave home at once or more acreage would have been affected. There wasn't even time to inform my family that I was leaving.

We've three children. I wasn't at home when two of them were born. When they were small, I was almost a stranger to them. Now that they've grown up, they understand why I was away so often. They love me and respect my profession. Yet, like most youths of today, none is going to follow my profession. "It's enough for our family to have one member in this field," my eldest son once said.

Small wonder. Even some young college graduates, who are interested in agronomy, have given up. What scares them away isn't the hard work. Many believe they can accept and readily handle that aspect of it. It's the lack of recognition after you've done so much that's unfair, especially when you compare yourself with high school or college classmates now in other profession.

For example, several middle-aged agronomists in my company still live in small apartments with two or even three children. They keep asking for new apartments. I've put their names on the waiting list. But this is hardly any help or promise.

The fact is our company gets few new apartments for our employees. Many companies can build apartment buildings on their own. They can finance them with their own money. We can't, because we've little money. Recently we got a loan and opened a hotel, hoping that it would be a source of more flexible income.

The government knows of all our problems. They've tried to be of help, and their policies are well intentioned. But they don't have the money to turn their good intentions into reality.

As a result, few youngsters nowadays want to be agronomists. It's said only people with no other choice become agronomists. Now in the Dalian area, there are only about 2,500 agronomists and agrotechnicians, far from enough. This shortage has some built-in dangers. The thrust provided by the contract system peaked some years ago. Further increases in grain production can only come from the use of new technologies. What will happen if we simply don't have enough people?

Unlike most other companies, ours is supposed to serve the farmers while charging them as little as possible. So we operate with only a marginal rate of profit. Our business is to supply farmers with quality seeds.

Usually the process involves four steps. First, we seek new species that are high in yield. We either develop them on our own or bring them in from other areas. Second, we test to see if they perform as expected.

This is called check culture. Two pieces of land, of about the same size and fertility, are selected. The check plot is sowed with seeds of the new species, and the "control" plot with the seeds of the ones already in use. They are given the same amount of water, fertilizer, and so on. In autumn, they are harvested separately and the per-unit yields are compared.

This step is crucial. Usually, tests are conducted at different sites at the same time. They may be repeated for several years in the interest of accuracy.

If these tests show positive results, then we take the third step, We produce seeds of the new species in large amount. Finally, we brief farmers on why the new strain is better and sell new seeds to them.

Usually farmers are willing to use them. It may

amount to an increase as high as 30 percent. We have kept some statistics. On the average, a new corn species can bring about 750 kilograms more per hectare. For rice, the increase is 500 kilograms per hectare. Compared with other yield-increasing methods, the cost is less, and the input of man-hours is about the same.

Yet, not all is rosy. In recent years, our speed in coming up with seeds of new species has slowed down. The whole area here can be divided into nineteen climatic zones. In the past, we had a site in each to do comparative tests. Now only ten still cooperate with us. This reduces test accuracy. Our second step, therefore, takes longer. No one wants to say that a new species leads to a higher yield, unless he is sure. The stakes are high.

Furthermore, the seed quality tends to decline. The third step is when we sign contracts with farmers to produce seeds for us. In the past, we dealt with about 370 "production teams." Now we've to do business with more than 15,000 individual households.

You can imagine how the workload has increased. Seed production is very delicate and certain rules must be heeded. What's more, if a single producer violates them, a whole region will be affected. Last year, when pollination drew near, a farmer left his corn fields and went fishing. Unable to find him, our agronomists had to rip off the stamens of his corn for him.

Seed production takes at least a year. Therefore, when a species is in short supply, eventually there will be no supply. So predicting is essential in our business. Yet, making a prediction has become increasingly difficult.

Now, farmers can decide what to grow on their contracted land. Usually they want to grow whatever is likely to earn them the most income. Like the tide, their need for a certain species ebbs and flows. Yet, unlike the tide, you can't foretell what will happen, and when. Once we prepared corn seed in a great quantity. Yet farmers wanted to buy peanut seeds. Soon we ran out of peanut seeds, and in the end farmers blamed us.

These problems we face aren't unique, for they reflect problems in grain production in this whole area.

It's a coastal area here. The economy is rather developed. The census still lists many people as farmers, but actually they are workers. Most of them work either in small local enterprises or in construction teams.

Even among those who remain in agriculture, many view growing grain as a sideline. They spend most of their time on more lucrative enterprises such as fishing, poultry growing, cultivation of fruit, market gardening and other things.

The morale of those who depend principally on the growing of grain for a living is on the decline. A farmer once told me, "I have to eat. But I don't want to produce more. What good is it when a cartful of sorghum is cheaper than a bicycle?"

As I indicated, part of this shift can be traced to agricultural economics. In recent years, prices of farm chemicals, diesel oil, farm tools, and other production necessities have steadily increased. Meanwhile, prices of farm produce have held stable. The net incomes of grain growers, on the average, have declined for several years.

Recently, the prices of meat, eggs, cow milk, fruits, fish and vegetables also have risen. This has made growing grain even less desirable. Many farmers have adjusted to these price changes by not growing grain. It's understandable. What's the point in working harder than others but getting less money?

Now, a typical household with five members has about 10 *mu* (about 0.67 hectare) of contracted land. If it produces corn, the net annual income will be around 500 to 600 yuan (US$ 135 to 162). If it grows rice, the figure will be nearly doubled. In either case, the reward is minimal, considering how much effort has been expended. If the household had ten times more land, its income would increase by about that proportion. But the input of man-hours wouldn't. As a result, the household is more likely to engage in grain production.

I think these problems exist nationwide. The difference is in degree. So, to secure a long-term increase of grain production, two policies are necessary. One is to raise grain prices. And the other is to allow grain growers to operate on a larger scale.

Part Twelve
Medical Care

Obstetrician: Yuan Fang

I place hope in my daughter, but I don't want her to be a doctor.

A medical doctor is highly respected in China, but not well paid, since hospitals are non-profitable businesses. For a forty-year-old man, who has been a doctor for only five years, things are even harder.

Yuan Fang (a pseudonym), an obstetrician in a gynecology and obstetrics hospital in a medium-sized city, is in such a situation. His college education was delayed by the Cultural Revolution. Although he is the main support of his hospital and does the work of a doctor in charge, his pay is only that of a resident doctor. He is a victim of situation where seniority is more important, seemingly, than performance.

The hospital in which Yuan Fang works has eighty doctors. Only two are men.

To be an obstetrician means that you've to be on duty at crucial moments at all times. If a doctor isn't prepared to accept these responsibilities, patients will suffer.

One Sunday last December, when I relieved a doctor on the night shift, I found that every one of the ten patients had a problem. That means the doctor on the last shift passed on problems to me which she herself should have handled. I told her that this wasn't a proper thing to have done, but she acted like she didn't care.

About ten o'clock, a patient suffered a sudden swelling of her abdomen. I thought immediately that her uterus must have ruptured. If a Caesarean operation weren't performed immediately, she'd die.

Meanwhile, another emergency popped up. A fetus had difficulty in breathing. All methods to remove the baby from the cervix failed. A Caesarean section was the only hope.

But it was Sunday, and there weren't enough doctors to perform two operations at the same time. On normal days, three operations can be performed simultaneously. The general medical practice is to try and save the life of the woman before that of the baby. So at ten, we started an operation to save the life of the woman. When I opened the uterus, blood spurted out from the swelling, confirming my diagnosis that her uterus had ruptured. Fortunately, both the mother and the child survived.

When the operation was finished, it was nearly noon, but we had no time to eat. We immediately started the second operation. But it was too late. The baby had suffocated. Naturally, I felt badly for the woman and her family.

Although such emergencies rarely occur, in this case, the life of the baby could have been saved if certain doctors had shown enough concern for their patients and done their duties properly.

I think it's ethical to treat your patients impartially. If a patient has serious problem, her own, or family background, is immaterial.

Recently the daughter of the provincial governor entered the hospital where I work, to give birth to her child. The woman's mother wanted a single room for her and requested that the head of the hospital, or the director of the obstetrics department, perform the operation. The infant was seventeen days overdue, and a bit too large. So a Caesarean operation had to be performed.

On the day of the operation, the head of the hospital took charge. The department head also was on hand, and the anaesthetist was most qualified. Outside the operating room, another doctor waited with the wife of the provincial governor.

In my hospital, the mother sees her newborn baby on the third day after birth. But the daughter of the provincial governor wanted to see her baby on the second day and was granted permission to do so. Ironically, the baby caught cold after seeing her mother. The baby had to be treated with special medication. That meant that the mother and baby had to stay longer in the hospital than in normal cases.

However, I don't think the daughter and grandchild of a provincial governor are any more valuable than those of "ordinary" persons.

Although my hospital specializes in gynecology and obstetrics, it's mainly known only as a place where women give birth. To my mind, in a hospital such as mine, gynecology should be a major determinant of the reputation of such an institution. There isn't a proper laboratory for even simple gynecological testing.

Test-tube babies? No, not possible in my hospital.

It's not only that my hospital lacks the proper equipment, but most Chinese aren't ready to accept the idea of this type of birth. Do you know there's a sperm bank in Hunan Province? But nobody volunteers to donate sperm.

Obstetrics may not be as complicated as artificial insemination, but it isn't easy when a pregnant woman develops complications. In such a situation, I feel we should seek the aid of experienced doctors from other hospitals for consultation. But my supervisor discourages us to do so. She would regard such a consultation as an indication of our hospital's incompetence.

One time, a pregnant woman suddenly died during the night. Normally, a postmortem examination should have been conducted, with doctors from other branches of medicine participating, to determine the cause of death. But the hospital didn't ask the patient's family for permission to perform an autopsy. Possibly her family might not have agreed to an autopsy, but they never were asked, and the hospital was happy to drop the whole matter.

A good obstetrician is judged by his or her ability to make firm and right decisions at crucial moments. It isn't like a surgeon whose skill depends on the use of the scalpel and whose operations are mostly prepared far in advance.

The skills I have are not only drawn from my own experience but also the experience of others. That means I've to read and keep learning all the time.

A few days ago, I was on the night shift. A woman in labor stopped her uterine contractions. I remembered a medical magazine I read a few days ago suggesting that under such circumstances, an intravenous injection of a tranquilizer would help to restore the contractions. As a doctor, I only offer advice. It's the nurse who administers the injection. I'd tell from the expression on her face that she didn't agree. She felt it was an extra burden on her. I said: "You don't believe it?" And then I produced the magazine which I luckily had brought with me that day. She mumbled a few words and went to do what I had told her to do. Two hours after the injection, the baby was successfully delivered.

In my hospital, if you follow previous procedures, it's easy and comfortable. But if you offer new ideas, you are asking for trouble.

Last year, I started a project to record the healing and restoration of the uterus after a Caesarean section. I think the subject is relevant to my work. The head of my hospital nodded his approval. I did the experiment by myself.

I started with 180 patients, but collected data on only twenty patients, because many left the hospital when I wasn't on shift and I didn't want to entrust other doctors with the task of carrying on my project. The crucial time of my project was the fortieth day after childbirth. Patients normally return on the fortieth day for an examination. Some on my list didn't come. Or even if they did, I might not have been on shift. So my experiment wasn't as complete as I'd hoped.

My pay? Oh, if you think of money, you don't want to do this work. My monthly salary is seventy-six yuan. If bonuses and subsidies are counted, I make a bit over 100 yuan. My wife is the head nurse in the provincial mental hospital. Her pay is a bit less than mine. We've a five-year-old daughter. My wife's grand-aunt, who's no children and no income, also lives with us. We aren't wealthy. But we are able to make both ends meet. So I'm quite satisfied with the way things are. A second job isn't possible at all for doctors, especially obstetricians. I know that engineers get extra income by providing services to rural enterprises in their spare time.

Money isn't that important to me. What I care most about is that the value of my efforts are acknowledged. However, that would seem to be wishful thinking in a situation where merit is measured according to seniority, instead of ability.

Last December, my hospital examined wage scales for doctors. This was to determine promotions. But I was very much aware that there were too many people with seniority over me and that, therefore, my chances for promotion were minimal. So I decided to take my yearly vacation to escape the conflict. Before I left, I said at a meeting that I hoped all of the qualified persons would get promotions so it would leave vacancies for us next time.

When I got back, I learned that none of us who started working after our graduation in 1982 got promoted. But one resident doctor, who cannot even write one complete page of diagnosis, and always likes to gossip, was promoted to the position of doctor in charge simply because of her longer seniority.

I don't think this system encourages people to work hard. I often remind myself that I don't work for money but out of conscience.

Sometimes I think of moving to another hospital. Of course, still as an obstetrician. What else do you think I'd become at my age? But I'm weighing over the advantages and disadvantages. My supervisor told me that they wanted to entrust me with an additional supervisory duty. That means I'll have more power, though my pay won't be increased. That shows how much I'm appreciated. So I'm undecided about leaving.

For a male, it isn't easy to work among women. I admit I get a lot of respect from my colleagues, but I have to be modest, tolerant and extremely careful when speaking. Otherwise, I might hurt someone unintentionally. I have to be careful to avoid involvement in gossiping. I often tell my friends that I've become "feminized." Before entering college, I was a worker, and all my colleagues were men. And now it's just the other way round.

I don't think I've had any problems treating my patients. I don't regard them as the opposite sex but as patients. When I started as an obstetrician, I was already thirty-five and married. I didn't find my work embarrassing. I did whatever my duty required of me without hesitation. If you hesitate, it shows you may have personal considerations which a doctor shouldn't have.

My serious attitude towards work has helped me gain the trust of patients. Some patients have even requested that I personally attend to them. One patient wrote me a letter after leaving the hospital addressing me as the "Director of Obstetrics Department." I never have written to former patients. I think my responsibility ends when they leave the hospital.

Ironically, my acquaintances seldom approach me except for emergency cases. I understand that. In the beginning, my wife wasn't too happy about my being an obstetrician. It wasn't that she didn't trust me, but she was afraid that my work might affect our private life.

Men have certain advantages over women in the field of obstetrics. They are less bothered by household chores and children. They have more time to read and work on self-improvement. Above all, they have greater physical strength, which is especially needed in cases of difficult births. Sometimes, it seems, men are more tolerant, and sympathetic, than women in the delivery room.

Six years ago when I served as an intern in an obstetrics department, my instructor, also an obstetrics expert, told me that giving birth is like dying. I remember well his words. I always try to be kind to my patients.

Medicine is a profession that deals with people. You have to be knowledgeable in many things. My patients range from rural residents to teachers, actresses, and salesgirls. When I talk to them about their business, they become interested and tend to trust me.

Obstetrics wasn't my first choice. There's a bitter story behind this.

I graduated from my province's best medical college with an excellent academic record. I was assigned to the provincial capital's central hospital. My first choice was to work in the department of internal medicine. At first it was agreed upon. But later, the daughter of a top-ranking official in the province was also assigned to the hospital from another medical college. And she wanted the same thing. So I was told to step aside. They put me in the post of anaesthetist and assured me of a quick promotion. But I was hurt, and left the hospital.

At that time, there were only two jobs available. One was to teach at a nurses' school, and the other was to be an obstetrician at my present hospital. I chose the latter.

I regard my life as a story of frustrations and setbacks.

Twenty-two years ago I was preparing to take college entrance examinations when the Cultural Revolution broke out. The middle school where I studied was the best in the city. My aim was to enter one of the nation's top medical colleges. However, that "revolution" shattered my hopes.

But at that time I wasn't conscious of the opportunity lost. Like many other students, I enthusiastically took part in the movement. I joined the Red Guards and became engaged in factional fighting. Later the faction I belonged to lost the upper hand and I was ordered to work in the countryside.

This time I didn't follow the tide. I stayed at home, with nothing to do. Just imagine a healthy young man of twenty who has no job and is being fed by his parents! I was lucky I didn't become a petty criminal. The only thing I enjoyed doing at that time was talking with my former classmates about social problems.

I finally got a job in 1971. It was with a mechanical engineering company. My work was to follow the derrick and fasten and unfasten the heavy weights. People say that no respectable girl would want to marry a person who does this kind of work.

Later the head of the company discovered the talent I have for writing. Often he asked me to write speeches for him to deliver at meetings. I later was promoted to do statistics.

In 1977, I heard that universities and colleges would soon, for the first time after the Cultural Revolution, admit students through examination. I was overjoyed at the news. Two of my old classmates and I decided to try. But the three of us were so poor that we couldn't buy the study aids that were essential in preparing for the examination. Nonetheless, we all managed to pass.

Unfortunately, we were barred from colleges because we were considered too old. At that time we were thirty. We felt we'd been deceived. We wrote letters to officials concerned. And our effort paid off. The three of us finally were admitted to different colleges. I went to the medical college that I'd chosen as my first choice.

Good things all came very late to me. I entered college at thirty, got married at thirty-four. Now I'm forty, but I'm only a resident doctor although my responsibility is that of a doctor in charge. At such an age and in such a position, I really feel I'm under a great deal of pressure. I've to be better in almost every aspect than my younger colleagues. That isn't easy because younger people have their own advantages. They are more energetic and inclined to try new things. I place hope in my daughter. But I don't want her to become a doctor. I think she's good at expressing herself and might make a fine college teacher or a journalist.

Nurse: Du Shuying

I don't feel a nursing career's that great, but it's hard to imagine hospital wards without nurses being on duty twenty-four hours a day.

Finally, the nursing care department of Beijing Xuanwu Hospital pursuaded thirty-year-old Du Shuying to make a recording about her profession. She is one of 500 nurses in this general hospital, which specializes in neurosurgery. Nine years ago she became a nurse in the ward of internal medicine, and now is the head nurse in the digestive ward which contains thirty-three beds.

She looks young and fresh. Her natural beauty has only been a little diminished by night shifts. With a sunny countenance, her bright eyes always seem to be smiling. Her voice is soft and gentle. She is a comfort to troubled people. As she says: "I'm well suited to being a nurse."

She is the eldest of four children. Her parents are retired workers. Her husband is two years older than she is. For five years, since they were married, he has been studying history at a night university. He will graduate this year with a degree.

The day shift in my ward starts at 8:00 every morning. I get up early, at about 6:30. I then wake up my daughter. I listen to the news on the radio while eating a quick breakfast. Meanwhile, mother helps me dress and feed my daughter. When everything's ready, I take my daughter to the nearby kindergarten on my bike. Then, I go directly to the hospital.

Nurses offer service to patients twenty-four hours a day. They share the work, and cooperate with one another. They work five different shifts in turn, one week at a time.

There're three overlapping day shifts, all of which start at eight o'clock in the morning. On the main shift (8:00—16:00), nurses give intravenous transfusions, injections, and blood transfusions; on the normal shift (8:00—12:00, 13:30—17:30), they perform general nursing care, prepare medicine for patients, observe the patients' conditions, test the vital signs of patients and record their intake and output volume, and then go around the ward; on the double-period shift (8:00—12:00, 14:00—18:00), they carry out the medical orders of doctors and observe the overall conditions of all patients in the ward. Then two night shifts follow: the first is from 18:00 until 2:00 of the next day, and the second is from 2:00 until 9:00.

I arrive at the ward at least ten minutes earlier, because I'm a head nurse now. There's a regular briefing between night and morning shifts. I listen to reports on the conditions of each patient and look at bedside charts. And then as a head nurse, I accompany the physician-in-chief as he makes his rounds of the ward. This takes an hour or so.

Then I make a routine examination of the condition of the patients and work and appearance of the nurses. Twelve o'clock is our lunch time. At 1:30 p.m., I continue my work. I never feel the need to take a nap at noon. At 5:30 p.m., the day's work is done. When that comes, I don't have to rush, because my mother can help me by picking up my girl at kindergarten.

Back home, sometimes, I help mother do some

cooking, or teach my daughter to write Chinese characters. After supper, I read, watch TV, or knit to time. At about 11 p.m., I go to bed. My day-to-day life's almost always the same, except when I'm on the night shift. The eight hours I spend on shift at the hospital are the most interesting and valuable parts of the day for me.

Our job's very hard. Each of us must work 100 to 150 night shifts a year. A month's average is ten.

According to our hospital's regulations, nurses must go on night shift from the seventh month after giving birth to a child, and nurses who're seven months pregnant are exempted from night shifts. Our nurses dislike night shifts, but I'm different. I don't mind going on the night shift.

I regard myself as no different from the other seven nurses with whom I work. I do more work and give few orders. I'm seldom in a bad mood, but I do feel my hospital's current service isn't as good as it was before, though I try to do as well as I can. When I was a nurse and not a head nurse, I tried to explain everything to my patients very thoroughly while carrying out my doctors' medical orders. But now I'm not as good as then. There're so many things for me to do. I'm not simply a nurse now. I must get medical orders directly from doctors and assume the responsibility for carrying out the treatment program.

Sometimes, patients won't cooperate with the nurses, which really creates a headache for us. Then the nurses oftentimes tell patients the head nurse asked me to do such and such. Therefore, patients think that it's the head nurse that's making the trouble. All in all, I'm not as good as before. I feel the pressure of my work.

After graduation from nursing school in January 1979, I was assigned to work in the internal medicine (a general one which includes angiocardiopathy), immunity, internal secretion, hematopathy, respiration, and digestion wards. Within nine years, I've spent time in all these wards. Finally I was named the head nurse in the digestive ward.

Our ward has thirty-three beds in four small rooms, and two large rooms. There's an emergency room to treat those who've attempted suicide by taking such things as DDVP (dichlorvos), overdoses of sleeping pills, rat poison, weed killer, or pesticides.

I'd prefer to stay in the angiocardiopathy ward. There I'd learn a lot of things, such as electrophysiology and electrocardiograms. Most of the patients there're older people. Their mood's somewhat steady. But most of the patients in our digestive ward are suffering from liver ailments. They're always ill-tempered. They really are hard to please.

One morning last fall, we'd an incident in our large male ward with nine patients in it. Generally, our nurses help patients make their beds twice a day—in the morning and in the afternoon. But our nurses' efforts in making the ward clean and tidy also calls for the cooperation of our patients. One patient made a mess of his bed after the nurses had helped him make it. Actually, the patient didn't need to use his quilt, so I asked him to fold it up. He refused. Then I told him that this was our hospital's regulation. He still refused. Another patient joined in the quarrel. The atmosphere became heated. Since there were so many colleagues with me, I thought I'd lose face if I was defeated. So I raised my voice to force the patient to do as I ordered. But the patient said "No!" The other patient again joined in, this time with vulgar language directed at me.

The dirty words really made me angry. So I said without thinking:"Watch it! One of your relatives slapped the face of our head nurse yesterday."

However, the director in charge of our day-to-day work stepped in and asked me to join her in the nursing care department. There, leaders criticized me for quarreling with patients.

The patients I like the most are generally common people or senior cadres who come from a simple family background or from workers' or farmers' families, as well as reasonable patients and family members. I dislike those patients and families who look down upon nurses and create discontent.

I still don't know how to cope with these hard-to-handle patients. In dealing with those unreasonable patients, I use two approaches, either turning a deaf ear, or trying to explain things to them, because nurses aren't supposed to lose their temper with patients. Also, I don't think there's any reason to be polite to family members of patients who make unreasonable demands. I'd had no problems with that patient before the quarrel. I only asked him to do as the hospital regulation required. Later, I gradually became aware of my error. If I'd changed my way of speaking, I probably would have achieved better results. Self-control for a nurse is very, very important.

Nurses must help those patients who've lost the ability to care for themselves. Some of their duties are to help patients take medicine, wash their hands, face and feet, brush their teeth, care for their skin, and trim their nails. We also help patients wash their hair once a week, and take a sponge bath once a week. It's easy to do all these. But most of our nurses feel embarrassed taking away the stool and urinating equipment in front of patients' relatives. So in these cases, our nurses let the relatives do that instead.

I know that our nurses, especially unmarried young girls, are embarrassed to wash a patient's perineum, or insert a urinary catheter. Some even feel degraded in doing so. But I do all these things with no problem. Sometimes, I help patients suffering from constipation.

Besides physical nursing care, we also do some psychological nursing which includes having free-ranging talks with patients.

Before surgery, nurses must have the patients' hair cut. If doctors want to do some examination such as sternal puncture, nurses must get the puncture bag, anesthetic and have a sample bottle ready.

There're five doctors in our ward, one physician-in-chief who's responsible for the quality and program of the medical treatment, two experienced doctors, and two young doctors who've been out of medical college for only a year.

Cooperation with doctors directly affects our clinical work. Sometimes, young doctors aren't familiar enough with their jobs, and sometimes they give incorrect medical orders. No matter what happens in my association with young doctors, I always show my respect for them, especially in front of our patients. I prefer to discuss any problems I've with them in private. I think I keep a good relationship with these young doctors and we've mutual clinical goals. When off shift, I'd like to be on good terms with them. As I always say, "You must respect other people if you want other people to respect you."

To carefully observe patients is a very important joint operation between doctors and nurses.

Once I gave some medicine to a patient, and he said he'd rather wait until the hot water got lukewarm. When I came back, the patient had finished taking the medicine, but he looked embarrassed. I opened the drawer of his small table and found out why. There were some twenty tablets in it. The tablets were hormones. The patient admitted that he was worried about the side-effects of the drug since his beard had become heavy and since he was putting on weight. I tried to reason with him, and in the end he agreed to cooperate with me.

I still remember the words of our teacher in charge of our class, when I was in nursing school. She said that young girls should be dignified in behavior and appearance, but she didn't tell us how to do it. I learned all these things in my clinical practice. I trained myself to walk in a naturally elegant manner and speak in a gentle voice. The colors of my clothing match. I pay attention to my behavior when I speak to male doctors.

I prefer light make-up. Most of the nurses look pale after so many night shifts. If they lightly apply make-up, they make themselves feel better, and the patients also feel better being nursed by a nice-looking person. I daren't apply make-up while on shift, because our hospital nursing care department doesn't encourage us to do so. But off shift, I surely do so.

Today's society pays great attention to a diploma. But I'm not a degree-winner of any kind. When I was in high school, my study was affected by the Cultural Revolution. When I graduated from high school, there was no opportunity for us to take part in the college entrance examination. When I was in the nursing school, there was no laboratory and I never learned biochemistry. It's no use complaining now. However, I still want to learn something. But I don't have the confidence to compete with young nursing school graduates and to go to the nurses' college to do further study. The college requires a student to have a good basic knowledge of mathematics, chemistry, and other fields related to a nurse's job. I know my limitations.

No diploma means no hope. I've to find a way out. I'm now trying to write an article, perhaps a kind of work review on nursing service in our ward. I'm doing this in the hope of getting a higher professional position. I'm now in the stage of collecting material for the article.

Nurses sacrifice a lot—youth, time, and energy. They cannot live a regular life. They must have an almost unnatural self-control when they're cooperating with doctors, and dealing with patients and patients' relatives. Our nurses seldom make complaints at the time, but they do complain afterwards.

Nurses're underpaid. My monthly salary's only seventy yuan, and my bonus is twenty yuan. Another three or five or ten yuan are paid according to your nursing seniority. And we get no overtime pay. Some nurses want to leave clinical work because they think that they're doing a hard but thankless job. Young husbands try to persuade their nurse-wives not to go on night shifts.

In recent years, fewer amd fewer young girls in urban cities are willing to enter nursing schools if they can find a better job and earn more money.

On the contrary, young girls in rural areas are anxious to receive such training and to get assigned to urban hospitals so that they'll have greater mobility later in changing jobs and so that they become city residents.

Our labor should be recognized by people throughout society. People should know that if doctors want to carry out their treatment program, there must be nurses to observe the patients' condition the whole day. Only nurses take direct care of patients. Without nurses, you can't imagine what might happen in hospital wards.

There's prejudice against nurses in our society. Sometimes it can be very open. From the way the patients talk, we can see that the patients respect doctors more than nurses. Whenever patients have a chance, they'll express their appreciation to doctors, but never to nurses. After recovering, some patients come back to the hospital with gifts—wine or cigarettes or film tickets—for doctors, but never for nurses. We feel the difference, as well as the unfairness. We do much more than doctors as regards the treatment of patients. Since I'm a head nurse now, sometimes patients send me film tickets which I share with the other nurses.

But our young, unmarried nurses have no difficulties finding spouses. Today's young men seem to take a fancy to nurses. Perhaps they reason that if nurses are good at taking care of others, surely they'd be good at taking care of their husbands, and managing household things. But when they get married, these young men don't want them to go on night shift.

Sometimes, emergency cases require that our

nurses stay on the job longer. Under such circumstances, I'd rather stay and do all that I can, because young nurses in my ward need time to meet their boyfriends. So I sometimes take their place. My husband never complains about it because he owes me a debt of gratitude. For five years he's indulged himself in self-improvement, and never done any housework.

Almost every Spring Festival (Chinese lunar New Year), from the eve through the whole festival, I've been on the night shift. I've never felt used because my mother's always helped me to take care of my daughter, and because my husband understands me and supports my work.

On Sundays, my husband joins me in taking our daughter to a park, cinema, or theater. My husband's a cadre in charge of Party affairs in a governmental department. If I'm working on Sunday, my husband'll take my daughter out without me.

When I complete a shift, I always wash thoroughly. You've to take good care of yourself if you serve as a nurse. Sometimes, patients suffering from liver cancer in an advanced stage spray blood on our clothing. I'm really afraid of bad things happening.

I enjoy a great deal talking and laughing with my colleagues. I like theatrical performances. I've never missed a good TV series. If I'd a choice between watching a TV series and doing some self-study, I'd choose the former. I want to relax in my spare time.

I selected a nursing career myself. There's nothing for me to regret. My job as a nurse is important. Overall, I like it. We nurses, after all, are always needed by patients and their relatives.

Part Thirteen

In the Service and Catering Trades

House Maid: Zhang Yexiu

The city is nice, but isn't where I belong.

In cities, it's common for a family to hire someone to take care of the elderly, or the children, and also handle household chores. But they are not normally known as "servants" or "house maids." They are addressed to as *Ahyi*, a Chinese version for aunt. Up to the 1970s, most *Ahyi* were middle-aged or older ladies who came from poverty-stricken rural areas to make a living in cities. Since service facilities have lagged behind population growth in cities, there always is a need for *Ahyi*.

In recent years, an increasing number of younger *Ahyi* from the countryside have come to cities. Most of them are about seventeen to twenty years old, and they are more interested in experiencing city life than in making money.

Big cities, such as Beijing, Shanghai, and Guangzhou, have set up several service centers to help those families in need in making contacts with these girls. Beijing Chongwenmen Family Service Center has placed in house-maid positions 28,160 girls in the four years since it opened in 1984. But there is still a shortage of *Ahyi*. Many newcomers find their employers through other *Ahyi* who are from the same areas.

Zhang Yexiu, twenty, was taken to Beijing by her village friend from Anhui Province in East China. She has been an *Ahyi* in Beijing for three years and has worked in six households.

I'd never left home before I came to Beijing. My mother wouldn't allow me even to go to the county town, which was 20 kilometers away. I didn't go to school either. At thirteen, I began to help my mother make string bags as sideline work. It was dull. I used to envy some of the girls in our village. They were *Ahyi* in big cities and they looked so nice, dressed in fashionable clothes, when they returned for holidays. One day, I met a girl named *Meizi* in a shop. She was home to visit her fiancé and was going to leave for Beijing the next day. She asked me to accompany her. I knew my mother wouldn't agree, so I didn't tell her about my plans. I borrowed some money from my sister. My father saw me off at the bus station the next morning. I didn't shed a tear. I was so happy and excited to leave home. It was the first time in my life I'd taken a long-distance bus and a train.

The first few days in Beijing were terrible. We stayed in a little hotel. *Meizi* spent a few days of her holiday before returning to work, taking me to parks and to department stores. Being almost out of money, I needed a job. Once at an intersection, I found I was left behind, I started to run. A speeding truck made an abrupt stop before hitting me. I was frightened and cried out. *Meizi* blamed me for not seeing the red light. I started paying attention to traffic lights after that.

I finally found a family which needed an *Ahyi*. I was asked to look after a one-year-old baby. The family wanted to pay me twenty yuan a month. Three days later, *Meizi* came to see me. She said the pay was too low and that I should get forty yuan a month. But my employer said she couldn't afford more. So *Meizi* escorted me out without even saying "good-bye" to my employer.

Then I began to take care of an eighty-one-year-old lady who was dying.

She died a week after I began the work. It was an awful experience. I've always been afraid of death since I was a child. I hope I don't have to attend such an old one again. But I simply didn't have a choice then.

I then went to work for a doctor's family. At home I had been looked after by my sister when I was small, and I looked after my younger brother and sister when I was growing up. But I was wrong in thinking that I knew how to look after a baby. I was corrected all the time by the baby's mother. For instance, the diapers didn't get enough sunlight. The baby's milk bottle had to be disinfected with boiling water. I don't say that she was a bad lady. But she really had a quick temper. I know I'd room for improvement, and I always controlled myself even when she shouted at me.

I'd a day off every other week. Once I returned from my day off on Sunday, she was angry and nasty to me. I said to her: "You are a doctor, but your words aren't clean." The next morning when she called to ask how her baby was, I told her, "I quit, right now." I was in tears when I murmured "good-bye" to the baby, who was asleep. I came back to see him several times after I left.

The next employer, a school teacher, was very

nice to me. As I had never been to school before, she taught me to read and write. I learned my first 500 characters from her. I stayed there for seven months. Another *Ahyi* found an easier job for me with a family that needed a cook. I persuaded the teacher to let me go. After I left, she put her little daughter to the kindergarten.

I cooked for a family of four for three months. The parents were often away from home on business. Their twenty-seven-year-old daughter was a very liberated girl. She'd many boyfriends.

She invited her friends to parties where everyone sang and danced until late at night. I had to clean the littered floor after the party was over. The girl asked me not to tell her parents what she did. I didn't want to be in the middle. So I quit again.

Now I'm taking care of *Hanghang* and I'm enjoying the work. He is three, a clever and healthy boy. Hanghang's mother said they used to have a middle-aged *Ahyi*, who was a diligent and quiet worker, but didn't know how to play with *Hanghang*.

I teach him to sing songs and tell him stories. *Hanghang*'s mother is a researcher at an art institute. She often works at home. City people don't have much space at home. To avoid the boy disturbing his mother, I usually take *Hanghang* out to parks during the day. *Hanghang*'s parents teach me reading and writing. They buy me textbooks. I also learn from *Hanghang*'s picture books. When I spot a new word there, I look it up in the dictionary. I read the story before I try to tell it to *Hanghang*. Every evening after *Hanghang* goes to bed, I read for almost an hour.

I keep a diary every day. *Hanghang*'s mother says it's a good way to learn. I write letters to my friends and my family. My mother has changed her mind about my leaving, since she knows now that I'm doing okay and can write letters. She told me in a letter she dictated to my father that arithemetic was useful to learn. My father is an accountant in our village.

Hanghang is going to go to kindergarten this September. His mother wants me to stay on. But I'm thinking of going home. It's been more than three years since I left home. I've experienced almost everything here: toured all the scenic spots, shopped at every big department store, and met many different people. The city's nice but it's not where I belong. I'll go back, but not empty-handed. I'm going to learn a skill.

I've contacted a tailor, who'll teach me how to make clothes in exchange for chores I'll do for her. I'd like to return home with a skill. My sister's recently set up a tailor's shop in her husband's village and is doing very well. Rural people are more concerned about clothing now.

I've a boyfriend. He comes from my neighboring village and is also in Beijing, making cakes. He's a happy, funny guy and at the same time practical and hardworking. He asked me if I'd any wishes, I said I only hoped to have a house of our own, so I don't have to live with my future parents-in-law. We can save money to buy electrical appliances together.

I want to have a child, but only one. I'm the fourth child of six. I'd seen enough of my parents arguing with each other when we children were disobedient. I think we'll be happier with only one child.

Roast Duck Chef: Cai Zenglian

I'm good at roasting ducks. I like to eat duck and I can never get enough of it.

Cai Zenglian probably is the best Beijing roast duck chef in Beijing. He has prepared this delicacy for more than thirty years.

He has the typically robust figure of a cook and a keen sense of humor in his character, an uncommon quality in many Chinese.

At sixty, Cai is a top grade chef at *Quanjude* Roast Duck Restaurant in central Beijing. The restaurant is the largest of its kind in China and can serve 2,000 people at a time. It's where Chinese leaders often take visiting foreign heads of state to taste this famous dish.

Of the restaurant's 600 employees, there are more than sixty cooks that do the roasting work. The kitchens are "off limits" to visitors.

In Beijing, there're around 100 restaurants that serve roast duck. But I feel the roast duck in my restaurant's the best. Last year, we served half a million customers, and sold a record high of 210,000 ducks.

I heard there's a saying popular among tourists that you cannot miss two things if you go to Beijing. One's visiting the Great Wall and the other's eating roast Beijing duck. I'm so happy to hear this. I accept the words that "The customer is always right." If a duck isn't properly roasted, or my customer isn't satisfied, I cannot sleep well.

I've tried to be better than others. I like to spend time improving my professional expertise. One can never learn enough about cooking. So, when other people are preparing dishes, I observe, and then come back to do it myself. In this way, I've learned the recipes of many famous Chinese delicacies.

One reason I do well in my trade is because I use my brains. For example, in addition to roasting ducks, I also have made improvements in the use of traditional utensils and in the stove used for roasting ducks. My improvements make the roasting work easier, shorten the time needed, and save firewood.

Now I can cook dishes with different flavors. Cooking, just like anything else, is a process of observing, trying it over and over again, and finally mastering it.

I've eaten many delicacies, but roast duck is the best. Unlike mutton, which has a very distinct taste, roast duck is a dish that most common people can accept.

Chinese cuisine has become a favorite of many foreigners. Some years ago, I was contracted to work for more than one year in a Chinese restaurant in Toronto, Canada. My skill was highly praised there. Since 1981, my restaurant has sent over 100 experienced cooks to work in restaurants in countries such as the United States, Canada, and Japan. We're happy to have more people taste roast duck and to earn hard currency for our country.

Here's the history of roast duck and my restaurant.

Quanjude, meaning "assembly of all virtues" in Chinese, was founded in 1864 by Yang Quanren, a peddler who sold chickens and ducks. But roast duck itself originated in the royal kitchens 400 years ago. Historical records state that "no delicacy is better than duck roasted in Beijing."

Ducks are usually roasted in an open oven using fruit wood. Roast duck is crispy orange-red on the outside, and tender inside. It's delicious as well as nutritious. It may sound as if I'm advertising it, but this's really how I feel.

We buy force-fed ducks from a farm in suburban Shunyi County. Each uncooked duck costs about ten *yuan*. And we sell it roasted at about eighteen yuan. There're a dozen steps in roasting a duck. We put twenty ducks on a stove at a time and we roast them for forty to fifty minutes. After that, we use a sharp knife to slice the meat which then is served to the customers.

My job is very challenging and demanding. I never thought of being a cook when I was young. I'm a native of the Jiaodong Peninsula in China's eastern province of Shandong. My hometown's a heavily populated place and land is relatively scarce. Many people used to go to other places to earn a living. My father was a fisherman, and my mother sold fish. My family'd hardly make ends meet before 1949, so I'd to leave my home and make a living elsewhere. In 1943, I came to Beijing to ask for help from my brother-in-law. He got me a job at *Quanjude* as a handyman the next year. So, I've worked at this restaurant for forty-four years.

When I started work, the restaurant employed forty people. I was given free meals and boarding. But I earned nothing else. We'd no set working schedule. We got up and started working when the sun rose and we quit when the sun set. We worked at least twelve hours a day. And we'd no holidays. When other people were free, we were even busier. Many of us dozed off during work. Now I sleep less. Perhaps age makes one need less sleep.

As an apprentice, I worked hard and did everything my master asked me to do. I often did errands for the restaurant. After that, I became a cook.

I've followed three masters and I've also taken on some apprentices. I think I'm an easy-going and open-minded person. Some time ago, a young apprentice wanted to *kowtow* to show respect to me, but I refused and told him it was unnecessary.

My years of work have taught me that one's to be keen and quick in his work if he wants to be successful. I earn a monthly salary of 180 yuan, much higher than our general manager, who earns 139 yuan. With bonus, I've a monthly income of 240 yuan.

Though my hair's still dark and I look young, my health is worsening. I suffer from diabetes. So I ride my bike to work every day. I live in the eastern suburbs and it takes me thirty minutes to come here by bike. I get plenty of exercise this way.

As for my family, I've a lot of stories to tell. When I was only seven, my parents arranged a marriage for me. My would-be wife was only five at that time. We didn't really marry till I was twenty-two. That was in 1950 when I went back home. When I got back to Shandong, everything for my wedding had been arranged. At that time, there wasn't the freedom of marriage such as young people today have. Everything was decided and arranged by the parents of the two families. Young people had no say in their own matters.

The day of our wedding, my wife came to my home in a sedan chair. Our relatives and friends were invited. It was an unforgettable experience for me. I found my wife very nice and pretty.

We've four children: two sons and two daughters. My oldest daughter's a farmer in Shanxi Province. My younger daughter's a salesclerk in a grocery in Beijing. Both of my sons're cooks. They've followed me and maybe even have surpassed me. My elder son is good at preparing Shandong cuisine, and my younger son's specialty is Sichuan cuisine. Early this year, my elder son won first prize in a professional cooking competition held in Beijing, and I only got a second. I was both elated and disappointed.

Cooks used to be looked down upon in our country. Things are getting better now. I'm a member of the China Association of Cookery and I've been invited to give lectures on cooking. The general manager of my restaurant, Wang Yiren, has been very kind to me. Not long ago he gave me preferential treatment in getting an apartment.

At home, my wife usually cooks the meals. But when guests come, I do the cooking. My wife fries fish very well and I enjoy the food she prepares. We seldom dine out or entertain guests in restaurants. It's too expensive.

I'd retire now. But the restaurant has asked me to stay on. At present, I mainly supervise the work of younger cooks and give them suggestions. If I went to work in a privately-run eating place, I'd be a rich man. People who roast ducks well are really scarce now. And many private restaurants have offered me high salaries to work for them, but I've refused. I'm proud to be at *Quanjude*.

Studio Photographer: Shen Yutang

I've been a portrait photographer for thirty years.... I hope one day before I can't work any more, I'll have a chance to take a nude picture.

With a history of sixty-seven years, Wangkai Photo Studio is among the best of Shanghai's 127 studios. Nearly everyone in Shanghai knows about it. Its speciality is portrait photography. Although the studio is well known, few have any idea who was responsible for bringing this about.

"I don't care if the public ever hears of me or not," said Shen Yutang, a top-grade photographer of the studio and who has contributed his efforts to furthering Wangkai's business. "Wangkai gets famous. That's enough," he said.

Thin as a stick, with a straight back and wearing a grey tunic and trousers, the white-haired man, with serious eyes, looks more like a retired army officer than an experienced photographer. Now sixty-three, he actually is the number one photographer at Wangkai Photo Studio.

Although born in Suzhou where he lived until he was nineteen, he has no trace of a Suzhou accent. And his sense of values, his life goals and his view of family life are typically Shanghainese.

Why do you come to me instead of others? Am I that famous? I don't think I've anything special to tell, because I haven't done anything heroic.

In fact, I've never been specially trained as a photographer. I've been learning it all by myself since I started an apprenticeship in a photo studio in

Suzhou at age thirteen. I've been a portrait photographer for thirty years.

It was in 1958 that I was sent to Wangkai. I've worked here for thirty years. Since then, I've done restoration work, photography, and worked in the darkroom. An all-rounder, you might say.

It's no easy job. There's so much to learn that you can never say you're perfect. Take portrait photography for example. A good photographer should accurately capture the character of the person he's photographing. But most people don't care for that. As often is the case, in some photo studios, a customer is asked to sit in a chair and smile when told to. And within seconds it's all over. You can imagine the second-rateness of the picture.

As for me, I first of all try to communicate with the customer. I'll ask him how he wants to present himself, what his occupation is, and what he's going to do with the picture. Then we discuss how his picture should be taken.

Experience's taught me that customers want the photographer to determine their posture, touch-up their hair, and readjust their collar. They think getting their photograph taken is a special treat and that after such attention it will be better.

To let every customer have this special treatment is what I've been trying to do for years. As a result, I've many customers as well as new ones that have been recommended to me by the old ones.

However, good service is only one of the factors that attract customers. Quality should be at the top of the list.

As you know, I feel that I'm a good portrait photographer. In fact, I've won various national awards. Last year, I was awarded a silver medal for portrait photography by UNESCO.

Some customers are quite shy. Feeling awkward in the artificial studio light, they find it hard to smile. Even when they did manage to force one, the smile isn't pleasant to see. In this case, we photographers have to try to get them to relax and make them feel they are with a friend who won't laugh at them for their awkwardness and who is really lending a helping hand.

Some people believe a smiling face is the true essence of portrait photographing. I don't think so. Indeed, some people look more handsome and more lively when they smile. But some don't. A serious face sometimes adds a gentlemanliness and an authority to those who'd otherwise look older if smiling. But pointing this out to the customers directly concerned is useless. People tend to stick to their original practice of smiling when before a camera.

Customers in the old society were mostly rich people. Actresses and prostitutes came, too, as their occupations required. Poor people seldom came except when they needed pictures for new identification cards. Today, the customers are from all walks of life. Comparatively speaking, I prefer film stars, actresses, and singers. I think they've the instinct, talent, and experience to make themselves look good.

We're quite busy. Even during the Cultural Revolution, Red Guards crowded into the studio to have "revolutionary pictures" taken. A standard "revolutionary picture" portrayed a Red Guard holding a little red book of Mao's quotations, wearing a green army uniform with a leather belt tightly around the waist, and with almost a scowl on the face.

During that period, customers weren't allowed to wear Western suits or laced shirts because it was regarded as an outward expression of "petty bourgeois thoughts." Girls or women couldn't bring a bunch of flowers. Even newly-weds couldn't hold flowers. Curling one's hair wasn't permitted, not to mention putting on make-up.

I remembr a young man who came to our studio to have a roll of film developed. When he came again to pick up the film, he was taken to the police because he was wearing sunglasses in the pictures. That poor man! I don't know what became of him later.

It wasn't until 1979 that Western-style wedding picture was taken again. Now about fifty couples come here per day.

I think the most noticeable change in customers is the clothes they wear. In the 1950s, people wore Lenin suits, only to be followed by Mao suits in the 1960s. After 1978, Western suits became popular. In recent years, all kinds of free modern style have become popular. As a result, more people are taking color pictures.

In other words, I think, the change lies in the customers' much more flexible sense of beauty and their pursuit of beauty in life.

With living conditions much improved, many people've taken up photography as a hobby. When going on a picnic, or having a family reunion, or on other occasions, amateur photographers have a good opportunity to show off their skills. Still, people come back to us to have a portrait taken.

I seldom have a picture taken of myself. Having gotten used to standing behind the camera, I'd find it ridiculous to sit before it and be photographed. It'd be as if the world were upside down.

I haven't felt well recently. I often have a stomachache, an illness prevalent among photographers. But I don't want to see a doctor, because I think it would be a waste of time. What you get from the doctor's just a few tablets and fear of cancer. I'd rather stay at home for a day and drink as much hot water as I can. If anything happens, it's God's will—you can do nothing about it.

People say winter's the season to nourish one's body by eating ginseng and other Chinese herbs known for their tonic effect. But it's a luxury I can't afford.

As for fame or things like that, I'm not interested. When it comes my way, however, I'll have no choice but to accept it, right?

For years, I've worked hard and have been careful not to offend the leaders and colleagues in my work unit, or my customers. I've always tried to keep away from any conflict of interests. You can say I hold myself aloof from the world.

My desire in life has been nothing more than a comfortable home, and a nice family in which love and peace are shared.

But the painful fact is that though busy as a bee for years, I've failed to reach that goal. Perhaps it's because I've a big family.

I've three sons and one daughter. My wife, who died of liver cancer last year, was a housewife. They all relied on me.

Money was always a problem. If we planned to buy only ten yuan worth of food, we dared not spend a penny more. We had to save a little for our children.

And we managed to give one thousand yuan to each child to help them buy things for their wedding.

Then, just when my wife and I were planning for our senior years ahead, she became ill and left me.

Perhaps I was destined to live a bitter life from the day I was born.

At the age of nine, I lost my father who died of an unknown illness. My mother had to do embroidering everyday for rich families so as to feed the four children—three girls and me. Sometimes we didn't have enough to eat.

Still, mother managed to save a little to send me to school, hoping I'd become an educated gentleman later. But she couldn't afford to support me any longer when I was thirteen. She had to send me to a photo studio. At least, she thought, there I'd have something to eat.

Today, young people cannot imagine how hard a life we apprentices had then.

The sleeping quarters of the studio were so small that only one bed could be placed there. So I had to sleep on the floor with three other boys. The boss taught us nothing because he felt that when we learnt his trade, we'd become competitors. So what we did daily was just household chores. The money we got each month was only one yuan, just enough for a haircut. Often we'd to make do with having our hair half-cut to save half of our salary. In fact, we were no different than long-term hired hands.

Now looking toward the future, I've no confidence. I'm afraid the rest of my life will be a lonely one.

People have advised me to marry again. I've carefully thought about it, but cannot make up my mind. I don't believe in match-makers. They can talk you out of your mind. And I don't trust myself, either. What if I was ensnared by a bitchy woman? What would I do then?

My children often come to see me. My daughter never forgets to bring me a portion when she cooks a good dish.

I've no hobby really. I just read newspapers, watch TV and listen to the radio in my sparetime. I don't go out. All you see outside are crowds of people and all you hear is noise. I'd rather stay at home.

Sometimes I go to the movies, mostly comedies. I remember someone once said that life was a tragedy. I've the same feeling. Finding humor and fun in life is an accomplishment.

I don't want to retire yet. I hope some day, before I'm too old to work, I'll have the chance to take a nude picture. Last year, I took a half-nude picture of a girl who said she was going abroad soon. As the picture wouldn't appear in the country, I said yes.

A year has passed and nothing has happened. Nevertheless, I'm sill apprehensive sometimes.

I've talked to no one but you about that wish of mine. Many people in our country still regard nude pictures as pornography, although we occasionally see exhibitions of nude photography.

Chiropodist: Tang Yongqun

People are interesting. They look down on this profession, but once they've trouble with their feet, and need podiatrists, they change their attitude drastically.

Unlike their counterparts in other countries, pedicurists in China do not have their own clinics. They usually work on their patients in public bathhouses. Public baths are common in this country, where hot water supply is scarce and few apartments are furnished with a bathtub or a shower. It is convenient to pedicure people while they are fresh from the bath. Yet the trade tends to be despised. Although many people could not do without pedicurists, few would consider them medical doctors.

Tang Yongqun, fifty-two, is one of two veteran bathhouse chiropodists in Hefei, capital of Anhui Province. He has been engaged in this type of work for thirty-two years.

When we meet, Tang, and his apprentice, are busy working in a special clinic attached to the Xinhua Bathhouse in downtown Hefei. Some clients are waiting inside the clinic; the others are in the corridor.

From the corridor, which leads to the big communal bath, it is impossible, because of the clouds of steam and smoke, to determine how many people are in the clinic.

In the ten-square-meter room, a stove provides warmth. There are two wooden deck chairs, opposite which are two plastic-coated sofas. Close to the door is a white cupboard containing ethyl alcohol, tincture of iodine, absorbent cotton, and other medicine for external application. Some are made by Tang himself from Chinese medicinal herbs.

I'm getting old. I feel more tired than ever before. The work before was sometimes a bit tiring, but now I often suffer from real fatigue.

People who come to bathe in the bathhouse often seek a chiropodist's services. My clients vary in age and sex, as anyone can suffer from foot disease. Some of them simply want their toenails trimmed, and some have ailments that need two hours of cleaning and cutting. On the busiest days, I treat sixty patients.

While bathers lie talking and laughing over tea, I bend working, a naked foot in one hand and a special knife in the other. Oh, the mixed smell of steam and foot odors used to repel me. But that doesn't bother me now because I've got used to it. I worked this way with ease when I was young, but now, oh,... If I go on working for two hours, my eyes become blurred, my arms sore, and my back hurts.

Chiropodists must pay special attention. I don't exaggerate. It's no easier than doing a fine piece of embroidery. In fact, it's harder, since they work on a piece of cloth while I work on flesh. On the one hand, light cleaning and cutting won't cure the disease. On the other hand, heavy cutting causes bleeding.

Last year one of my apprentices—only nineteen years old—cut too deeply into the foot of a patient. The boy was so frightened that he couldn't say anything when he saw the wound bleeding. I kept on telling the patient we were sorry. Not saying anything, he let us bandage his wound. But he never came back.

If a thing like this had happened to me, it would be very embarrasing, because I'm considered the best and most experienced chiropodist in the opinions of my fellow workers. They'd laugh at me.

There are as many as dozens of categories of foot diseases. Each requires a particular treatment.

If you can't distinguish one from another then you can't cure it. In addition, you must have some knowledge of psychology, or you won't succeed. For example, with children, you must be quick at cutting. When treating the old, it's important to be gentle and tender. As for women, being oversensitive to pain, may never come to you again if you hurt them.

The most common ailments are corn and callouses. Their treatment isn't difficult. First, I've the patient soak his feet in a basin of hot water. The water makes it easier to distinguish the corn from surrounding tissue. Then I sit down, wipe the patient's feet, and put them onto my knees, where a dry towel has been placed. I've to hold my breath while digging my knife into the corn. Finally, I apply ointment, and dress the wound.

I must work quickly because I don't use anesthetics. I remove a corn in minutes. Some of my clients say: "Foot illnesses departs at the very touch of Master Tang." That's true.

You can never guess how many corns there may be in the feet of a single person. Once I dug more than 200 corns out of the feet of a truck driver! This was new even to me. It took me two hours. According to the pricing—which is twenty-five *fen* for a corn—the driver should have paid at least fifty yuan. But I only charged him ten yuan because he didn't have enough money with him.

The most difficult foot disease to cure is what we pedicurists call *huayin* disease. The fungus infection covers quite a large area. Outwardly, it looks semi-transparent and feels hard. Underneath, it looks like a stalk of wild rice—a mixture of black dots and white tissue—and feels soft. Its treatment requires extreme carefulness. I slowly cut between the hard layers until the soft part is visible. During the process, any slightest overdoing leads to bleeding. Then I apply medicine to destroy the soft tissues. This kind of foot disease is stubborn to cure. It's not easy to get rid of it once and for all.

As our jargon goes: "Pedicure depends 30 percent on a master's skill, and 70 percent on his knives." I'm very fastidious about my knives. The first thing I do when I come here each morning is to sharpen my knives.

A typical pedicure knife looks like a chopstick but shorter. One end, which serves as the cutting edge, is a little bit wider and thinner than the other. I hold the knife in my right hand between my thumb, index and middle fingers while the other two fingers support my hand against the client's foot.

The work is disagreeable, tiring, and demanding —it really requires fine skills. When I see people who had foot trouble walking briskly after my treatment, I'm pleased because I feel that my efforts have been repaid.

My treatment is different from doctors in hospitals. Liu Mingfang, a worker in her mid-forties at Hefei No. 3 Radio Factory, is an example. She'd a swollen toe last year, and she was told by the doctor that she had paronychia, and that she had to have an operation to get the troubled nail removed. Fearfully, she turned to me. After examining her foot, I assured her that I'd cure the toe without taking off the toe nail. But all I'd do was disinfect her toe and bandage it because she screamed as I was probing.

After just one treatment, her toe had been cured. She was very grateful and now often comes to see me.

I don't think I'm more skilled than hospital surgeons. Obviously, they've their superiorities. But we pedicurists also have our advantages. We know foot diseases very well. To us, many foot ailments don't really require drugs or operations, notwithstanding assertions to the contrary by many surgeons. And it's more convenient and comfortable for foot sufferers to go to bathhouses than to see a doctor.

My philosophy is to do everything possible to help my patients. I often ask myself: If I were the patient, what kind of treatment would I want to get? So I work devotedly. I think that's why I'm popular with my clients.

People look down on this profession, but once they've trouble with their feet, and need chiropody, their attitudes change drastically. A nearby shop assistant was very unfriendly to me before I treated his foot corns. Now he never forgets to smile or offer me a cigarette whenever we have a chance encounter.

Society, however, never lacks people who hold pedicurists in scorn. Young men often tease me by saying, "Why, come, your father is waiting for your service!" Damn! Some people outwardly say my work is very important, but inwardly they are reluctant even to shake hands with me.

That kind of disrespect was rare until after the Cultural Revolution. I was annoyed at first, but later, I got used to it. I always comfort myself: those guys will certainly change their views when they come to me for help. I'm sure of that. And more importantly, I make a living through my own labor.

Fortunately, my family—my wife, two daughters

and two sons who are all employed—has never ridiculed me because of my job. One of my sons-in-law, a high school teacher, once said to me, "Dad, I admire your skill. Let me be your apprentice, OK?" I knew he was joking, but it was nice to hear.

My workmates respect me, both because I've worked longer than anyone else in the bathhouse and because I'm good at chiropody. I get along well with them—whether they are old or young.

Since Chinese Central Television Station included me in a special news program last year, more people have come to our bathhouse for treatment, and the bathhouse has set up a special clinic with me as head. I was promised I'd get 40 percent of the clinic's income in bonuses.

I told our bathhouse boss that I'd work hard for the clinic but refused to share in the income. My colleagues said, "What a fool you are! The share is considerably higher than the bonuses other workers get." I knew that, but I wasn't ready to make a bit more money at the risk of alienating myself from other workers. It wouldn't have been worthwhile. On the average, I get 180 yuan a month. That's enough. Compared with the 1960s, when my family's combined income was less than 100 yuan, we are doing well.

Public bathhouses are busy from October to May; the rest of the time is pretty slack. During this slack period, all bathhouse employees are assigned to other units in the service trade. I've served as a sanitation worker, a warehouse keeper, a waiter, and so on. However, I found chiropody suits me the best. I love it though I don't know why. I guess it's because it's a pleasure to relieve people of pain.

Hobbies? *Taijiquan* (Chinese shadow boxing) is my favorite. I began to learn it fifteen years ago, and now I do it every day. When one of my regular patients learned that I was physically weak, he advised me to do it. Still a bit skeptical, I studied it under a well-known local coach. The exercise really works. Soon I stopped taking medicines. Now I make it a rule to get up at five in the morning and go to *Xiaoyaojin* Park to practise. I once had a desire to raise flowers and goldfish, but I've no time to do such things because I've to work from eight a.m. to eight p.m. every workday.

I began to work in a bathhouse when I was fourteen. I've done all kinds of work. Now, most of my old workmates have retired, and been replaced by their sons and daughters.

Times are changing, workers are different. In the past, people worked with enthusiasm. They didn't care very much about money. But young workers now refuse to work more than eight hours a day unless they are paid overtime. Old workers continue to try to offer the best service, because we fear bad service would keep the clients from coming back. Young fellows never worry about that. They say, "They won't come? Ah, that's OK!"

I've had three apprentices. Two work in other bathhouses now, and one still works under my guidance. In terms of their skill, none of them is my equal. An important reason is that they are less committed to this profession. When I was an apprentice, I was eager to master the technique, which I believed was my only means of making a living.

My parents had ten children. I was the second. In the old days, my family lived in the countryside not very far from Hefei. My father was in poor health, so the whole family was living on what my mother could make laboring in the fields.

In 1947, when I was ten, I remember, we were very poor. Mother told us children to get up late and go to bed early every day, for she could provide us with only one meal a day—not rice but thin wheat porridge! On the eve of Spring Festival (Chinese lunar New Year), we "feasted" on two boiled eggs each.

As a teenager, I began to herd cows and make beancurd for the wealthy. Though I worked hard, I still couldn't feed myself.

In desperation, I left for Hefei, where one of my relatives was a partner in a bathhouse. I begged him for a job, saying that I'd do anything to avoid going back to the countryside.

So I began doing odd jobs at my relative's bathhouse—washing towels and spittoons, shining leather shoes, drying wet straw sandals, and running errands for the bathhouse operators. In this way, I received tips, which, though not much, were enough to support myself.

Zhang Yonghe, a chiropodist in the bathhouse, was well known for his skill. Whenever he worked, I'd stand nearby watching. He'd no children and was fond of me perhaps for this reason. One day he joked to me, "Boy, do you want to learn chiropody? If you do, go and buy me a package of cigarettes." This was a good chance to learn, I said to myself. When I returned with the cigarettes, he was astonished. "You can't break your promise to teach me," I told him. So he took me on as his apprentice. In the daytime, I followed my master and watched. At night, I practised by paring chopsticks.

In the 1956 campaign in which private enterprises and businesses were transformed into state-private ownership, I became a regular chiropodist at the Feifeng Bathhouse. Since then I've worked in several bathhouses in the city. I feel fortunate to have left the countryside and learned chiropody.

My apprentices haven't had such experiences because they don't know what it is to be hungry, they only think about changing jobs.

TV Relay Station Technician:
Feng Chaoneng

When I was sad, I'd sing and shout in the woods. That helped pull me through.

He is only twenty-one years old, but he thinks of himself as a man of great willpower. Living at a TV and broadcasting relay station on top of a mountain with a sullen companion, the isolation could be very depressing, but he has found many ways to amuse himself.

He is of slight build. Tattooed on his chest is a flying dragon. One of the some 60,000 Bulang people living in the mountains of Yunnan Province in Southwest China, he is proud of his Bulang nickname *A'aiyue*, which means "little rabbit."

Although from his mountain-top relay station, he can see the town below, he has come down the mountain only twice since he started the job a year and a half ago.

I was born in March of 1967. My father is a Bulang. He's been head of the weather station in our township since he left the army. My mother's of the Han nationality. She's no outside job. I've been able to speak both Mandarin and the Bulang dialect since I was young. People of the Bulang nationality don't record dates of their birth. My father says that I was born on the day "when our house caught fire."

I graduated from junior high school in August 1986. When the county broadcasting station was recruiting workers, I applied for a job and took an exam which I passed. After being offered a job, I reported to the station on December 15, 1986. The next day I climbed Buodao Mountain and began working at the relay station.

At the foot of our mountain is the county seat, only 900 meters above sea level. It's tropical climate suitable for growing bananas, papayas, and other tropical fruits. The mountain top, where the relay station's located, is 2,340 meters above sea level, and has an entirely different climate. It begins snowing in October.

The mountain's covered by forest, and it's often possible to spot wild animals. To get to the top of the mountain from the bottom, a person has to climb seven to eight kilometers, which would take even a healthy young man more than five hours.

There're only two of us at the relay station. My colleague is a fifty-year-old man of Han nationality. He doesn't play chess or poker, nor does he tell jokes or sing. So sometimes I'm lonely. On the mountain you can get a clear view of the houses and buildings down below. You can see people below moving about in the square. The contrast between the bustle down below and the desolateness surrounding you is striking. I've thought about leaving many times, but I haven't put in a formal request yet.

The relay station's two tasks. One's to receive TV programs from the provincial TV station. The other's to relay the programs of the county broadcasting station to various parts of the county. China Central TV (CCTV) programs are received by satellite at the county broadcasting station. This isn't part of our function.

I get up at six o'clock in the morning. At half past six, I turn on the machine that relays what's being received from the county broadcasting station. This includes the half-hour newscast by the Central People's Broadcasting Station (CPBS), and the county's own programs. I turn off the machine at eight, and cook breakfast. After that, I read or do whatever I like.

In order to relieve boredom, my colleague and I grow vegetables and raise twenty sheep and a pig. I'm also keeping thirty chickens. The feed for some of the animals has to be carried to the mountaintop from below, oftentimes by other people. But we've to cut grass ourselves for the pig and sheep. There're leopards and bears on the mountain. Two of our sheep have been killed by leopards. Yellow weasels also prey on my chickens. However, since I brought two dogs here, I haven't lost a single chicken.

The chickens and dogs are affectionate companions. Whenever I've free time, which is often, I play with them.

I'm also raising a beautiful pheasant. At the beginning, I put it in a cage. Later, I let it roam about freely in my dormitory. I enjoy watching this beautiful bird walking and flying about.

At 1:40 p.m., I go back to work, since the programs from the county broadcasting station resume. They are mainly music and announcements. At 2:10, I turn off the machine.

We've free time in the afternoon. I bought a shotgun. I go *chuanshan* (hunting) almost every afternoon. Although there're a lot of animals here, I cannot shoot bears, leopards, or hedgehogs, because they are "protected animals." I only hunt pheasants, other birds, and deer. *Chuanshan* (hunting) is a custom of the Bulang nationality. No matter how hard and dreary life is, hunting relieves many tensions. I enjoy the sport itself far more than the booty.

We begin to cook supper at half past four.

At six, I turn on the machine to receive programs from the provincial TV station and the county broadcasting station. The TV programs usually lasts until eleven.

I go to bed very late. After I turn off the machine, I begin practising *wushu*, or shadow boxing. I took a liking to *wushu* when I was a youngster. When I was in primary school, I learned a form of Bulang boxing called *Benquan* from an elderly man of the Bulang nationality. After the evening workout I read until falling asleep around one o'clock in the morning.

I don't feel tired although I only sleep about five hours a night. If I'm sleepy during the day, I just lean against something and take a short nap.

The books I read are technical ones related to my work here. We don't have teachers on the mountain so I've to teach myself. Self-reliance is a good thing. After more than a year's study, I've mastered the skills that are required for a station-relay man. I don't think I'd have made such progress if I'd been down below, where you can achieve nothing without connection. So, in this sense, I'm quite lucky.

However, I've had my share of hard times. I broke up with my girl friend. A high school classmate of mine, she became a worker in the county sugar mill after graduation. We were close friends for four or five months. We even exchanged letters through others after I came here to work at the relay station. However, by and by, we drifted apart.

Last May, when my grandmother died, I asked for

a two-day leave. My girl friend told me then that she no longer wanted to continue our relationship. She didn't want to work on the mountain, for once you are there, you cannot go home even if you've one.

Naturally, I was very sad. But I made up my mind not to leave just because of this. If I felt depressed, I'd walk into the middle of the forest where I'd shout and sing. *Chuanshan* (hunting) also helped.

My job here is quite hard, but I get a monthly salary of 160 yuan, which is higher than that of an engineer in the city. However, I haven't saved much. I don't spend a lot on food—only about thirty yuan a month. I've smoked a lot since breaking up with my girl friend. I smoke two packs of cigarettes a day. And that costs forty to fifty yuan a month. Besides, I drink one or two small cups of liquor before going to bed. I guess that's part of my Bulang heritage.

The tattooed dragon on my chest also is part of my ethnic heritage. All young boys have a design tattooed on their chests. It may be a snake, a dragon, or a hawk. Some also tattoo their names. I've had this dragon since I was a second-year pupil in primary school. Our fathers say that a dragon tattooed on the chest wards off evil spirits.

At the relay station, there are only two of us, or occasionally only one. I'm not afraid of "devils" or beasts, but I'm concerned about the thunder. The weather is strange up here. The thunderstorms in the summer are formidable, and the dry thunder in the winter is even more frightening. On New Year's Eve last year, a light snowstorm was accompanied by thunder. Our machine wasn't functioning, the lightening rod being bent.

Last year there were seven or eight thunderstorms. Our windows were smashed twice.

I've been here for a year and a half. Everything's okay. I don't feel as lonely as I used to. Now, I'm looking forward to taking a training course to improve myself.

Part Fourteen

To Mend and Repair

Antique Restorer: Zhao Zhenmao

I was once a beggar. Now I'm a research fellow and a restorer of antiques in the Forbidden City.

He represents a Chinese success story.

At seventy-three, Zhao Zhenmao has witnessed many of the joys and sorrows of life. He was once a beggar in the streets—a social outcast. Now he is a research fellow and topgrade restorer of antiques.

Zhao has repaired a variety of ancient Chinese artifacts, including some collections in the Forbidden City, where he has worked for the past thirty-six years. As China's most prestigious antique restorer, he also is a veteran connoisseur of cultural relics.

He has a rectangular face. His hair is white, and his hands are rough because of years of work. A bit hard of hearing, he speaks with a strong Hebei accent.

Zhao and his family live in a two-room apartment in the suburbs of northeast Beijing. His home is modestly furnished. There is a 12-inch black-and-white TV set, a washing machine, and an electric fan. On a bookshelf, there is a replica of a tri-colored glazed horse of the Tang Dynasty (618-907). There are no apparent signs of wealth.

He likes old things, such as bronzes, yet he wishes he had modern appliances such as a color TV set or a refrigerator.

I've just retired from the historical relics repair department of the Palace Museum (formerly the Forbidden City). I'm a bit old. But the shop hopes to benefit from my experience, so they've employed me as an advisor.

According to regulations, people with special skills retire at the age of seventy instead of sixty. Although it sounds egotistical, the shop cannot do without me. As a Chinese proverb says "An old horse knows the way."

I'm currently writing a book entitled *The Techniques of Repairing Ancient Bronze Ware* which will be a summation of my work. It will be published by the Palace Museum Press.

But I feel sorry on account of my lack of a formal education.

In 1953, though skilled as an antique restorer, I was also totally illiterate. Fortunately, the government allowed me to attend a part-time school to learn how to read and write. Now I can read newspapers and books. For this, I'm grateful to the new government. I don't worry about my book as an editor will take care of problems having to do with the manuscript.

In the field of antique repairing, there're very few people like me in China. You can probably count the number of them on two hands. I repair ancient bronze ware, frescos, handicrafts made of gold, silver or jade, lacquerware, porcelain, pottery, and tortoise shells with ancient inscriptions. As they are all a priceless part of our cultural heritage, I'm proud to be helping to preserve them. Some years ago, Pu Jie, the younger brother of the last emperor of China, asked me to repair a small quadripod for him because he knew of my skill.

In my repair shop, our job is to maintain, preserve, and restore numerous collections of the Palace Museum. There're more than fifty of us. A dozen copy and mount ancient pictures. There're also four men who specialize in fixing a large collection of clocks and watches.

To fix a bronze artifact, over a dozen techniques and various materials have to be employed. Most bronze wares have been buried for thousands of years and are badly damaged when unearthed. To restore them, we have to remove the rust, figure out the original shape, and weld the broken pieces. This is a time-consuming job. Take for example, the world-famous "Flying Horse of Gansu" a brilliant centuries-old bronze sculpture. Originally, there were holes in the horse's neck, and its mane and tail were missing. It took me a week to fix it. Repairing a broken *bangui*, a kind of container used during the Shang Dynasty (16th—11th century B.C.), took me the longest time of all-four months. Furthermore, you have to restore an object to its original shape. It should be what it was; otherwise your work will destroy the artifact rather than restore it.

The restoration of antiques is an art in itself. An antique fixer has to be well versed in art, history, and metallurgy. He also must have the discriminating qualities of an art connoisseur.

So I ponder for a long time over what I can do and should do with a particular piece of art before I actually start to restore it.

Bronze ware, with its history of over 4,000 years in China, played a very important role in our ancient culture. Bronze ware over the different dynasties evolved into many different styles and periods. I recognize differences. I have been invited to be a member of the Cultural Relic Evaluation Committee under the Ministry of Culture.

Apart from restoring antiques, I'm also good at copying them. Our factory makes reproductions of ancient artifacts for display and teaching purposes.

I've trained many apprentices who now work in various provincial museums all over China. In 1973, I even took on an Uygur girl as my apprentice. She came from a museum in Xinjiang in Northwest China. I taught her and others for a year. During this time they mastered the basic techniques of antique restoration. Before I retired, I'd nine apprentices. But as they didn't work hard, they are not skilled in doing delicate, more exacting work. Young people today don't listen to you.

Although I'm an old hand of my trade, I'm completely ignorant in dealing with modern things. I know nothing about bikes, radios, or TVs. When my own radio goes wrong, I have to take it to the mechanic, which costs money.

As a retired person, I'm beginning to feel old, and my health is deteriorating. I no longer care about success the way young people today do.

I know nothing about keeping fit. Having always been in good health in the past, I never worried about it. But I know I've to take care of myself now.

I've no particular hobbies. Having spent so many years working with ancient and dead objects, I myself became somewhat introverted and taciturn. Some of the retired people in my neighborhood love to play chess or listen to Beijing Opera. But I don't like mixing with people. I like to be by myself.

I can't afford to collect antiques myself, as my

limited salary goes to support my family and I've very little money left. But I've kept some photos of the antiques that I have restored.

I've three sons and two grandchildren. My wife is a housewife. My eldest son is a Party leader in a factory. My second son has been mute from birth. He ploughs fields in my native village. My youngest son is now a worker in a factory that makes kitchen utensils. My sons are dutiful and respect me. Some time ago, the eldest bought a washing machine for us.

My father was a horse-cart driver. He lost all his money when he went into business and left. My mother had to cook meals for a landlord. My eldest brother was forced to join a local warlord's army in the 1930s and was killed in a fight. In 1930, when I was fifteen, I left my native village in Hebei Province with a few others to try to make a living. As it turned out, I had to beg for several months before finally making it to Beijing.

I was introduced to Zhang Wenpu, a skillful antique restorer and owner of an antique shop. He accepted me as an apprentice, although he, in reality, used me as a cheap laborer. Zhang took on many apprentices as well. However, only seven people later became masters in this trade. Of these seven people, all are dead, except me and one other man who works at the Museum of Chinese History.

Under Zhang, we worked from morning till night. Sometimes he beat us. Zhang made a fortune by restoring antiques and owned six houses. Later, he indulged in gambling and heavy drinking. He died not long ago.

Zhang didn't intend to pass his skills to us. We were only given heavy manual work to do. But when

Zhang was restoring antiques, we stood and watched, trying to take everything in by heart. Sometimes, when Zhang was happy, he might give us some instructions. As time passed by, we tried to restore antiques ourselves. A master can only point the way for you, and then you've to go down the road yourself.

In 1938 I started an antique shop myself, which I ran for twelve years.

In 1952 I was employed by the Palace Museum because many cultural relics in the Forbidden City were in poor condition and needed repairing. I've been there ever since.

Now I'm a senior antique restorer and research fellow, with a title equivalent to that of a professor. I earn a monthly salary of 160 yuan, plus some bonus, which brings the total to about 200 yuan.

If you asked me to sum up my experience, I'd say: Restoring antiques, like anything else, is no easy job. You've to be steadfast and concentrate before you can do it well.

Bicycle Repairman: Ren Wenming

I've been working all my life. I'd feel uneasy if I were idle all the time.

Many foreign visitors call China "a kingdom of cyclists" because of the important role bicycles play in the daily life of the Chinese people. Townspeople ride bicycles to get to work, to send their children to creches and kindergartens, to do shopping, and to go sightseeing. Farmers ride their bicycles to the fields and to markets. They use them also to visit relatives in other villages. In the south, farmers even use bicycles to transport live hogs and coffins to the market.

In Beijing during the rush hours between 6:30 and 8:00 in the morning and between 4:00 and 5:30 in the afternoon, hundreds of thousands of bicycles pour into the streets. Statistics show there are more than six million bicycles in greater Beijing (which includes ten suburban counties).

The mammoth number of bicycles poses a serious maintenance problem which the state- and collective-run repair shops can never hope to cope with. Fortunately, an increasing number of individual repairmen have been setting up repair stands at major street intersections or opening small shops. Ren Wenming, a sixty-seven-year-old retired mechanic, is one of the new group.

Ren usually makes ten *yuan* daily from his repair work. This comes to about 300 *yuan* a month equivalent to the salary of a senior college professor. This income, plus his and his wife's pension, has enabled Old Ren and his wife to lead a comfortable life.

Except for his house, Old Ren had nothing to complain about. He, his wife, and his son originally lived in a spacious room with a small bathroom. But nine years ago when his son got married, the old couple had the bathroom refurnished into a bedroom and moved into it, leaving the bigger room to the bride and bridegroom. But there is still hope for Ren as regards housing. When the municipality decides to pull down the dilapidated one-story houses to make room for highrise apartment buildings, Ren may be allotted a flat.

I retired in 1981 after working for thirty years in an electronics factory. The idea of repairing bikes come from my nephew, who was good at this work. I spent a little more than 100 *yuan*, about the monthly salary of an ordinary worker, to start the business.

The beginning was interesting. I asked the help of a relative who worked in a ministry and knew someone in the department that issued licenses. They asked me why I, at this age, wanted to enter a business. I just smiled, and they seemed to understand.

For those entering the bike-repair business, there's an examination which consisted of having would-be do certain repairs in order to demonstrate their qualifications. But since my relative knew someone in that license department, I obtained the license without taking an examination. That was in late 1985. In addition, people knew I'd worked as a mechanic for a long time, and they didn't doubt my skills.

It's not difficult to have a bike repaired or cleaned. Lots of people nowadays complain about the charges of repairmen. But this isn't a problem for me. I've never overcharged a customer.

Once a man came to me with a broken spindle on his bike. He left the bicycle for me to repair. The next day, he picked up his bike. Several days later, he brought it back, protesting that I'd overcharged him and that I hadn't changed his spindle. I examined it and found that the spindle hadn't been changed. I didn't do the job. It was done by my nephew, and he was away when the customer was there. I didn't know whether he'd had installed a new one or had the previous one repaired. The man was angry. But I tried to remain calm, saying that the cost being only 4.5 *yuan*, there was no need to shout. I told him I'd give him back two and a half *yuan*, which he accepted. Later, I found out he was living in our neighborhood, and I think he knew that too. He was embarrassed, and didn't look at my repairshop when he passed it.

Since I started business two and a half years ago, I don't like to see bikes that don't work. I prefer having them repaired. I can tell you what's wrong with your bike after riding it for a while. A satisfactory thing for me is to see satisfied customers ride away.

Another thing that inspired me to start the repair business was to make a living. One can't do without money. As a Chinese saying goes, "You can have nothing but money, and you can have anything but disease." My monthly pension is ninety *yuan*, and it's difficult to live on this with rising prices. I don't seek to make big money. Just enough to support the family. My wife used to be a mobile worker at a pharmaceutical factory and her retirement pension is only sixty-five *yuan*.

I want to be self-supportive. That's why I decided to repair bicycles. People are different from one another. Some couldn't understand why I started a business at my age. But I wanted to do it. And this money helps me a great deal. I've a son who's a worker. He's married and has an eight-year-old daughter. I can make a contribution to the family, and am proud to be able to do so. I want my family to benefit from the money I earn. Members in my family take care of, rather than depend on, one another.

I want to express thanks to the community committee. They certified my application to start the business. However, I'm not happy with my housing. It's dark and dirty, but I can do nothing about it. I hope to live in a cleaner and brighter house.

I go out to a place about 300 meters away from my home. It's located at a crossroad and I find that many people are very considerate of me because of my age. They often go out of their way to my stand so that I've some business. But there're times when young men steal tools when I'm busy with repair work. On the whole, society's friendly, but it's unfriendly sometimes.

No matter what season it is, I always go out. In the cold winter, I go out when the sun shines, and get back home at four or five in the evening. The cold wind's the most unpleasant. Just look at my hands. They're so chapped. Some cyclists're very symphathetic, and send me rubber gloves. But they don't last. Besides, you've to take them off when doing delicate things like patching up broken inner tyres. The work'll be ruined if there's any dirt in the glue.

I've thought of buying a big umbrella that'll shade me from hot sunshine, or rain. I also want to get a big bench, since that'll make my stand more impressive. But the city environmental committee won't permit it.

I've to pay 5.3 *yuan* as a market administration fee

each month, and 15 *yuan* for tax. The administration fee used to be 2.3 *yuan* but in the past month it's risen to 5.3 *yuan*. I don't know whether tax or other fees also will rise.

People come to us individual bike repairers because we're located throughout the city. We do repairs which many state-run repair shops won't do. For instance, they refuse to repair broken tyres since the fees are low, and the work's difficult. They seem to neglect their duty to help customers.

I've no weekends off, and go out only if it doesn't rain. The repair work's interesting because you can help people. And you can meet new people and talk with them while you're working. It's a lot better than just sitting in a tiny room all by yourself. I've been working all my life, and would feel uneasy if I were idle all the time. My wife takes care of the housework, such as shopping, cooking, and looking after our little granddaughter.

Repairing a bike isn't very difficult. But still you'd always try to improve your skills. Once, a veteran repairman came to my stand to borrow some tools. I learned from him how to round out the rim of a bicycle wheel, and how to adjust the spikes.

Fortunately, I'm very healthy. I'm not a drinker. A glass of beer will put me under the table. I smoke a few cigarettes, but I'm not addicted to nicotine. My spare time entertainment's watching the news programs on TV. Weather forecasts are important, but I don't understand the foreign movies and TV series. Local Chinese dramas, such as Beijing Opera, Pingju Opera, are interesting, and I love comic cross-talk.

However strong I may be, I'm tired after a long working day. I hope to work another two or three years. I don't know whether I can go on with the business after I'm seventy. I'll quit if I don't feel strong enough to go on.

Watchmaker: Liu Pinyi

I only hope that someday people will say: "I have a watch for him to repair, but he's dead." It would be too bad if they said: "why's the old fellow still alive?"

Liu Pinyi, sixty-six, runs his "Jingshi Watchmaker's Shop" in East Beijing's Chaoyang District.

The walls of his room are hung with at least fifty framed letters of appreciation and souvenirs from his customers, in addition to a business license and a price table.

The letters, both in Chinese and English, praise the shopkeeper for his excellent craftsmanship and service.

"They represent only a small number of my customers," said the grey-haired Liu in a strong Northeast Chinese accent. Wrinkles stretch above his square jaw as he smiles.

Liu, who is dressed in a blue Mao suit as most ordinary Chinese of his age, has repaired watches for forty years. He was born into a rural family. He couldn't afford to go to school. At five, he began to tend cattle for a landlord. In his early teens, he washed dishes in a small restaurant. As a young man, he learned watch-repair skills from an itinerant watchmaker in his hometown of Yichun, Heilongjiang Province in Northeast China.

He came to Beijing in 1953 with his wife, a fellow villager, hoping to improve his skills and lead a better life. He worked in a state-run watchmaker's shop until he retired in 1979.

He came out of retirement and opened his own shop three years later when the government began to encourage individual business.

He has repaired more than 70,000 watches of all brands

and types. Three fourths of the watches he repaired were done free of charge.

He and his fifty-four-year-old wife, also a retired worker, have two sons and two daughters, all married and working in Beijing.

I was a senior watchmaker before I retired. As a retiree, I'd have been living in ease and comfort, enjoying my pet birds, and playing chess and cards like many other old Beijing people. But, instead, I returned to my trade.

There's no special reason that I did so. I'm a faithful reader of the *Beijing Evening News.* An article the newspaper carried one day in 1981 caused me to resume watch repair. I still remember the main points of the article. It went something like this:

More and more peole nowadays can afford a watch given the improved economic conditions in the country. They, however, have difficulty in getting their watches repaired. City-, state- and collectively-owned watch repair shops usually don't bother with watches that have only minor problems, because it isn't profitable. And if people take watches with only minor problems to these repairmen, they are charged heavily.

How can a watchmaker sit idly when he's aware that many people are in need of watch repairs? So I decided to resume my old trade and set up a shop to help those in need.

I provide service guarantees. That is, if your watch breaks down again within half a year after my service, you can bring it back to me for free service. I also don't charge for adjusting, repairing watch straps, fixing watch hands, or clearing water from the watch.

To customers, it's an annoyance to have a watch that is always slow or fast a few minutes. That's easy to correct. It takes just a few minutes. I'd feel guilty if I charged for such a minor repair.

Free service takes up much of my working time and certainly results in a lower income. However, I feel I've done something worthwhile when I see customers come in worried but leave happily.

I've no skills except for repairing watches. Why not use this craftsmanship to serve the people? This, to put it in a formal way, I consider to be a contribution to society.

In China there's an old saying that "persons of the same trade are enemies," meaning that one'll take some business away from the other. I don't agree with that. Competition between counterparts is inevitable. But I think friendship and cooperation are more important.

To put my feelings into action, I made a rule: any customer can have a free service in my shop within six months after he had his watch repaired in another shop, no matter whether state- and collectively-owned or individually-run. I do this because other watchmakers are charging for repair work even if a watch breaks two days after they repair it.

Don't you think it's better that customers use the money saved to buy other commodities?

My service has won more customers. However, it's resulted in resentment on the part of a few of my counterparts.

One morning when I got to my shop, I found a piece of paper stuck to the door. It was an anonymous letter which warned me to be "careful" if I continued to offer free services.

I was so angry that I tore it up. I paid no attention to the threat. So far nothing has happened to me. There's nothing to fear now even if misfortune happens to me someday.

My business is booming. More and more customers, Chinese and foreign, are coming to my shop. Some even send me their watches by mail.

I was very busy and assistants were badly needed.

In the winter of 1982, my eldest son was discharged from the navy and was at home waiting for the government to assign him a job. I persuaded him to join me.

I told him that if he worked with me, he'd leave a job vacant to others looking for employment. At the same time, he'd earn more money than an ordinary worker in a factory.

He finally agreed. Several months later, one of my daughters resigned from a state-run factory and became my second apprentice, again at my urging.

Every morning I get up at 6:30 and go out to run half an hour for exercise. After eating my usual breakfast of two eggs and milk, I ride a bicycle to work, which takes about fifteen minutes.

I arrive at the shop at around 8:00 and begin to clean the room, sort through the watches I worked on in the previous days to see which should be ready for their owners. And lay out tools and spare parts for that day's work. I'm ready to receive customers at 9:00.

Business hours are from 9:00 to 12:00 in the morning, but I often work until 1:00 p.m., or even later, because of a long queue of people with broken watches.

I devote the morning mainly to those watches that

can be repaired quickly. I deal with the difficult ones in the afternoon, and at night.

I go home for lunch if I can close the shop at 12:00. If I can't, my wife, an amiable woman who never takes issue with what I do, brings me my lunch.

After lunch I take a one- or two-hour nap, and then start a closed-door operation on the watches I received in the morning. The day's work ends at around 10:00 p.m., and I go home to eat supper.

I usually drink three glasses of boiled water before supper. I never drink water during work time, even in summer. My philosophy is that excessive water puts an extra burden on the stomach and, in the long run, damages one's health. A person should learn to take care of himself.

However, I don't drink liquor. Neither do I smoke. I like fish, shrimps, and fresh vegetables. I never touch meat. Any kind of meat.

Let me tell you my childhood story.

I was stricken with typoid fever when I was two. One day I was breathless. My relatives, assuming that I was dead, carried me to a wilderness area to bury me. As I lay down, a dog circled my body, smelling me.

My mother, who was in deep grief and sorrow, noticed the strange behavior of the dog. She put a hand on my chest and found that my heart still was beating. I was taken home. So I wasn't doomed to die early.

Upon recovery, I asked for meat. My mother cooked me a lot. I don't know where, or how she got it. But I'm sure she must have sold the most valuable things in our poor family. I ate so much meat that I grew sick of it. I've never touched it again.

Now I'm in good health. Medical check-ups show my internal organs are working as well as my watches. If I didn't look into the mirror, I wouldn't admit that I was over sixty. I still feel as if I were in my thirties. A day's work comes easily.

Most of the difficult jobs involve old or foreign-made watches. Spare parts for them are in short supply. Watchmaker's shops, in general, refuse to repair such watches, which consume time and aren't profitable.

To help customers, I decided to deal with the difficult problems.

Clients come here because they still think their watches are useful although watches nowadays are something even rural residents can afford. On the other hand, they won't seek your help if they don't trust you. So why should you turn a cold shoulder to them?

I accept watches that have been refused by other watchmakers. I also try every means to repair it, particularly when other means have failed.

A Beijing customer has a watch that stopped because of a broken spring. Many well-known watchmaker's shops in major Chinese cities had either failed or refused to repair it. I repaired it by changing the spring. The cost was only 2.1 *yuan*.

I'm not saying that my craftsmanship is better than that of my counterparts at home and abroad. Still, it's really far from easy to master the skills needed to repair watches. I cannot remember how many days and nights I've devoted to this profession. In the early days, when I was recruited by the state-run watchmaker's, I even moved to the shop so that I could devote all my time to master the skills.

However, excellent craftsmanship isn't the only decisive factor. It's the spirit of serving the people, heart and soul, that helps make things go. As a matter of fact, there's nothing one cannot do if he really wants to.

Professor and Dr. Heinz Herlinger, a textile and chemical fiber expert from Stuttgart, West Germany, lecturing in China, came to my shop with an old pocket watch. He told me, through his interpreter, that the watch was from his father. In Europe it was impossible to repair. He wanted it repaired, whatever the cost.

Even without examining it, I knew it would be a tough job to deal with a 100-year-old watch. But since the professor was here to help us in China, I felt I'd help him in return.

I spent three nights cleaning the dirt from the watch and with tools I made myself filing the springs to replace the broken ones.

With the repaired watch in hand, Professor Herlinger was delighted. He offered me 6,000 *yuan* in Foreign Exchange Currency as the repair fee.

That's more than two years' income for an ordinary Chinese worker, but I declined the offer. I told him I did the repair work for the friendship that existed between our peoples. Money can never buy friendship.

Some people don't understand me, however. They say I'm a fool who's ready to run a business at a loss. But I think differently.

You see, a man should have brains: a big one and a small one. The former should concentrate on the country's interests and the future, while the latter should pay attention to personal affairs and the present. The big one should control the small. This time my big brain told me not to take the FEC offered. I didn't. Even if you put gold before me, I'd never touch it.

Still some people ridicule me for seeking publicity. My answer is: I must take the lead in letting every foreign friend feel the warmth, hospitality and friendship of the Chinese people.

Professor Herlinger wrote some articles in praise of China's individually-run businesses and its open-door policy after he returned to West Germany. When I learned about it, I was pleased. It was an indication that my work is related to the country's reputation.

Sometimes I go to repair watches in schools, universities and other institutes where intellectuals work, if weather permits.

I didn't have the opportunity to go to school when I was young. I hope all of today's children receive a good education. Teachers, as treasures of the country, ought to be respected. They've much to take care of. They cannot afford to go from one watchmaker's to another to correct a minor problem with their watches. I want to save precious time for them.

You can hardly imagine how they need services offered at their door. Last month I did repair work at the Beijing Teachers' College. I'd planned to work there for one day. But I had to be there again the next day, for the queue of staff with broken watches waiting for repair seemed to be endless.

As I was about to leave, some of them, holding my hands, tears in their eyes, told me, "Mr. Liu, I appreciate your kindness. Thank you very much."

I'm not an ambitious man. I only hope that someday when I'm dead, people will say: "I have a watch for him to repair, but he is dead." It would be too bad if they said behind my back: "Why is the old fellow still alive?"

Part Fifteen

To Beautify

Hairdresser: Ahua

I want to make a name for myself

On a secluded street in Beijing is the small Dafang Beauty Parlor, which can accomodate only three customers at a time. Ahua is attending to a young man, whose hair is shoulder-length. The young man asks that his hair be done in the style of the hairdresser. He smilingly tells the customer that the way his hair is done is no longer stylish.

The hairdresser is Wang Zhihua. His boss and close friends call him Ahua according to Guangdong custom.

Now at the age of twenty-three, he has worked for a number of beauty parlors in Guangzhou, Shenzhen, Changsha and Zhuzhou in the past four years. He came to this small parlor in Beijing three months ago to establish his identity and make a name for himself. He made this job contact through the introduction of a friend.

It's a practice for Beijing's private parlor owners to hire master hairdressers from fashion-conscious Guangdong Province in the south. It is said that every beauty parlor has at least one hairdresser from Guangdong employed there. And there are 1,300 parlors like Dafang in Beijing.

I never expected to become a hairdresser, but the whole thing seems to have been predestined.

I found it enjoyable to style hair for my friends when I was a high school student. I observed people's hairstyles as I walked the streets or, looked at pictures in publications. If I noticed something new or something unusual, I would be anxious to try it out myself.

The first time I styled someone's hair was in the ninth grade. Once a classmate and I saw a man whose haircut was very attractive. It was a short, straight, pseudo-punk haircut. My classmate wondered how it was done, and I offered to do one for him.

Back home, I clipped his hair in the style I remembered seeing. Then I sprayed some water on his hair and combed it backward. The hair seemed to stand straight. Since it was my first try and was, to a considerable extent, based on my memory, the work was naturally far from perfect. In some places I cut a bit too much, while in others, I cut too little. Now, as I look back, I marvel at my boldness. As the saying goes: newborn calves aren't afraid of tigers!

Cutting hair for my friends became a hobby of mine. Usually I did it at lunch time or after school so it wouldn't affect my studies.

However, some of the teachers were opposed to certain styles. They thought that men wearing long hair were "hippies," who should be criticized.

That thinking's absurd because we shouldn't judge a person by his appearance. What's more important is what he does. I love having my hair long, because short hair dosen't fit the shape of my face.

Since I left school, I can wear my hair as long as I please.

In 1983, I took entrance exams to qualify for higher education. But I didn't pass it, so I remained idle for some time at home, hoping that I would be assigned a job as a result of the exams. Yet no job was offered. My father suggested that I learn a trade. He believed that one should earn his living through the use of skills. So I went to work in a beauty parlor run by a friend of mine in Guangzhou. He had hired a man who had been to Hong Kong.

I started as an apprentice, the lowest of the three grades of hair-stylists. My work was to shampoo and place hair pins.

The next grade is barber, who clips and sets simple hair styles, under the guidance of a master. Once you become a master, the top of the three grades, you are entitled to share profits with the employer. The length of each period depends on the individual's talent. For some, it may be very long. Since I had learned some basic skills in the past, it took me only eighteen months to become a master, which is quite fast.

My parents are workers. My father is a truck driver. My mother is a retired pharmacy worker. They don't object to what I choose to do, as long as it's good for society. I've been working as a hairdresser for four years, and I enjoy doing it.

When you're an apprentice, you learn very basic skills. To advance, you've to be innovative. This trade of ours challenges one's perceptions. Some people want to follow what is fashionable. They want certain hair styles whether or not they are actually suitable for them. In fact, one style doesn't fit everyone. It should be determined by the configuration of one's face, features and age. For instance, a crew cut isn't appropriate for a person with a round face, while long hair is unsuitable for a person with a long face.

Each person has his own tastes. My policy is to

meet the client's request. I'll fix his hair according to his wishes. Of course, I'll let him know if I think the style he wants doesn't fit him, and I'll offer my suggestions. But if the client persists in his preference, I'll follow his decision, and try my best to make him look good. After all, the client is our god. The existence of a beauty parlor is to let everyone who goes out look their best.

People in North China and in South China have different preferences when it comes to hairstyles. Many northerners prefer to wear their hair long, while nowadays more southerners tend to choose a shorter haircut. This is probably a matter of climate. Short hair is certainly not suited to the long, cold winters in the north. It's different in the south. Besides, the south sees more, and faster, changes of hair styles. Perhaps it's because the south is geographically closer to the outside world and more subject to its influences. I guess this is a reason that Beijing's beauty parlors love to hire hairdressers from Guangdong. And we Cantonese love to travel.

I have worked in several parlors. I prefer bosses who are easy-going and humorous. Like the one I'm working with now. He doesn't put on airs and lends a hand when we are overburdened.

What I consider to be the most important is to be in good spirits. That way, the workload seems to be less heavy. If the boss is hot-tempered, even a doubling of your salary won't make the job worthwhile. I always select bosses who are to my liking.

While in Beijing, my employer provides board and lodging, and we share profits, normally a seventy/thirty split between my boss and me. Among the parlors I've worked with, this one is medium in terms of income. Yesterday, for instance, the four of us made 200 *yuan*. That sounds OK, doesn't it?

Since our parlor isn't on the main street, it cannot be compared with those in the downtown area, which have become famous. But this is the only parlor on this street. So long as we do a good job and establish a reputation for our skills, I'm sure more people will come to us.

I work from 9 a.m. to 9 p.m., twelve hours a day. But I'm not busy all the time. There are periods when few customers show up. At such times I'll have a cigarette and take a break. If it rains or snows, it is likely that there will be no business. So I'll take a day off.

How do I spend my days off? I go to other parlors to chat with my friends and to keep myself abreast of the latest hair styles and new skills brought by those fresh from the south. Sometimes I go sightseeing. I've been to the Great Wall, Ming Tombs, Summer Palace and many other sites in the Beijing area.

I also like reading. I've collected quite a few books about new trends in hair styles. Some of them are published here in the mainland, others come from Hong Kong. I also like to read books about motoring and car maintenance. I have a driver's license.

Yes, I do read novels. My favorite novelist is Jin Yong of Hong Kong. His stories about ancient heroes are fascinating. Every night, I spend at least one hour reading before going to bed.

I won't say how much I make every month. But I can say it's enough for me to enjoy life. From time to time I dine out. I went back home by plane during the Spring Festival (Chinese lunar New Year) holidays. And every month I have some surplus and send it home. My parents don't need the money, so they put it in the bank for me. We usually don't use cheques or credit cards in China, and it's not safe to keep cash with me, since I'm often on the move.

A girl friend? That hasn't come to my mind seriously. I had a former classmate who used to be close to me. We were on good terms. But since I had to make a living away from home, I said goodbye to her. I don't want to keep anybody waiting for me. Maybe I'll marry someone with whom I can get along well. I don't know. That matter is too far away for serious thinking. I'm not yet ready to settle down.

So long as society values my efforts, I think I'll continue to be a hairdresser. If it appears that my skills are no longer required or appreciated, I'll do something else. Probably I'll become a taxi driver. But personally I prefer hairdressing. I think it's an art since it requires creativity.

I don't want to run a parlor of my own. I love to be mobile. It's boring to stay in one place too long. I seldom stay with a parlor for a long period, because I want to see more of the world. Although the employer here is good to me, I will be leaving soon. I'll go to Shenyang or Harbin in the northeast. Later I'll go to Xinjiang and Inner Mongolia.

It never has occurred to me that the current policy may change. If there is a change, I think it'll be for the better.

I don't understand politics and I'm not very much interested in it. My judgement of a policy is to see whether it allows individuals to use their talent to the fullest. As far as I'm concerned, the current policy has allowed me to do this, so I think it's good.

Fashion Designer: Song Fusheng

Some young ladies want good taste in clothing, but many of them don't know what good taste is.

The short, thin, elderly man is one of the top ten garment designers in Shanghai, China's leading fashion center. Now sixty-four years old, he has received many honors.

His is a "garment making" family. His two daughters, one of his two sons and his son-in-law also are in the garment industry. He has trained a large number of garment designers, including some gold and silver medal winners in the national garment designing contest.

But he is saddened sometimes, since neither of his two sons has met his expectations. One is a welder, and the other has just begun to learn the ABCs of design under his tutelage. And he is separated from his family—he lives alone in Shanghai, while his family still lives in his hometown, Chuansha County 25 kilometers east of Shanghai. He returns home every weekend and on major national holidays.

I never thought that one day I'd be a prominent woman dress designer in Shanghai. I got only a primary school education. Though I was a top student, my parents couldn't afford to give me higher education. They owned a small piece of land that just barely supported our family of five members. They sent me to my uncle's family in Shanghai in order to make a living. I was then fourteen years old.

My uncle helped me a lot. He got me jobs in factories and shops as a bookkeeper or junior clerk. But I was fired time and again because I came from the countryside and spoke Shanghainese with a very thick local accent. Finally my uncle found a "suitable" job for me which didn't "require a mouth"—working as an apprentice in a tailor's shop. In the old days, tailoring, bricklaying and carpentering were regarded as the three "best" businesses for the poor, because they didn't require higher education.

I was short and thin then, as I'm today. I'm only 1.62 meters tall and weigh only forty-nine kilograms. I still remember the day my uncle called me: "*Afu* (my petname), my poor thing, I'm sorry I can't find a better job for you. If you like, you can go to a tailor's shop to learn a trade. You see, since you're short and thin, it might be a good job for you."

An indoor job was ideal for me since I couldn't do heavy work. Tailoring, therefore, was my first choice.

But at that time, things were quite different from the way they are today. As an apprentice, I learned almost nothing about tailoring in the first two years. I just looked after my master's children, cleaned the house, and did cooking and other chores for the master. The master was the boss and also the only tailor in the shop. My boss was at least ten years older than I was. After two years, the boss began to teach me how to cut out garment patterns and sew them into pieces of clothing. At that time, everything was done by hand. A sewing machine was luxury, even in a tailor's shop. But actually the boss didn't like teaching me and often lost his temper on this account. At other times, he swore at me and beat me for no reason. I didn't like him. However, years later, when

I worked for a big clothing shop and had an apprentice of my own, I began to understand him better. Who would want to pass his knowledge and skills to others and thus create competitors for himself?

After serving out my apprenticeship for five years, I went to work at a Russian-owned garment shop on Maoming Road in downtown Shanghai. I learned how to make Western-style garments, especially Western-style women's dresses in the shop.

Since then, I've worked for several clothing shops and factories as a garment designer. But earlier, we were looked down upon as "tailors" or "craftsmen."

In 1949, New China was founded. I was then twenty-five, and was a fairly well-known Western-style garment designer in Shanghai. I started to work at Shanghai Garment Company in 1958, specializing in designing women's dress for export.

Now I'm regarded as the number one "women's dress designer" in Shanghai. The honors I've received are due to the Communist Party of China and to the state. Without their help, I couldn't have become a first-class designer. The state sent me to study at the Central Academy of Arts and Crafts in Beijing in 1960, where I majored in garment design, adult body structure and garment structure for ten months. The state also sent me abroad to exchange ideas on garment designs with my counterparts and to study local styles in different countries.

I've been to the Soviet Union, Syria, Kuwait, Iraq, Lebanon, Bahrain, and Japan. At present, the Chinese-made women's dresses I've designed are selling well in those places. A wider range of women's clothing I've designed also have been exported to the United States, Hong Kong, Australia, Canada, Cuba, Czechoslovakia, and Poland, as well as to Southeast Asia and the Middle East. I've designed all kinds of lady's wear, ranging from pyjamas, skirts, blouses, summer dresses, overcoats, two-piece suits, to cheongsams (a traditional Chinese-style women's dress with a slit skirt and a mandarin collar).

I probably designed 200 types of women's clothing a year before my retirement in 1981. I was supposed to stop working as a lady's garment designer after that. However, my employer—the Shanghai Garment Research Institute (the predecessor was the Shanghai Garment Company)—asked me to serve as an advisor to the institute's design section. So I've never stopped working for even a day, except on holidays. Now I do have more free time than before, because the institute has placed no limits on my working hours. I can go to work later and come home earlier than others. In fact, I've never done that since I retired seven years ago, except on Saturdays and Mondays. Since my family is in Chuansha County in the suburbs of Shanghai, I've almost nothing to do at my "home" in Shanghai proper.

I go home to the countryside every Saturday afternoon and come back every Monday morning. It takes two and a half hours each way. At home, I play with my grandchildren, and offer advice to my daughter-in-law who's also a designer at a local silk garment factory.

I got married in the late 1940s to a woman my parents had chosen for me. My wife stays at home. She does household chores, looks after children and now her grandchildren, and has a small vegetable garden as well under her wings.

We've four children—two daughters and two

sons. My eldest daughter is now a fairly well-known tailor in my hometown. She works in a local clothing factory. My younger daughter is a worker in an embroidery-garment factory in my hometown. The factory produces embroidered garments for export. My elder son is a welder. His wife is now a designer in the silk garment factory. She's a very nice daughter-in-law and treats me and my wife very well. I try to teach her a lot about garment designs. She's very perceptive and learn things quickly.

The only child who's still single is my youngest son. He's twenty-six. He left the countryside for Shanghai to "replace" me in the institute in 1981 when I retired. He's now my "apprentice," learning garment design under my tutelage.

Now, I lead a "utopian" life, compared with my childhood days. I get up at 6:30. Then I go out to a street garden near my home to "breathe wholesome air"—*Taiji* (a traditional Chinese shadow boxing) or jog for half an hour. After that, I go to a snack bar for a simple breakfast—a cup of soya-bean milk, with a flatbread and a deep-fried dough stick. I go to work at 8:00. I'm luckier than others. I work seven hours a day, one hour less than others, from 8:30 to 11:30 a.m. and 12:30 to 4:30 p.m., because I was re-employed by the institute as an advisor after my retirement. Sometimes I work extra hours in order to make arrangements for work the following day. After work, I walk back home, which takes fifteen to twenty minutes. My room is 12 square meters. I've lived alone since I came to Shanghai and I've grown accustomed to it.

My night life is very simple. I watch TV, read newspapers and books, and sometimes help neighbors cut out garment patterns, if they ask me.

Despite my retirement, I'm busier than ever. I'm the only advisor in the institute's design section, which is composed of five designers. They all are my former apprentices and well educated, having graduated from either higher-learning colleges or polytechnical schools, majoring in fine arts. I'm in charge of examining and approving their draft designs, doing technological designs, and cutting out paper-based garment patterns. In this case, I design an average of twenty new styles of garments a month, of which fifteen are put into production.

My favorite apprentice is Chen Shanhua, a thirty-one-year-old woman garment designer. She works hard and has achieved remarkable success in designing women's garments. Her masterpiece is a black cheongsam with a red cloak which won a national gold medal. Three women's garment designs she made were selected by the China National Garment Industrial Corporation to be shown at the Second International Fashion Fair and the 54th International Women's Clothing Fair held last September in Paris. The fair attracted a large audience when the Chinese models, wearing the fashions, appeared on French television. I hope one day one of my apprentices will become China's Pierre Cardin.

Generally speaking, China's garment industry is still backward. China's export garments are either popular models or low-grade ones. In my opinion, this is partly due to China's low living standards. Women in the West usually have a variety of clothing. They don't want to have two garments of the same style. But Chinese women, even those in big cities don't have good taste in clothing, because they either don't have much to spend on modern-style clothing or don't like the styling. Some young ladies want good taste in clothing, but many of them really don't know what good taste is. Anyhow, things are getting better now. Garment research institutes have been set up in many large cities including Beijing, Dalian, Guangzhou, Shanghai, and Tianjin.

I plan to work as an advisor for another two or three years instructing a dozen new garment designers. I hope my son will be one of them. After that, I'll "officially" retire and return to my home in the countryside to enjoy being with my family.

When I return home, I give lectures or on-the-spot demonstrations to a few garment design workshops, if asked. And if conditions permit, I'd like to help them to cooperate with each other to set up a garment development company so that they can improve their technical standards through exchanging experiences with their counterparts in big cities.

A person should do good things for mankind and enjoy a good reputation. Why not I?

Goldsmith: Nan Zhigang

They said I was a treasure to be preserved.

Nan Zhigang, fifty-one, has been a goldsmith for thirty-three years, a craft his father had practised. He works now at the Beijing Arts and Crafts Research Institute. There are three main jewelry factories in Beijing, employing about 2,000 workers. Nan Zhigang is one of a few senior jewelry masters.

My colleagues called me "Grandpa Nan" as soon as I'd finished my apprenticeship thirty years ago. That was a title of honor for highly skilled master workers. People don't address me like that nowadays. Some of them call me a researcher. No. I'm just a worker, although I hope that I'm a skilled worker.

Five years ago, I requested a transfer to a factory closer to where I live. The institute where I now work heard about my request and immediately invited me to join them. They said I was a treasure to be preserved.

At first, I went to the institute and offered advice to the young, thought up processes, or added finishing touches to some pieces. There was always time for tea, newspaper-reading, and talking.

This bothered me. I asked for a private room where I could work. For two months, I worked on a gold ornament which weighs 500 grams and stands

11 inches. It was a figure of an ancient lady playing a *pipa*. The *pipa* (a pluck instrument) was inlaid with 140 pieces of diamonds which could be taken out and worn as a brooch. I won a prize for this "*Pipa* Lady" at the Southeast Asian Jewelry Competition. My father would have been proud of this honor. He wanted so much for me to be his equal. He went to Mongolia to teach his jewelry skill for several years, but never won an international award.

My father earned much money even before Liberation. We'd have been wealthy, but he spent a lot on opium and gambling. My step-mother treated me badly and didn't send me to school.

After the founding of New China, I entered a night school. Without training, I couldn't have gotten a decent job. My father left me in the care of his workmate when he went to Mongolia. He said: "If you cannot be better than I am, I hope you'll be no worse. You've all it takes to develop a skill."

He worked in a cooperative formed by individual craftsmen. People withheld their secrets of skill. For instance, my master never told me how he made his tools. He'd say, "The master only shows you in, and then you do your own thing." I lived in the workshop. After my master went home, I examined his tools and the jewelry he was working on.

Near the end of the 1950s, we all became workers of a state-run jewelry factory that was a combination of many cooperatives. I was a bit cocky when I entered the factory's big gate. On the doorway were displayed pictures of ten honored workers, one of whom was me. Thanks to my master's conservativeness, I became more curious and innovative. I began to improve old tools and invent new ones.

I've good skills because I've good tools. I've been told, that in Western countries, there're specialized tool factories. We've to import most of our tools. But I've made 80 percent of my tools. Having no place to mass-produce them, I spend a lot of time making them for myself and for my apprentices. The director of my workshop used to complain about this. He preferred that I work on the products. I asked him, "Do you know how the products come about?" They, of course, were made using tools. I felt he was too stupid to understand this. That's why he'd become a workshop director, but never a great master.

I've taught nearly sixty apprentices. I'm not secretive. I tell them everything they want to know. The pity is that the apprentices aren't that eager to learn nowadays. With a proper schooling, they'd find other attractive jobs. One of my favorite apprentices, who was with me for four years, has recently become a manager of a company. I'm a bit worried about the successors in this trade.

I haven't been able to teach my son. Wearing jewelry was banned as a kind of bourgeois luxury during the Cultural Revolution. Our factory produced capacitors for almost seven years. He's now a mail carrier and has a family of his own. My daughter is employed as an attendant in a four-star hotel. Both of them earn good salaries. My daughter is particularly proud of her position. How can they be satisfied? They didn't get enough education during their school years. And they don't have a skill such as making jewelry or something.

I've a skill. People come to me when others can't handle the job. So I'm respected. On my name card, I'm called a "Senior Jewelry Technician." As a member of Beijing Jewelry Development Committee, I attended the Hong Kong Jewelry Show last spring. I met there with the managers of two jewelry companies. They saw what I produced, and, on the basis of this, wanted to employ me. My children kept telling me: "Try it, daddy, why not?" A big chance to make money, of course. But I never thought of going there. Who'll pay me a pension when I run out of energy? There's free medical care here. I'll get the same amount of money after retirement as I do now.

I don't really care about money. When I see people approve of my work, I'm satisfied. Sometimes I'm asked to repair rings or necklaces for the wives of foreign ambassadors. If I'm happy with the work, I'll say, "Don't pay. Get me a carton of cigarettes."

I'm really hurt when others don't respect my work. When I was twenty-two, I made a miniature reproduction of the Longevity God. A photographer came to take a picture of it for a production sample. Instead of me, the maker, a grey-haired man was asked to pose with my work. I was irritated, and went to the head of the factory. He explained that clients would be more satisfied if they thought it was a work of an experienced person. Absolutely ridiculous! I insisted that the pictures taken not be used. They agreed in the end.

I'm not boasting when I say that because I was skillful, lots of girls expressed their appreciation. That made me dizzy for a while, and even sometimes absent-minded at work. My master would warn me, "Concentrate on your work. Don't daydream about girls." Then his own daughter arrived from a suburban county, and started working with her father at our factory. I married her a year later.

My wife still works at the factory, doing surface treatment. She spends three hours every day commuting between our home and the factory. We'd be just as well off if she didn't work. But she loves working and being with others. My daughter takes care of all the family chores, and I cook the evening meals. People outside know my skill in making jewelry. But my family appreciates my cooking.

In these few years, people keep coming to me to make rings, earrings, or necklaces. I don't know how they get so much gold and silver. Every month, I make two or three things at home. The extra money that I get from doing this just about equals my salary. I don't think I work too hard. I spend a lot of time with my grandson. I take him to parks and sit with him watching television. Sometimes, I think I'd teach him to make jewelry when he grows up. But his parents might have their own plans. He'll have a good education, and possibly will become a professor or scientist some day. Who knows? He's only four.

Latrine Cleaner: Zhang Jianzhong

My mother said: "What you're doing is a job a worthy man doesn't bother to do and one that a worthless man can't do well. Do it well if you do it."

His name is Zhang Jianzhong. This thirty-eight-year-old Beijinger does the dirtiest job in his city—cleaning public latrines. He has been doing this for six years. He works five hours a day, six days a week, with occasional overtime. He now is head of an eleven-member cleaning squad of the Third Cleaning Team of the Xuanwu District. His squad is responsible for 135 public latrines in central Beijing.

He married seven years ago and has a six-year-old son. He does most of the house chores ever since his wife became crippled by polio. He spends three hours a day on tricycles—two hours on his own tricycle taking his wife to and from work, and one hour on a company tricycle carrying such tools as brooms and spades as he goes from one latrine to another.

With a round face and shaven head, he looks much younger than his age. At 1.625 meters (about 5 feet 3 inches), he weighs only 53 kilograms. He wears dark blue work clothes throughout the day—old ones on duty, and new ones when off duty.

I first worked as a lathe turner at the Beijing Heavy Machine Tool Plant for fifteen years beginning in 1968.

In 1983, I took this job. I liked my former job.

It's a profession that no one looks down upon. It's quite different from my current one. If my family hadn't been hard up for money, I wouldn't have joined this cleaning team.

I was married in 1980. My handicapped wife had no job. The next year we'd a child. Counting my mother, I'd four mouths to feed. Someone told me that latrine cleaners earned more, and therefore I decided to change to this job.

One of my supervisors in my previous job liked me because I worked hard. He asked me to stay and said: "We can give you more money if you stay."

I shook my head and said: "I want to earn my own living. I want to earn more so I can enjoy such luxuries as a TV set and sofa."

My parents-in-law, both workers, also tried to dissuade me from taking this job because they were ashamed to have a son-in-law who was a latrine cleaner. But I'd made up my mind and accepted the new job.

The first month I earned a salary nearly doubled that of my previous job. I earned only eighty *yuan* at the factory.

I came home and told my mother: "Look! I got so much last month." I handed it to her, but she refused to take it. I said: "Please keep it just for awhile. It didn't come easily. It was earned by smelling stink and swallowing sneers."

My mother took the money and said: "Don't be discouraged. What you're doing is a job that a worthy man doesn't bother to do and one that a worthless man can't do well. Do it well if you do it."

As a latrine cleaner, there're few happy days.

Your difficulties may include a long wait outside a ladies' room. Some women never seem to mind how long they keep a cleaner waiting, and they chat inside without end. That's very irritating since there are fifteen latrines to clean in the morning and only fifteen minutes can be alloted to each one. If you don't fulfill the assigned quota, your bonus will be less.

Sometimes dirty words are hurled at you. This angers me. One day I bumped into a young man outside a latrine. As soon as he saw me, he screamed: "Damned! What lousy luck!"

If bumping into a sanitation worker were such lousy luck, people'd avoid such bad luck by not emptying their bowels.

I remember once a woman punched me because she was spattered with cold water when I took a hose off the tap. It wasn't my fault. She came into the ladies' room before I'd finished my work.

Such things are common, since people look down on sanitation workers even more than before. In the past, newspapers and broadcasts made efforts to educating people to respect us and our profession. But now they devote their pages and programs to such things as the economy and advertisements. Most of them have no interest in us because they cannot make money by promoting respect for us. Thus our problems are increasing.

We've no time to quarrel with impolite people. Many of us try to think of ways to reduce conflicts. I've a big "tolerate" character written on the back of my hand to remind me to keep calm when I run into trouble.

Of course, there're people who show respect or

concern for us. One wintry morning, an old woman saw me cleaning outside a ladies' room and said, "Your clothes have frozen. Please come to my home to warm yourself and have a cup of hot tea." Although I was too dirty to go to her home, her concern and offer warmed me. I told myself that although what I did wasn't the greatest job, it was still appreciated by some people.

To show their understanding of our work, some people talk with us and ask such questions as: "Are you well paid for this work?" and "Does this dirty work have a bad impact on your health?"

These questions make you understand that there are people who care.

Yes, we're exposed to infectious diseases. We deal with nightsoil all day and sometimes we've to use our hands to dredge out soil pipes. That's why most of us pay special attention to personal hygiene. We always take showers and change into clean clothes before going home.

We've a general physical examination every two years. I've no problem with my health except for a backache. I got that working in the factory. It bothers me now as my current job requires a great deal of stooping. I've to have a one-or-two-minute rest every so often.

That's my only problem. But I've no reason to complain since I chose this job. What's more, I always try to do a good job. By "a good job," I mean to keep my latrines as clean as my own home. I always keep my house tidy and clean.

There're some people who lack a spirit of public morality and purposely make latrines dirty. But the latrines are to be clean when you finish your work.

There can be no nightsoil left in the pits, no urine stains in urinals, no dust on the walls and windows, no trace of phlegm outside, and no cobwebs in corners if you want your work to get a high rating.

A high rating requires much effort and provides only a two-or-three-*yuan* bonus a month. However, I still try hard to do a good job. When people enter my latrines and say "Oh, it's so clean," I'm pleased and take the words as a great compliment.

The heads of my team like hard workers. That's why I was promoted to be a cleaning squad leader. To be quite honest, I didn't want to be a leader. I'm a person without personal ambition. I only accepted the job after being urged to do so.

There're eleven of us in the squad. All are married, two of them came from factories which had closed down. They were attracted here by a higher salary, just as I was.

As the squad chief, I do the same amount of cleaning as other workers. The difference lies in that I schedule replacements when squad members have a holiday. As a head, I've to work harder and more carefully, since other workers will follow my example. I'm always the last to return home from work.

I don't mind the hard work. What bothers me are the unavoidable disputes which usually are caused by misunderstandings. When someone in the squad is discontent with my decisions, he'll be at odds with me.

One of my squad members commented that I'm too obedient to the team heads. But I can't see why I shouldn't be obedient. They've treated us well. Nowadays many young people have developed a rebellious psychology, which I can't sympathize with. I neither want to lick the boots of the team heads nor be a trouble-maker. I don't want to have conflicts with anyone. I don't like quarrels.

We seldom quarrel now, but we did argue a lot in the past, mostly over money. At that time we'd so little money that every cent counted. Sometimes when I wanted to buy a bottle of wine, my wife wouldn't allow me to, which resulted in quarreling. But now she doesn't mind my buying a bottle of wine since we earn more.

She also is working now. Her job is a temporary one as an accountant at a parking lot. She earns about ninety *yuan* a month.

I earn nearly 230 *yuan* a month now. If I were still at my former job, I'd be getting only 140 *yuan* a month.

When I worked there, I was so short of money that I'd afford only an eight-cent dish and some steamed corn bread for lunch. I had to borrow decent clothes when I had dates with girls. None of the six girls I went with wanted to marry me because of my impoverished condition.

At last I married a paralysed girl. I told myself that even if my wife were a person physically sound, she might become crippled in an accident. I've never cold-shouldered my wife because of her physical condition.

Everything's changed now. Before I came to the cleaning team, we had to have the cheapest vegetables each day. Stuffed meat dumplings were a luxury for us at that time. But now, we've good dishes every day and dumplings often.

My dreams have come true. We've a black-white TV set and a sofa now. We've also saved a small sum of money.

My son's well dressed. He can compete with other children in the kindergarten. A pair of his leather shoes cost me fifteen *yuan*. When I was at his age, the shoes I wore could hardly be called shoes at all because they were so shabby.

There were six members in my family, my father was an actor in an opera troupe. He had to quit his job in 1964 because of ill health. My family had to depend on the forty-*yuan* salary of my elder brother. To help the family, I quit school and began to work when I was only seventeen.

Compared with the past, I'm now in heaven. I'm content with my lot. I've a good wife, and a lovely son. Next year, we'll move from this small one-room house into a new flat with two rooms, plus a toilet and a kitchen. We've enough money.

I'm also satisfied with my current job because it gives me enough money and time. I need more time to take care of my family. I've no other great wishes. I'll do this job until retirement. I can retire at the age of sixty.

Wishes for my son? He's talented. I don't want him to follow in my footsteps. I hope he'll have a chance to receive a good education and then become an architect, my childhood dream. Even now, whenever I see a high building, I'm attracted by it very much. It's a mystery to me. I wonder how the things in the mind of an architect are transformed into reality.

What's more, to be an architect you'll leave behind a lot of permanent things. Your buildings are towering there after you die. But a cleaner leaves nothing, and therefore he disappears totally. If I were well educated, I'd never have taken cleaning as my trade.

Mortician: Ma Yanlong

To many people, the respect and fulfillment they get at death is what they've hoped for all their lives. It's a pleasure to help them realize their last dreams.

Ma Yanlong works at the Beijing Hospital where he has handled dozens of China's top leaders of the past, including the late Chairman Mao Zedong, Premier Zhou Enlai, Madam Soong Ching Ling, and hundreds of lesser known VIPs. He is a cosmetic mortician. At fifty-four, he is one of some 2,000 in his trade throughout the country. He often smiles when he is not working.

No, I'm not famous. At least not in the usual sense of the word. Not many people know me. Or if they do, they don't want to. They think my job is terrible.

Some people even hesitate to shake hands with me.

I don't talk much the first time I meet a person. It wasn't until recent years that I acknowledged to others that I was a mortuary makeup man. I always felt that I'm only a part-timer.

In the past, when asked by a stranger what I did, I'd usually tell them that I was a pathologist at Beijing Hospital. Last year, I received the title of "director pathologist," which meant that I could enjoy the status and salary equal to that of an associate professor at a university.

My work in mortuary makeup is no worse than the kind of work one does in conventional laboratory testing. But they don't offer any title for my kind of work. I want to be recognized. That's why for over thirty years, I've been reluctant to become a full-time makeup man, although I've had some success in this work.

I go to the mortuary on assignment. The job is neither easy, nor pleasant. There's always the threat of infection. There's no extra money unless I exceed my eight hours of work. I get the same income as most other medical workers of my age, around 150 *yuan* (about 40 U.S. dollars) per month. And the advanced age of the leadership has kept me busier since I entered my fifties four years ago. Nevertheless, I feel rewarded by the mere thought of having served so many great men. In fact, I've made up the human remains of almost every high leader and noted public figure since the founding of the People's Republic in 1949.

I've fourteen photo albums. But they can't hold all the photographs I've of my work.

Here's a picture of Madam Soong Ching Ling in the 1960s. Here's another one of her when she died in May, 1981, when she held the post of Honorary Chairman of our country. Her appearance represented one of my accomplishments. The method of putting the dead in a pool of flowers, half-covered with the flag of the Chinese Communist Party—which I first introduced in the 1950s—has become a formula for such occasions. What pleased me was that I managed to keep Madam Soong's fine composure, since her body had been donated to pathological autopsy according to her last wish.

Usually the work of the mortuary involves four steps. First, put the remains into an approriate posture. The head must be lifted. The chin must be postured to protect appearance, and the legs are spread a bit apart to facilitate dressing. Second, antiseptive measures.

Third, and the most difficult part, is the makeup. As a matter of fact, it can be called a combination of makeup and plastic surgery. My portable workbox is filled with scalpels, scissors, absorbent cotton, bottles of ethyl alcohol, razors, clippers, combs, greasepaint and brushes. The corpse often doesn't resemble the living person. I often request a good picture of the person taken, say, ten or twenty years before.

The last step is the simplest and most pleasant. The flower-and-flag formula. In addition, the bier should be well placed so that beams of two 500-watt spotlights meet at the dead person's breast. At first, this was done from the viewpoint of being able to take better photographs. But, later, even as a Hong Kong newspaper stated, it was found that "with well-arranged lighting, the dead can be made to appear breathing."

I've collected news clippings as well as letters of appreciation from relatives. I treasure these because they are from those who understand and respect my work. For example, one letter said: "Mother and we children felt so relieved at seeing father's body so peaceful, as if sleeping." This makes you feel good.

I've kept a letter written in English by the family of a veteran foreign expert who had worked at Xinhua News Agency.

(The letter, dated December 10, 1986, reads as

follows:

"We wish to extend our heartfelt thanks to Dr. Ma Yanlong for his marvellous post mortem work on Michael Shapiro. Michael died on Sept. 29 and at the viewing on Oct. 21, many commented that his corpse had received the very best attention of an experienced mortician. Michael looked so peaceful and still alive as a result of Ma's efforts. The entire family felt he would be forever with us. This was and is a great comfort which has eased, to a great extent, our sorrow in losing a dearest husband, brother, and father.)

I'm emotional. My late parents used to be pious Catholics. What has always moved and inspired me is that most of my clientele have donated their bodies to medical study. Our hospital mainly receives the very well known recently deceased. This is unusual in other Chinese hospitals.

It never occurred to me that I'd become a mortician on my graduation from a one-year army medical school in 1951. I did my first makeup job that year at the age of seventeen. A general had died of illness. The hospital assigned me to prepare this last salute to him. So I painted his face and arranged the flag and flowers. My leaders praised me. After that, they chose me as the mortician for important people.

I wasn't frightened by the dead. The veneration for great people overcame my fear. Yet for years, I didn't like the job. It wasn't enjoyable. By and by, however, I gradually came to accept it. To do it better, I made efforts to broaden my knowledge of plastics, painting, aesthetics, and psychology. As a result, although I was labelled a "reactionary" during the Cultural Revolution (1966-1976) simply because I'd been born into a comparatively wealthy family, I was sent for every time an important figure died. In fact, the two most important missions in my career occurred during the Cultural Revolution.

One was the death of Chairman Mao.

It was September 9, 1976. I was working on a farm in the northern suburbs of Beijing. Suddenly a car came from the authorities high up and took me to Zhongnanhai (the living compound of China's top leaders in the center of the city). I awaited orders in a very large house, which seemed to be the residence of a very important person. In the strained and repressed air, medical workers, some of whom I knew very well, bustled about in the courtyard. Soon I was told that the Chairman had passed away and that I had been listed as a member of the group who'd prepare his corpse for its state funeral.

The procedures were done in the big house. First, however, they gave me a photo of the Chairman taken with U.S. president Richard Nixon. Fortunately it was a good picture. Nonetheless, I was so nervous that my hands trembled throughout more than an hour's work. When I finished, they took the body to the Great Hall of the People.

Another memorable experience was on January 8, 1976, when the people's beloved Premier Zhou Enlai died. The Premier was emaciated and unshaved since he had been suffering from cancer. Zhou's barber shaved him, and I did the makeup. We wept after the work was done.

Sometimes doing this job brings you much grief. I've taught four students, three from Dalian and one from Shanghai. I told them: "You should use your heart as well as mind to do this job well. For we aren't only putting the dead at peace, but, more importantly, immortalizing them in a sense. We need to have love, love for human beings."

I'm not a Catholic. I'm a member of the Chinese Peasants and Workers Democratic Party. Why haven't I joined the Chinese Communist Party? Quite a few people have asked this, since I've treated the corpses of so many Communist leaders. There're two reasons. One is that the Democratic Party has attracted a large number of medical workers. Therefore I've lots of opportunities there to mix with my fellow workers. The other is, that the Democratic Party has a more friendly and, perhaps, more democratic atmosphere among its members.

Although I've provided services for many high officials, I've never asked their relatives to do anything for me except sending me a few pictures of the deceased—to keep as souvenirs and files for my study. I've accepted some books written by those who've died. The most expensive gift was a Qingdao-6 camera (worth 200 *yuan*, the equivalent of about 53 U.S. dollars), provided by a relative of an overseas compatriot last year. Now I take pictures of the dead myself.

Sometimes, ordinary people use my services, too. Once, the parents of a twenty-one-year-old woman worker timidly knocked on the door of my lab. Their daughter had just died in an accident. They said they had read about me in a newspaper and that they wished to have a last look at their darling.

Three days later, when the parents—both workers—went to the hospital to get the girl's body, they knelt down in gratitude before me, tears rolling down their cheeks.

I'm sure the couple paid a good sum of money,

probably several dozen *yuan*, to the hospital. The hospital paid me one *yuan* (about 38 U.S. cents) for my work. But certainly you cannot charge parents who're so grief-stricken.

Open my own business? I've never thought of it. The crucial problem that a mortician suffers in China isn't the lack of money, but the lack of recognition and respect. I've three daughters. One is an office clerk, one a worker, and the other a gymnastic teacher. The two older ones are married. But none of the girls, nor their husbands, or, in the case of the youngest, boyfriend, shows any interest in mortuary activities. If they've indicated anything, it's a fear of infection, although I've never been infected. They aren't to blame. However, I believe that once you do a job, you should do it well.

My greatest regret is that my wife's sacrificed too much for me. She studied acupuncture at a hospital of traditional Chinese medicine. But now she does most of the housework.

For all the wages we're paid, I'll continue to be a mortician and, perhaps some day, a specialized one, if I've the qualifications to train more students. My retirement years will be spent on disseminating my knowledge and feelings about my work, which I consider significant.

To many people, the respect and fulfillment they get at death is what they've hoped for all their lives. It's a pleasure to help people realize their last dreams.

Fashion Model: Yu Qin

The biggest problem we models have is a fear of the future. While we're unqualified for a higher position, we're unwilling to take a lower one.

Yu Qin, twenty-four, was one of eight models chosen in 1984 to join the Fashion Troupe of the Shanghai Garment Company. She has participated in more than 100 performances at home and abroad.

Since childhood, she has loved singing and dancing. Her childhood dream was to be a singer or a dancer, but she never thought of being a model.

Even now, after having been a model for nearly four years, she still is wondering at what she calls "fate's arrangement."

If it hadn't been for the encouragement of my fridnds, I never would have had the courage to apply after reading a newspaper advertisement in 1984. "Take a chance and try," they told me. Why not?

I was 1.72 meters (about 5 feet and 6 inches) tall, 0.02 meters taller than the minimum height required. But I was the shortest in the troupe.

About 1,000 people applied, but only seventeen were chosen, including myself, after they'd passed a series of tests on music, acting talent, and good health.

When the news of my acceptance into the troupe was received at our factory, Shanghai Jinsha Handkerchief Mill, the factory director was concerned because he considered modeling to be a degrading profession. He attempted to persuade me to give up the idea. He said that I'd have brighter future if I stayed there as a statistician.

Mother was more flexible. Although she complained about the short-skirts that were worn in the streets and frowned when I used make-up, when I told her I wanted to become a fashion model, she didn't object. Looking at me, she said: "All right, as long as that's what you want to do."

Training was hard. Everybody worked hard for fear of being one of the nine that would be eliminated after the training, which lasted for six months. We walked four hours a day in high-heeled leather shoes. As a result, we returned home every day with painful blisters on our feet. Since then, I've never worn a pair of such shoes. Since we're taller than the average, we've no need to increase our height by wearing high-heeled shoes.

Some people believe that having an attractive face and a good figure is all that a model needs. That's not true. More important is a natural understanding of the beauty in music and action. What you present on stage represents your understanding and expression of the beauty of the clothes you are exhibiting to the audience. The job isn't as easy as it may appear.

At first, I'd put all my time and energy into concentrating on how to walk up and down the stage, and into changing my clothes between scenes. It seemed that I was doing things in exactly the way the director had told me to. It hadn't occurred to me that by simply following directions I never could hope to become a competent model.

Now, I'm one of the few who can assume postures

and gestures of my own.

I often appear on stage in cheongsam, or formal dresses. I think they suit me better than many kinds of so-called fashionable clothes. I'm not aggressive or outspoken. People say, I'm a typical Oriental woman: introverted, gentle, and soft in nature. Possibly they're right. Once, I tried on fashion leggings when we were rehearsing. The effect was awful: no matter how hard I tried to be aggressive, I wasn't in the least at ease. From then on, I've stuck to wearing formal dresses both on and off the stage.

The first time I performed on stage, I didn't ask any friends to attend because I wasn't very confident. Later, my mother came several times, which gave me some needed encouragement. One day she asked me how we changed clothes so quickly. I had wondered the same thing before I became a model. Every model has an assistant to help her change, fasten the zipper, and do up the buttons. When a model performs abroad, her assistant needs to have stockings ready that match the color of the dresses. But as an experienced model, I can do many of these things myself.

What's difficult is that stockings are easily torn. No matter how careful you are, a hole or two always seems to be there. Most of the time, we just go on with the torn stockings, hoping that the strong stage lighting will help conceal them. But if the troupe leader finds out, we're in for it.

Even though experienced, we make mistakes. I remember once when a colleague went on stage wearing a black shoe on one foot and a white shoe on the other. By the time we discovered the mistake, it was too late to do anything about it since she already was on stage. To our surprise, and relief, there were no complaints. Because she was wearing a white blouse and a black skirt, the audience thought the black and white shoes represented a new fashion and that they, therefore, matched the blouse and skirt. My colleague was lucky. Most of us aren't that lucky. We often make mistakes, such as wearing wrong-colored stockings, forgetting to put on necessary accessories, or buttoning dress contrary to the requirements. If the audience is observant, they can detect these.

We prefer foreign-made cosmetics, which we usually buy when we go abroad, to those made in China. Foreign-made cosmetics have more subtle colors and are water-proof. With such cosmetics, even when I wash my face, the make-up is still there. If I'm wearing make-up made in China and it rains, my face is a mess.

Perhaps to be a model you have to be original in matters of dress and style. You can see that what we wear—sweater, skirt, and shoes, and even ornaments—are different from others. I paint my eyelids blue. I don't think many Chinese girls do that. So it's only natural that people stare at us wherever we go. Anyhow, we've gotten accustomed to it.

What troubles me the most is having to push to get on and off the bus every day. The beautiful clothes I wear often are like dirty wash rags after each bus fight. Taking a taxi is a luxury I cannot afford. Even if I could, getting a taxi isn't easy. Sometimes, you've to place an order for it three days in advance.

Contrary to some people's belief, we don't earn a lot of money. With a salary of sixty-four *yuan* a month, and five to ten *yuan* for each performance, we're by no means millionaires. And since we love nice clothes, we spend most of our money on them.

If the object was to make money, none of us would choose modeling as an occupation, I'm sure.

Diet? Almost all the reporters we meet ask that question. Once in Japan, reporters came to our dining table to see what we were eating, and how much. The fact is that none of us ever has been on a diet. Business trips require a great deal of energy. Some theaters have no air-conditionings in summer, and we're often covered with sweat after every performance. It's hard to put on weight with that kind of a schedule.

Of the countries I've visited, I prefer Italy because of its ancient, varied culture and its picturesque cities. The Italian people are very friendly. When we were there, they'd stop their cars to let ours pass first and sound loud horns to greet us despite regulations prohibiting such noise. I hope we can go there again.

I liked my former work as an accountant in the mill. But if I were to choose between two jobs, I'd rather be a model. As a model, you can go to a lot of places and experience many things. Having traveled, I'm anxious to do it again. Mother reminded me recently that I was out of Shanghai on business trips for nine months last year.

I've no special friend in the troupe. But I've some male friends outside. I guess as a child I was considered a "tomboy."

The biggest problem we models have is a fear of the future. Modeling is for the young. When you grow old, you no longer are desired in this profession. The question is that we're unqualified for a higher position but unwilling to take a lower one. As a solution, the troupe has famous dress designers give us regular lectures in the hope that some of us will join their ranks some day.

I plan to learn fashion design in Holland. Probably for two years. I've relatives there and they've promised to help me. But my boyfriend wants me to stay here. He said he doesn't want me to leave him alone.

He's a male model in our troupe. We've been together for two years now, although we've been careful that no one else in the troupe knows about it.

I don't want to get married, not for at least several more years anyway. We don't have time to make wedding preparations and I've Holland to consider. But I don't think marriage is a detriment to modeling. A married woman has a special quality: the beauty of maturity.

Part Sixteen

On the Market

Kebab Vendor: Abel Emitti

I think I won't quit the business of selling kebab, unless I find a better job. I don't know what I'll do in the future, but I want to live the way I like.

Abel Emitti, a twenty-two-year-old Uygur from Urumqi, capital city of the Xinjiang Uygur Autonomous Region, is busy roasting and selling mutton kebab at his tiny barbecue stand about 80 meters north of the front gate of Beijing Institute of Economics. The slender young man, wearing black jacket and blue jeans, looks happy and energetic. Now and then he calls out to passersby: "Come on, my friends. Have a look and try it. Don't pay me if it's bad. Twenty *fen* each, or fifty *fen* for three."

People cluster around him, holding skewers, eagerly eating the sizzling mutton cubes, which is Uygur's favorite food, and which has become popular in Beijing and all over the country since the early 1980s. The kebab vendor has brown hair, a brown moustache, and brown eyes—a strange appearance to most inland Chinese.

I'm from Xinjiang. I'm a Uygur. I can speak very fluent Mandarin, though with an accent. At home, we'd many Han neighbors. We're good friends. They taught me Mandarin. I learned a lot from them about the people and life in the inland. Since I was very young, I've dreamt of traveling across China. Now, this dream's come true.

My name is Abudu. It's my Han name. You know, many of us Uygur have Han names. When we come out and deal with Han people we use our Han names. All my Han friends call me Abudu. They always say, Abudu, have a drink. Abudu, have a cigarrete. I like it. My Uygur name is a bit too long for Han people to remember.

My home is in Urumqi. It's beautiful and clean, not like Beijing where there's always a mess, and it's too dusty. If you go to Urumqi, I'm sure you'll love it.

I've a mother and father. My Daddy used to be a high school teacher, and my mommy was a shop assistant. Now they're both retired. I've six brothers and sisters. All of them have jobs. The reason I'm in this business is simple: I couldn't find anything else to do. When I finished high school five years ago, I couldn't get a job. I was very upset, idling around, with nothing to do. Some of my friends also were jobless. We wandered about the city, chatting, laughing, drinking, and fighting. Nobody helped us. My mother could do nothing about me but weep. My father told me to leave.

One day, when we were at one of my friends' home, drinking big cups of beer, someone suggested that we try our luck in another province. It's been said that quite a number of Uygurs and other people from Xinjiang were doing brisk business in other provinces. I had an idea. I'd sell mutton kebabs. We Uygurs like it. In Xinjiang you can find it everywhere. I thought that Han people might like it as well. So I told my parents of my plan. They said they'd pray for good luck. But I wept when I was alone on the train heading for the inland. It was the first time I'd gone so far away from home.

During the past five years, I've traveled around the country. I've been to Xi'an, Shanghai, Guangzhou, Tianjin, and lots of other cities. I came to Beijing early last year, sold kebab, and make a lot of money.

To make mutton kebab isn't as hard as one might think. You get an oblong iron box to serve as a barbecue. Then burn charcoal in it. You get some fresh mutton, slice it, and then pierce the pieces of mutton with skewers. The skewers are placed over the burning charcoal to roast while you sprinkle salt and ground chili on them, turning them several times over until a fragrant aroma comes out and the kebabs are ready. It's so nice to see the kebabs sizzling over the fire. It's like listening to music. The fragrant smoke also attracts people. They come and buy, and buy again. They keep paying until they eat their fill.

Every morning I buy mutton and spend several hours preparing it. I start selling kebab in the afternoon, at about three o'clock, and finish at seven, or a little later. Usually, I can sell around 250 skewers a day. I'm a good kebab maker, and people like to buy my product. I've many regular customers—workers, students, and private vendors. Many of them come up to me and say: "Give me ten skewers," and then after a while, a young guy would ask for another ten. Of course, not all the people like it. Some Hans even hate the smell of it, I know. There're also some people who make trouble for me. Those whom I dislike the most are tax-collectors or sanitary inspectors. I don't know why some of them treat me in such an unfriendly manner. When I first started my business in Beijing,

I used to sell kebab at a crossroads not far from the Temple of Earth Park (in north Beijing). One day, several people came and wanted to fine me for some ridiculous reason that I didn't understand. I refused to pay them. They got very angry, and overturned my little barbecue and ordered me to leave. I left.

But still I think Beijing is the best place to sell kebab. People come to Beijing from all over the country. We find many kebab lovers here, including some foreigners. People here are rich and generous. What surprises me most is the fact that many Beijing girls like mutton kebab. In the other cities where I traveled, girls seldom eat kebab. But in Beijing, it's quite different. Many girls come and buy. They can eat as much as men can. Sometimes, their boyfriends have to stop them, cautioning them not to eat too much.

I love making kebab. I love this business. There're many Xinjiang Uygurs doing this business in Beijing and many other cities. People like us. They jokingly call us the Tianshan Kebab Company. So we're selling Tianshan brand kebab (laugh). You know the Tianshan Mountains. It's the most famous mountain range in Xinjiang. But some bad dealers are ruining our reputation. They sell bad mutton, even non-mutton meat.

I've made quite a few Han friends here and there. They've given me much help. They helped me find a place to live, told me where to buy fresh mutton at reasonable prices, and have taught me to speak fluent standard Mandarin. But I haven't made friends with any Han girls. I don't know why.

It's about time for me to go back to Xinjiang. I've been away from home for more than five years. I've sold hundreds of thousands of kebab, and I've made a good deal of money. I think I'd quit my business soon, but I'm reluctant to do so because I love it so much. I'll go home in the near future. My parents have written me many letters asking me to come home. I also miss them. I'm still single, so I probably will get married when I go back.

I think I won't quit the business of selling kebab, unless I find a better job. I don't know what I'll do in the future, but I want to live the way I like.

Part Seventeen

Communication and Entertainment

TV Reporter: Jia Yuxiang

If I were given another choice, I still would choose to be a TV reporter rather than a newspaper or radio reporter.

He is so busy that he seldom arrives home before supper time. His eight-year-old daughter loves having dinner with her father.

Although he has been working at Beijing Television Station (BTV) for less than five years after his graduation from the People's University, Jia Yuxiang, thirty-nine, has been the director of BTV's news department—the principal department of the station—for more than two years. His duties now are to assign reporters to cover daily events in Beijing.

Of BTV's twenty programs, Beijing News, produced by Jia and twenty-eight colleagues, has the largest audience. Statistics show that almost 75 percent of BTV's audience watch Beijing News.

I'm proud to be a TV reporter. This profession enables me to meet people from all walks of life, from a top leader in the central government, to a dustman on the street.

Among all my former schoolmates now working in journalistic circles, I'm one of the few who've been promoted to be director of a news department. If I were working for China Central Television, I'd still be an ordinary reporter. Why? Because the news department of CCTV has more than 200 reporters, and it's impossible for all of them to have frequent chances to conduct TV interviews outside. You can get lost in the shuffle there. In contrast, BTV's news department has less than thirty reporters, and each reporter must film twenty news events a month. I thrive in this environment.

It's really a tough job to do TV coverage in Beijing. CCTV is a strong rival. They've more access to important occasions. But being a local TV station, we take advantage of our location. We can film and report more news of interest to those who live here. CCTV cannot match us in this respect.

For instance, in the summer of 1984, I learnt No.344 bus had no canopy at its Deshengmen terminal. No.344 bus has a long route and passengers usually have to wait about half an hour to get on one. Without a canopy, the passengers waiting, often numbering more than 100, including women and children, had to stand in the hot sun or in a heavy rain. They all complained about it. I felt obliged to report this. So I went there with my camera. The broadcast had good results. Ten communities, including factories and shops, donated 20,000 *yuan*, and a Beijing building company voluntarily built a canopy for the bus-stop.

Another thing worth mentioning is our coverage of a blocked underground sewer line on a noncommercial street. With the sewer line blocked, foul-smelling water rose up aboveground. People living by the street couldn't open their windows in the summer. Some of the citizens wrote letters to newspapers and authorities for help, but the letters did no good. When we heard about this, we went there to film. While we were filming, a number of citizens offered us glasses of boiled water. I remember one of them said, "Thank you for coming here. We've nothing but a glass of water to express our appreciation." I was really touched. I'd never felt so strongly before that ordinary people need us so much. Ten minutes after the news was broadcast, Mayor Chen Xitong phoned the municipal construction bureau telling them to solve the problem in three days. Although our TV station has no real official authority, we can let high officials know what's happening.

Of course, we're unable to know everything going on in Beijing.

We've more than 200 special correspondents, all with television cameras, working for us. When there's a traffic accident, our special correspondents, who're police officers, will go to the location in a police car, with the siren blaring. If we go there in our own car, it'll often take us hours to reach the spot. Beijing is notorious for its traffic jams.

Last year, three of my reporters went to cover a ceremony praising the absence of incorrectly written words on sign-boards on Wang Fu Jing Street. But at the ceremony, they found six incorrectly written words on the sign-boards. They shot a close-up of the six words. I was pleased with their work. In the evening, Beijing audience saw on their TV screens the coverage of both the ceremony as well as the six incorrect words. The commentator noted that "Wrongly written words do exist on Wang Fu Jing Street." You've to be courageous when criticizing red tape and unhealthy social tendencies. As often as not, somebody will telephone BTV, complaining and even cursing our reports after we've exposed something nasty. But I think a journalist must, above all, be faithful to the facts. We must serve the masses, not the minority. But there is one exception. We don't criticize the Beijing municipal government or Party committee. They're our immediate superiors.

Through our efforts, Beijing News, produced by our department, has attracted the attention of a wide cross-section of Beijing citizens. The mayor of Beijing watches Beijing News. Ordinary people living in the alley-ways also watch Beijing News. Our work is a bridge of communication between the authorities and citizens.

The work a director does is not just merely giving instructions. There're a lot of miscellaneous things. For example, visiting reporters who're ill in a hospital; distributing subsidized articles to subordinates; attending meetings, etc. I really regret that I've less time to go out and cover events myself.

Here's my work schedule. I arrive at my office at 8:15 a.m. At about 8:30, the telephone starts ringing and continues to do so until noon. I answer all of them because they provide us with news tips and I assign reporters to cover different stories. By one o'clock—that's our deadline—all reporters should be back with news pictures on their video tapes.

The duty editor compiles all the pieces of news in the studio and writes a commentary. Then I compare the narrative with the pictures on the screen and do some editing. When I'm satisfied, I sign my approval. Then it's the work of the broadcasters. Before the news goes on the air at 6:45 p.m., I'll look at the program again with BTV's director to make sure there're no problems. We've to be that careful, because Beijing News is BTV's most important program.

Our news programs are all taped. We don't do live broadcasting as our Western counterparts do because we don't have anchor persons who host TV programs. What we have are five broadcasters who merely dub the pictures filmed by reporters. They just read scripts written by others. Their perfomance is far from satisfactory. One of them was previously a dancer and didn't have the necessary education and training. But we don't have a proper training program for TV anchors yet, and we lack the technology to do live broadcasting. Besides, in China, we tend to expect everything to be perfect, and a slip of tongue from the broadcaster is regarded as an unpardonable offense. The practice of taping alleviates the pressure on the broadcasters.

I have to admit that BTV is in its preliminary stage since it's only nine years old. However, we're aware that live broadcasting is a trend we must someday follow and as the first step, we're going to recruit some good broadcasters.

My home is an hour and a half's bus journey from the office. By the time I reach home, it's often past 8:00 p.m. My wife and my daughter have already had supper. I feel sorry for my daughter. Other fathers have more hours to spend with their daughters than I do.

Before seven o'clock in the morning, I leave home for work. The traffic in Beijing during rush hours is very bad. From home to BTV and back again takes three hours on the bus every day, which can be as exhausting as a whole day's work.

BTV's coverage of important events, such as meetings between municipal leaders and foreign officials, are usually produced by me or my deputy director. On these occasions, English is very useful. I studied English in college and now listen to Radio Beijing's broadcasts every morning on the bus. So it's not difficult for me to converse with foreign friends who are seated next to me at a banquet. Journalism is becoming international and it won't do if a qualified reporter doesn't know English.

If I were given another choice, I still would choose to be a TV reporter, rather than a newspaper or radio reporter. I believe television will take the place of newspapers and radio some day because it's a medium which combines sight with sound.

I think TV reporters and editors are professionals. Why? We reporters and editors produce fruit, and broadcasters pass this fruit to the audience. Although a broadcaster appears on the screen and enjoys popularity, I'd rather be the authority behind the screen.

Pollster: Chen Chongshan

I hope to poll top Party leaders five years from now. Then I'll retire happily.

Chen Chongshan is a research fellow with the Journalism Institute of the Chinese Academy of Social Sciences. She is the first to conduct an opinion poll in China after such polling was banned for decades. Her survey on people's reactions to the Chinese media in 1982 was called a breakthrough in Chinese press history, although it resulted in some trouble at that time.

She is fifty-five years old. Her diminutive figure seems to contain inexhaustible energy. For one thing, she can talk with a person for several hours without a break.

Her one-room apartment in Southwestern Beijing is simply furnished with a pair of armchairs, a wardrobe, a double bed and three large book shelves, all old-fashioned, with faded colors. The only modern appliances are a television set, a radio-cassette tape recorder, and a refrigerator.

The apartment is the property of *Economic Daily*, where her husband works as a senior editor. Her only child is a student at Beijing University. The couple has a monthly salary of 400 *yuan*, which she believes is well above that of the average Chinese family.

There are many kinds of polls conduted in china these days.

Only six years ago, however, when I conducted the first poll on readers' response to China's mass media, I had to avoid using the term "poll." Many people, especially some high-ranking officials, sensed something "bourgeois" and unacceptable in the term "poll" and didn't approve at all of its use. So I used the term "survey of readers" instead.

I hit upon the idea of conducting a readers' poll because I wished to provide a factual and reliable basis for China's press reform, which had been first proposed by such senior journalists as Hu Jiwei and An Gang in mid-1982.

As a research fellow, my special interest is the function of the mass media and its impact on the public. I was disturbed to see, during the Cultural Revolution, that people tore in pieces or burned some newspapers in anger because they felt the newspapers were full of distorted facts. During the reign of the Gang of Four, the press and the audience were pitted against each other, and people refused to believe what appeared in the mass media.

With the downfall of the gang, the atmosphere began to change. You could imagine how encouraged I was by the idea of press reform, with its implication that mass media should serve the readers. I decided to go to the grass-roots units to investigate people's reactions to, and specific requirements of, the press. This, I thought, was my way to contribute to press reform.

But the idea was hard to accomplish. Apart from the psychological alienation prompted by the mere mention of the word "poll," we were ill at ease with what the survey might show. It would touch on the readers' faith in China's mass media, such faith (or lack thereof) being a very sensitive subject at that time. Should the majority of the responses be negative, I, as the poll conductor, would more than likely get in trouble myself. Because the mass media are considered the mouthpiece of the Party and government, their credibility must not be questioned.

Also, I then lacked the necessary funds or trained assistants to help me, nor did I have the modern equipment to conduct the survey.

Fortunately I received firm support from Hu Jiwei, the then editor-in-chief of *People's Daily*, and An Gang, director of the Institute of Journalism. An Gang was my former teacher at People's University in the 1950s. I couldn't have gone ahead with my survey without their support.

I also had enthusiastic assistance from some reporters of the *People's Daily*, *Workers' Daily* and *China Youth News*. Soon I was able to set up a seven-member survey team. We also trained ninety-five volunteers to visit the pollees at home, and thirty graduate students of journalism at the Graduate School of the Chinese Academy of Social Sciences joined us on Sundays.

We focused our poll in Beijing, and respondents were readers of the three newspapers I just mentioned. In order to reach a representative group, we decided to use random sampling. With the help of the Beijing Statistics Society, we selected 2,430 respondents, representing 295 work units or occupations.

The next step involved an enormous amount of work. We designed a fifty-four-item questionnaire for the respondents to fill in.

As we didn't have telephones to talk to our pollees, so we had to visit them by bus or bike. They were located all over Beijing. Some of them lived so far away that it was necessary to take a long distance bus to reach them. Once, I got off a bus at its terminal, then walked fifty minutes to meet a respondent. He was a farmer and was deeply moved. He said that a survey was a good idea; under ordinary circumstances, a farmer like him wouldn't have a chance to have his opinions on mass media heard.

It took us almost two months to finish the survey in September 1982. Then we had the problem of calculating the results. It was almost impossible to do calculation by hand. But we had no computer. The format of the questionnaire was designed so that an analysis of the data could be done by computer. I turned to the Beijing Computer Center for help. They agreed to help us as a first experiment in using computers to do an analysis of social science data. But the cost they quoted was beyond our ability to pay. I pleaded and negotiated, and finally the fee was reduced to 1,000 *yuan*, which was provided jointly by the *People's Daily*, *Workers' Daily* and my institute.

Unexpectedly, it was extremely difficult to communicate with the computer programers, because I knew little about computers, and they didn't understand journalism. It took more than two months to finish the programing. So the result of the first newspaper readers' poll didn't come out until early 1983.

This first poll indicated that 22.2 percent of the readers completely believed what they read in newspapers, and 55.1 percent believed most of what they read in newspapers. The results were quite positive. *China Daily*, China's sole English-language newspaper, reported on the poll in Associated Press and the overseas branch of the Xinhua News Agency, and Hong Kong's *Wen Wei Po* reprinted it. But other news media in China didn't mention it, probably because the idea of such a survey was too "foreign."

Despite my relief at the "positive" results of the survey, I believe some of the respondents didn't answer truthfully. Some, if not all people, were unwilling to tell the truth for fear of getting into trouble later. They had suffered in the past for their outspokenness in political movements such as the Cultural Revolution. The lingering fear of political reprisals kept them from being totally candid in responding to my questionnaire.

The fear of telling the truth, in fact, is the biggest obstacle in the four media surveys I've conducted. It's no wonder that we've had so few outstanding journalists in China in recent years. One big problem is that many reporters are afraid to write the truth, or are contrained from doing so. Some of them do write good and truthful stories, but they aren't published for one reason or another. If they'd several stories so printed, their chances for promotion would be adversely affected. So they write "safer" stories. As the reforms deepen, and the country opens up more to the outside world, I hope the reporters will become bolder. I hope my surveys will act as some sort of spur to action by indicating to newspaper reporters and editors what readers want to read and know about.

At present it's beyond my ability to eliminate various objective factors from influencing the way those being polled answer my questionnaires.

One thing that I can do, however, is to conduct my poll at a time when possible political interference is minimum. For instance, in 1983 I conducted an audience survey in Zhejiang Province from October 12 to October 25. That was a quiet period, and I believe the results of the survey were basically correct. A similar survey was conducted in Jiangsu Province slightly later, in November. The sampling was based on that used in the 1982 census, and was scientifically done. But the campaign to eliminate "spiritual pollution" had started in November, obviously affecting the results of the survey. They showed that as many as 80 percent of the people completely or basically had faith in the Chinese mass media. I don't believe such results are true. Many pollees apparently didn't tell the truth because of fear of getting into trouble.

I ran into different difficulties when I conducted a poll in Xinjiang in 1987. It was a "package" survey, in which TV, radio and newspaper audiences were polled. Xinjiang is a vast region, with some thirteen ethnic minorities residing in it. The survey was to provide up-to-date knowledge on the views of an audience as diversed as this.

But I hardly thought that I would have trouble getting the questionnaires printed. I was working for the *Xinjiang Daily*. When I sent the questionnaires to its press shop for printing, the press leader told me that the shop was too busy to print anything extra. He suggested I use mimeographing instead of relief printing. The mimeographed questionnaires would look so untidy and clumsy that respondents would be unwilling to fill them in. So I said if the printing workers were too busy, I could do the typesetting myself, since I had learned it at the university. One woman worker was moved by my insistence. She volunteered to help me typeset in her free time. Together, she and I spent five afternoons typesetting, proofreading and printing. She accepted no money for her work.

The results were interesting. It revealed that in that remote area, newspapers are the major source of local people's information. In total, 65.8 percent of the people surveyed completely or basically had faith in the mass media.

Since many ethnic people in Xinjiang are heavily religious, 10 percent of the pollees said thay also tune to Pakistani radios for broadcasts of the Koran. Regarding to the question "How do you plan to spend your money when you become better off?" the majority of those polled replied that they would send their children off to universities. And 11 Muslims said they would go to Mecca on a pilgrimage.

Over the past few years I've gained experience in designing questionnaires and learned to do some computer programing. Now we've a computer at my institute, one which was given to us by the academy in 1985.

I feel my fame is growing, but fame isn't what I crave, nor is money. I would rather be with the ordinary people at the grass-roots levels. I came from a farmer's family in Zhejiang Province. I joined the revolution at the age of sixteen in 1949, immediately after the People's Republic of China was founded. I worked for five years with land-reform work teams in rural areas before I entered the university. That experience acquainted me thoroughly with the conditions and the people in the rural area. I feel at home mingling with such people, and it's a pleasure to listen to their concerns, interests, and wishes.

I now have an unaccomplished wish. In the *People's Daily* national survey I conducted in 1987, I selected three kinds of respondents: ordinary readers, leaders at the municipality and county levels, and members of the Party Central Committee. To poll the Party Central Committee members, I planned to distribute the questionnaires at the 13th Party Congress. That action required a lot of courage.

Why did I plan to survey those decision-makers? For years, some leaders only wanted to hear good news, not bad news. Some media people, in order to please them provided only "good news" based on one-sided and unobjective reporting, for which China once paid dearly when leaders made wrong decisions. If leaders have a clear understanding of the overall situation as well as of specific conditions in different parts of the country, their decisions are likely to be better. I tried hard to talk *People's Daily* editors into agreeing with my plan.

But when the Party Congress was in process in October, 1987, Qian Liren, editor-in-chief of *People's Daily*, winced. He dissuaded me from circulating the questionnaires, saying that the major issue at the Party Congress was discussing further reforms and the open policy, and that we, thus, should not distract them. My plan was thus aborted. I was very disappointed. So people surveyed in that national poll were only ordinary readers and middle-ranking officials.

I hope to poll top leaders at the 14th Party Congress five years from now if conditions permit. Then I will happily retire.

Poet: *Yang Laishun*

I have a dream:
On everyone the sun shines,
without playing favorites;
To everyone innocence returns,
with a little honesty.

His hair is rumpled and his jacket is unbuttoned. The first impression of Yang Laishun, a member of the Jiangsu Branch of the Chinese Writers' Association, would be that he is untidy, and certainly not a man of letters.

Yet he enjoys fame in the literary world and is the recipient of several literary awards.

Yang's father abandoned his mother when she was pregnant forty-two years ago. Two years after Yang was born, his mother also left him, and he was cared for by his grandparents.

He lived for more than thirty years believing that he was an illegitimate child. It was not until he met his father in Hong Kong that this belief was refuted.

Eloquent though he is, Yang sometimes is inarticulate when he describes his childhood and the dreams that have sustained him through poverty and discrimination.

There're no words to describe the loss of one's parents. Nor are there words joyful enough to describe a reunion with loved ones after years of separation.

Several years ago when my father hoped I could be more demonstrative in my love for him, I was speechless.

I feel very sorry for my father for having a son who is a virtual stranger to him. The poor man wants company in his advanced years.

Only when I saw fathers and mothers in my neighborhood sending their children off to school early in the morning and meeting them after school was I aware that my parents were missing.

You'd say that orphans have better fortune than illegitimate children. The former are well looked after by the government, whereas the latter, though having legal rights, are usually victims of social prejudice. It was taken for granted that I was born to an unmarried mother. That stigma haunted me for years. Having no childhood friends or family except my grandparents, I'd often while away my hours in seclusion, until my grandmother noticed and made me associate with people.

Grandma was a knowledgeable lady who told me countless wonderful stories that captivated my young imagination. I can still recall the details of many of them today. Grandpa had an antique business. I'd often go into his dimly-lit store to look at the shelves full of strange things. The dilapidated pottery figurines, rusty daggers, and old battle axes both mystified and frightened me.

Those childhood years had contributed substantially to my later development as a poet.

When I reached school age, I applied for admission to a school in my neighborhood.

"Why haven't you come with your parents?" the school administrator asked me.

I went back with my grandmother, who persuaded the head teacher to accept me as an auditor. I was later told that a pupil formally admitted to a school had to be able to identify his parents.

My favorite class was writing. My Chinese teacher was an amateur poet who could make ideas dance like notes of music. My descriptions of nature grabbed his attention. He often took time to coach me in spite of my reputation.

It's writing that gave me something to base my life on.

There was a privately-run poetry institute near my primary school, where I'd often listen outside the window. Impressed by my eagerness, the teacher admitted me without charge since I couldn't afford the tuition.

Rhyme to Chinese poetry is what letters are to English. A rhymebook is a Chinese poet's bible. I used to hang around a second-hand bookstore in Nanjing, where the cheapest rhymebook I found cost 3.6 *yuan*, which was an enormous sum for me.

I suddenly hit upon an idea. Why not pick up cigarette butts and resell them?

So every day for a month I went to a dingy bus terminal, which was far enough from home to avoid recognition, and picked cigarette butts off the floor. Later I sold my "prize tobacco" to nondiscriminating smokers.

When finally one day, I put a bag of coins on the bookstore counter, the shop keeper, who'd always before shooed me away, stared in disbelief.

After I bought the second-hand book, a nursery rhyme of mine was published in *Youngsters' Journal*, and another poem, "I Bring Tea to South Mountain," appeared that same year.

Despite my achievements, I often was given a cold

shoulder at school. At a class meeting before graduation from primary school, when I expressed my hope of becoming a poet, most of my peers laughed at me, saying I was aiming too high.

Today parents fuss over the rearing and education of their only children who are usually so spoiled that they can be justly nicknamed "little emperors." Society supposedly treats everyone equally, but in reality doesn't.

I spent my childhood as an object of discrimination. The insults from my classmates became routine. I came to realise the only way to avoid their insults was to stay away from them.

At home the rumors about my origins enraged my grandparents. Whenever my grandfather heard that I'd been involved in a fight with someone, he beat me.

Grandmother kept reminding me of my family background because the latter was a matter of great importance to everyone at that time.

They discouraged me from writing poetry and even burned verses of mine that were written on cigarette wrappers. I was so depressed that I thought of suicide.

Although my personal circumstances in high school were no better, I never stopped writing. At that time I heard a broadcast about the Xinjiang Uygur Autonomous Region (located in China's northwest). I listened with great interest to the accounts of pioneers in that vast uninhabited land.

After careful preparation, I packed my belongings, including a bag full of books and manuscripts, and took a train headed for Xinjiang without telling my grandparents or anyone at school. Fifteen days later,

I reached Hami (in Xinjiang), only to be sent back because I was too young.

I was discouraged but not disheartened. The ordeals I had endured over the years had toughened me.

I tried a second time but again was sent back.

My grandparents came under political attack during the Cultural Revolution from 1966 to 1976. One day, my grandmother gave me what little they had, ten *yuan*, and told me to escape for fear that I too would be subjected to persecution.

Then I led the life of a tramp, wandering from place to place. My health deteriorated as a result. On the outskirts of Qingdao, a seaside resort city in Shandong Province, I lay ill in a shed for a week with a high fever.

A carpenter working nearby was kind enough to take me to a doctor, whereupon I made a speedy recovery. I felt obligated to join the local construction team headed by the carpenter. We were like a gypsy band, moving all the time.

The old man was very strict with me, especially as regards carpentry skills. He'd lose his temper if he saw me with a book.

But when I told him about the local customs and folk tales of the places, his attitude began to change. I soon felt I belonged to a "tribe," one in which the members helped each other. For the first time in my life I lived in dignity, something which I'd longed for for many years.

Notwithstanding the difficulties—manual work from morning till night, felling trees and sawing wood all day long—I enjoyed the work.

I traveled from province to province with the

team, always fascinated by new sights, sounds, and cultures. It's these bittersweet experiences that gave me a host of topics for my poetry.

In my off hours, I jotted down my reflections on these experiences. One poem recorded my feelings about my life working as a member of the construction team:

I have a dream:
On everyone the sun shines,
without playing favorites;
To everyone innocence returns,
with a little honesty.

Four years later, in 1972, I left the construction team to return to my hometown, Nanjing, where I got a temporary job as a carpenter.

A year later, several of my poems appeared in newspapers. This was followed by the publication of a collection of my prose poems, *The Nanjing Yangtze River Bridge*.

In 1981, my father, who had been in the United States all these years, made contact with an old friend in China, who eventually located me. When he offered to help me study abroad, I hesitated to accept. To my father, I'm merely a carpenter who doesn't know how to read or write. Unknown to him, I hold a bachelor of arts degree from the Chinese Department of Nanjing Teachers' University.

"It'd be ridiculous for a Chinese to travel thousands of miles to study his mother tongue in a foreign land," I told my father in a letter. I enclosed in the letter some twenty of my poems about my feelings for my country.

Since my background has become known, my days have been filled with visits from those who've had similar experiences. In one letter to me, a handicapped young man said my confidence and new search for a new self-image have offered hope for the troubled and abused.

These words drive home the point that you'd never get bogged down in the quagmire of remorse and despair but, instead, be up and doing something to prove your worth.

New–Wave Rock Star: Cui Jian

Rock and roll is a special kind of music. It's anti–tradition and anti–culture.

"Pop" is a new word that invaded the Chinese vocabulary in the late 1970s. For a decade some heated disputes over its definition gave rise to confusion and hindered its healthy development in China. While the orthodox classical musicians scoffed at its "deformation of music," hundreds of "pop singers" were crooning the saccharine love ballads from Hong Kong and Taiwan. Still others used "pop music" to shout about their lofty aspirations for a brighter tomorrow. Then came a heat wave of disco that has been pounding streets in almost every city and even remote towns and villages. Whatever it was, the surge in interest in "pop" music recording thrust overnight this "new–born baby" into the commercialized world.

Amid all the confusion, there suddenly emerged on the Chinese pop scene a long–haired young man donned in baggy trousers and heavy army boots who presented his countrymen with a song "Nothing to My Name," a new kind of "pop music"—he called it "rock'n'roll." It was something completely new at the time.

The man's name is Cui Jian, twenty–seven, of Korean origin, a former classical trumpet player from the state–run Beijing Song and Dance Troupe. He was expelled from the troupe in April 1987 for allegedly failing to fulfill his work assignments and "indulging" in pop music. He writes and sings his own songs and has his own band that includes a woman, a visiting student from Hungary and an employee of the Madagascan Embassy in China. After his departure from the song and dance troupe, he and his band, called Ado, continued to perform at Pierre Cardin's Maxim's de

Pekin restaurant and other big international hotels in Beijing as well as at private parties arranged by foreigners and their friends.

For some Chinese listeners, Cui's music is a bit too experimental. He is the first Chinese rock musician who uses the dissonant chords and syncopated beats of avant—garde Western rock music. His music, bearing very little resemblance to that from Taiwan and Hong Kong, has been influenced by such Western rock stars as Sting and Talking Heads and is a far cry from anything his contemporaries are doing.

Absent from the stage for a year, Cui's January 1988's comeback skyrocketed him to unprecedented fame. His first album of songs, all of which he wrote, is expected to be released soon by the China Tourism Sound and Video Publishing Company.

Getting hold of Cui Jian is no easy matter. He tends to shun reporters, who, he says, exhaust him. "I live for music, not for news," he said in his three–room apartment, where he lives with his parents and younger brother. The room he shares with his brother is stacked with musical instruments and the wall is plastered with pictures of Western rock stars. His desk is piled with music scores, tapes, and books (including an English textbook). He rounded off the interview with an improvisation on his Japanese guitar.

Earlier this year I was allowed to perform again by the Beijing Performing Art Agency. Some people working in that company liked my songs and had been dropping hints to their "leaders" about how good my music was and how much people liked it. Those leaders, somehow feeling they were falling behind, waved their big hands and said, "Okay, let him sing!"

My concert at the music hall of the Zhongshan Park on January 21 was something of a success. The atmosphere was really good. The audience were extremely enthusiastic and responded warmly to each of my songs. They danced to the beat and sang along with me. It was just terrific! But I didn't expect the curtain to fall before I finished my last song. I'd no alternative but to hold on to the end. Then a few policemen came and dragged me very rudely to the backstage and scolded me that I'd "incited" the audience to be rowdy. They called me a "hooligan."

Actually, there was no official ban on my performing in public. But no concert hall would accept me. Most people reckon this unannounced ban on my performance was a result of the song "Nanniwan." In January 1987, I was invited to perform at a charity performance at the Capital Stadium in Beijing. As there were senior officials attending, I chose to do this 1930s ballad to arouse their nostalgia about the Communist–led army's spirit of hard struggle and self–reliance. I thought it would suit their taste. But no! My modern rock–style rendition of the revolutionary tune apparently enraged a veteran revolutionary, a Long Marcher. So it has been rumored that he had someone later put a "ban" on my performance.

I don't agree with those who'd put the blame entirely on the higher–ups. What's most painful to me isn't that you're misunderstood by the older generation. I don't expect the generation gap be patched up, but it's real pain when you aren't understood by your contemporaries.

I wasn't allowed to give public performances for a year. I think I was lucky though. It wasn't a wasted year—I did a lot of thinking and was able to keep my mind on writing songs. I felt I was getting to know more and becoming more mature in many ways.

I don't remember how many times I've told reporters about my experiences. I get really fed up. There's been too much coverage of me—all sorts of reports. Some reporters are geniunely interested in my music. But some reporters have never listened to any of my songs or attended any of my concerts. I find them disgusting.

I started my trumpet lesson at three with my father, who used to be a trumpet player with a song and dance troupe. I never had any higher music education. I was admitted to the Beijing Song and Dance Troupe in 1981 as a trumpet player. But it wasn't until they pushed me out of the troupe last April that I really felt free. Now, I can concentrate on rock music and don't have to bother about completing the tasks assigned to me by others. I'm lucky in this sense.

My interest in pop music goes back some ten years when it first emerged in China. I learned to play the guitar while singing and used to sing pop songs from England and the United States. I'm particularly interested in European and American pop music. There wasn't any genuine Chinese pop music then. Later I tried to write my own songs. "Nothing to My Name" is among the first I wrote. I didn't expect the song to become so popular.

I like all the songs I've written except those written with unclear objectives. I do have songs of this kind and I regret them. Song-writing is something original and creative. As for "Nanniwan," though my rendition has been well accepted and loved, I still don't like it, because I did it only to suit someone else's taste and because it's not something heart-felt. I don't like the song "The Last Bullet" either. I was asked to write the song for a TV play about the

Chinese soldiers on the Sino-Vietnam border. I've never been to the Laoshan frontline. And I just imagined a war scene there and wrote the song. But I'd never been there, nor experienced life there; so I feel that the song's not genuine. That's why I haven't included these two songs in my first album to be published by China Tourism Sound and Video Publishing Company.

Rock and roll is a special kind of music. It's anti-tradition and anti-culture. It's the ideology of modern man. It needs brand-new dynamics. It's sometimes a manifestation of sexual drive. It's got to be satisfying. When I get down to writing rock songs, I found that what I'd learned before—so-called "orthodox" concepts and "professional" techniques —was totally useless. I've always been looking for what fits me the best. For me, there's no alternative to Western rock music. I've listened to many groups and singers, whether or not they're famous. I got very excited when I started listening to The Police and Talking Heads (both are Western rock troups) years ago. I didn't understand the English lyrics and didn't know the background, but I felt that they were real rock and roll. I listened to a lot of "punk" music. Do you know who punks are? They've fantastic hairdoes, no respect for society and terrific music! There's also a style called "funky." I sometimes have tried to imitate it in my music. "Funky" music has a unique and very satisfying harmony and beat, and sometimes the singer doesn't sing the lyrics but reads the words to the beat in a particular way. I like it very much. I used this "funky" style in my "It's Not That I Don't Understand." Do you know Tom Brown? He's the "funky" musician I like most. I don't like Madonna.

She's a good performer, but not a good singer or musician. I haven't come to like jazz. It just doesn't satisfy me. Su Rui (Julie Sue) is the only singer from Taiwan I like. But the instrumentation of her songs isn't imaginative and creative enough. I've heard about Luo Dayou (also a Taiwan rock star now living in the U.S.), but I haven't listened to his music.

When I write songs, the chords structure comes into my mind first and then the melody. The most difficult part of it is to write lyrics. But a song can't be written without lyrics and that's a headache for me. Sometimes the words I've worked out don't match the melody. But sometimes I do write satisfactory lyrics, such as "Nothing to My Name." It didn't take me very long to work them out.

I don't know why the idea of blending traditional Chinese instruments with Western ones occurred to me. It just came into my mind quite naturally. In my instrumentation I sometimes used a reed pipe, or a *suona* (wood trumpet), sometimes a *zheng* (Chinese harp), because I've friends who are good at playing these instruments.

All the members in my band are my friends. We've been working together for a long time. I don't know how long we'll still play together, but at the moment we're working very well. I've some foreigners in my band and we get along well with them. They give me rock tapes and music scores that are hard to find in China. They have a wonderful understanding and mastery of rock music and I've learned a lot from them. One of them is a great guitarist. The quickness and nimbleness of his fingers are something I'll never have.

I've tried to express my own emotions and problems—they just happened to be the emotions and problems of my own generation. I curse the pedantic. I believe in nature and worship Taoism though I don't know much about it. I like to be a kind of onlooker and not to get too involved.

Rock and roll should get rid of people's sense of shame. Say, if someone fell in love with me and I wasn't in the least disposed towards her, I wouldn't pay any attention to her. I'll reject her curtly. I like to be clear-cut. I'd want to make her feel I'm but a bad guy and don't deserve her love. Then her self-respect and confidence would be restored. That's what I've done and tried to say in my songs.

People are so different. To communicate with each other is very difficult—sometimes I even think it impossible. Even when you like my songs and we share much of the same feelings about music, we're still different, very different.

Things are now much easier for me. I can perform anywhere. In fact, I've had too many invitations, including invitations for me to record. I'd like to take them up, but I'm too exhausted. I've a contract with the China Tourism Sound and Video Publishing Company for an album of my songs. This is the only company I'll associate with and I've refused other companies, because they don't really understand the meaning of copyright and have produced too much inferior music. This is the first time that I realize the importance of copyright—in protecting both the musician and the company. I don't want to talk too much about my songs. I'd like to let the listeners judge by themselves.

I don't have a girl friend—that would be too energy-consuming and at the moment I'm just too tired. I don't have any clear future plans yet. Yes, I'd like to go abroad, but that seems pretty distant now. But one thing is certain—I won't stop singing and writing.

Dancer: Yang Liping

I'm nicknamed peacock, but I'm not proud like a peacock.

Born into a family of Bai nationality in Dali, Yunnan Province, Yang Liping, twenty-nine, joined the Xishuangbanna Song and Dance Ensemble when she was twelve. In 1981, she was selected by the Central Nationalities Song and Dance Ensemble in Beijing to become a leading dancer at one of the country's most prestigious performing arts groups.

Yang is one of the few dancers to have made dancing a life career. She has always tried to achieve excellence in her field. Her dancing is, as critic Huang Shujia once said, "visual expression of her experiences and show her understanding toward life and Mother nature."

Yang did not receive any formal training at a dancing school, but she strongly feels that technique alone is not a substitute for artistic creation. She has taught herself literature, history, folklore, and aesthetics, as well as basic dance skills.

During the eight years she has been with the Beijing-based ensemble, Yang has choreographed and performed more than ten dances of different nationalities. In 1987, she was invited to participate in the Philippines Dance Festival and was made a permanent member of the Philippines National Folk Dances Association. In April 1988, she gave a solo dance soiree in the Philippines, the first of its kind for a Chinese dancer. In June of that year, she became the youngest dancer to have solo dance performances in Beijing. Almost all the dances she performed during the soiree are of her own creation. Meanwhile, she was hailed as a peacock star in Hong Kong early in 1988 for her performance of "The soul of Peacock." Behind her success, however, lies a bittersweet story.

My hometown features dancing. Each dance tells a story. One I don't believe today is about the footrings. This story tells about a lovely girl who finds a pair of rings, which she puts around her ankles. As a result she finds herself dancing non-stop, until she reluctantly takes the rings off.

When I first heard the story at the age of six, I thought it was a tactic by older persons to discourage us from dancing. Instead of being scared, I wished I'd have a pair of such rings of my own. And even today I often wish for that in my dreams. Recently, I created "Magical Footrings," a solo dance based on the tale.

I'm the oldest of four daughters of my divorced mother. When small, I collected firewood, and picked edible wild herbs to supplement my mother's monthly income of around thirty *yuan*. To please mother, I cooked daily several dishes of wild vegetables.

There never was enough food to go around. When serving meals from a pot with a spoon, I was very careful not to make any sound against the bottom of the pot, because the sound would indicate that there wouldn't be enough food for everyone in the family, which would hurt mom.

When I was five years old, my family moved to Xishuangbanna, a tropical mountainous region in South Yunnan. Seven years later, I enrolled in the Xishuangbanna Song and Dance Ensemble as a trainee.

My admission there is a bittersweet experience. Practice was a joy, compared to life at home. What troubled me was my mother's disapproval of my dancing. She thought a girl should stay home and learn to manage a house. Besides, it pained her to see me bending, twisting my arms and legs, and tumbling. "You might as well eat wild vegetables rather than risk your life," she once told me.

Mom traveled 12 miles to the ensemble to take me back home. All I could do was grab the door of my dorm, and cry out for help. It worked. The director talked mom into accepting my decision.

For many years in Xishuangbanna, I trekked with my dance company through mountains to perform for people living in remote villages, which usually had so many fleas and bugs that we had nowhere decent to unpack.

Though I lived a secluded exsistence in Xishuangbanna because of its backward economy and primitive means of transportation, my experiences there provided me with the background to enter the dance profession.

The local customs, landscapes, and folk tales have inspired me. I'd often sit on a mountain slope in my leisure hours to watch the sunrise and sunset, trying to figure out why the local people had tanned skin. It was because we were too close to the sun, my grandma told me.

In my hometown people view the peacock as a symbol of truth, beauty, and good fortune. It's a shame for a dancer from Xishuangbanna, whose people are proud of their various kinds of peacocks, not to be able to perform a peacock dance.

Local people told me that if someone wanted to imitate the way a peacock carries itself, she should first watch the peacocks prancing near a lake in

Xishuangbanna. Ten years ago I went there but didn't see any peacock dance and I thought I'd never make a good peacock dancer.

In the years that followed, although I've devoted much of my time to the study of peacock dances by other famous dancers, I don't copy their styles. I want a peacock dance to be based on my own observations of the bird.

When I entered the second national dance competition in 1986, I choreographed and performed the "Soul of Peacock," which won first prize.

At the start, my efforts drew sneers from some professionals who said peacock dances had been perfected by Dao Meilan, a famous dancer of the Dai Nationality. But I didn't want just to imitate her style. In creating "Soul of Peacock," I stressed the beauty of the bird but by not using the traditional dance pattern. Instead, I used repeated short dotting movements. I tried to seek the beauty not only in the form, but also in expression and spirit. I made every joint of my fingers and limbs expressive. All this distinguished my peacock from others'.

Critics say I'm very precise about coordinating the movements of my arms, wrists, and fingers when I'm representing the breathing of a peacock. True. But I think a real dancer dances with her feelings and not just her arms or legs.

Most people can move to music, but everyone isn't a dancer. Every dancer can move gracefully to music, but not every dancer is an artist. To real dancer, every movement she or he makes should be her or his understanding of, or response to, the particular aspect of life being depicted.

To this end, a dancer must have a variety of

experiences, but that doesn't necessarily mean that he or she understands life. A correct understanding of life results from one's cultural heritage. Only in this way can he or she convey the meaning to her audience of dance through the visual expressiveness of the dance.

I'm fond of reading. During the time when poems of the Tang Dynasty weren't available in bookstores, I copied almost 200 of them in five notebooks. Literature, together with my study of folklore and aesthetics, has helped me a great deal in my dance creations.

In Xishuangbanna in 1978, I was assigned a leading role in a dance just a couple of days before it was due to be performed in Chongqing, Sichuan Province.

Stunned at the unexpected selection, I was extremely agitated. I never had heard the music or seen a performance by others. The drama was new to me.

During the three-day trip to Chongqing, an actor briefed me on the dance movements of the drama, but this wasn't sufficient, although I was quite familiar with the theme of the story. I remember once shedding tears when I read a novel about the episode.

With the key actress never having rehearsed her dance, the premiere turned out to be a flop. My depression soon was replaced by redoubled efforts to practice and rehearse during breaks. This proved to be too much for me.

Ironically, one day in Chongqing when the script required me to faint away, I really did lose consciousness. I was taken to a hospital. The next day, visitors who were in the audience came with flowers and told me they weren't going to turn in the tickets for the coming performances.

I recovered. During the show the following evening, the audience held its breath as I "fainted away," and then broke into prolonged applause when they saw me perform in the next act.

I didn't pass out, that time, but I was brought to tears by their consideration and concern. I was fortunate in 1980 when I was selected by the Central Nationalities Song and Dance Ensemble to be one of its dancers who would depict the lives of different nationalities in dancing. Because of some red tape, however, I couldn't join the ensemble officially until 1981.

My nickname is "peacock," but I'm not as proud as a peacock. I've worked hard to succeed in the Beijing-based ensemble, where there's no lack of college-trained dance professionals. Nowadays, having a college diploma means practically everything. I come from Xishuangbanna, which is synonymous with backwardness. I had connections in Beijing and had received no special dance education. Probably, because of this, I have an inferiority complex.

Some people think I'm reserved and hard to get along with. Some say I'm indifferent to all other things except my own personal success.

I've ignored all these things, I've my own business to attend to. Others may have their own opinions about what I do. I'm different from them. If everyone thought alike, or conformed in every way, then we'd be living in a non-creative world.

There's nothing wrong with achieving personal success, so long as it isn't achieved at the cost of other people's interest.

I don't impose my ideas upon others, nor do I necessarily accept other people's ideas. Everyone has his or her way of living. But when I find others speaking ill of me, especially professionals, of course I'm concerned. But I always tell myself that people are different from one another. They only consider you to be right when they agree with you.

I work hard, but it's difficult for a young person like me to be recognized when seniority is used to measure one's performance. There're some people who'd rather do anything except let those with an enterprising spirit advance. When I created the "Soul of Peacock," I had to do all the details myself. I paid musicians to have music recorded, rented theaters for rehearsals, and extended myself in the dancing.

When the dance was a success, and I was invited to give solo dance performance in the Philippines, jealousy resulted. No one would have blamed me if I had idled my days away and eaten from "the communal pot." But if I create something new, the gossip starts up. "So be it," I say to myself.

People may find it hard to understand that my recent dance soiree held in Beijing is an expression of my inner self. Most of the dances are about my past experiences. Some said in the audience in their letters to me that they were not only impressed by my appearance, but also by my ability to convey my own experiences, and my earnest efforts.

"Romance During Hunting," an episode of the *Wa* nationality I created and performed, portrays two young people who fall in love and their struggle against nature and animals. It conveys the meaning of life and the price of love.

When I perform this piece, I'm excited. When I dance, I feel like living with something that just happened to me yesterday. Through my dances I find an outlet for my feelings and share them with my fellow people.

I belong to the common people. What differentiates me from others is that dancing is my life, while others may have different interests.

In addition to the stage and rehearsal halls, I'm a housewife. I've the responsibilities that burden all Chinese women—shopping, cleaning, doing laundry, budgeting, cooking, and so on.

My husband is a music composer at my ensemble. He was born in Beijing and was sent to Xishuangbanna to receive what was called "reeducation" during the Cultural Revolution. We have the same background in art and share many bittersweet memories.

A female dancer's professional career is usually short. In China, giving birth to a baby means the dancer has to end her dance career. To prolong my "dance life," I'd rather not have a baby in the immediate future. But when I'm too old to dance, I may also be too old to give birth. It's a difficult choice for a woman. I won't say that I won't compromise some day, though. On the other hand, I might not have children if bearing and rearing of the child would destroy my figure. Now I put my maternal love into a toy cloth baby I bought. But sometimes, seeing it makes me sad. Often I weep when I hold it in my arms.

I said to the audience at my dance performance in the Phillipines: "When I face an empty theater after you shall have left, I'll feel lonely. But I'll continue my search for the sun as I did in my childhood and resume my unfinished dream, my pursuit of art. I hope there'll be no end to that dream and I hope I won't lose my way in my pursuit."

Part Eighteen

On the Farm and in the Country

Farmer in the East: Wu Fengqi

I was as poor as a church mouse ten years ago. Now I've a new problem—a surplus of grain.

Dramatic changes have taken place in rural China since 1979 when a new system, the system of household-contract responsibility, was introduced in agricultural production. The yearly per capita income of farmers increased from 153 *yuan* (the equivalent of 41.4 U.S. dollars) to 463 *yuan* (125 U.S. dollars) in the 1978-87 period. Many formerly poor farm families have become well-off. Wu Fengqi's family is typical.

The fifty-year-old farmer was born in Yandangtou village in Fengyang County in Anhui Province in Eastern China. After he graduated from a middle school in the county, he went to work in the Yumen oilfield in Northwest China. In 1960, he lost his job and came home to till the land as a member of a collective.

In the eighteen years after he returned home from Yumen, his family often went hungry. His mother and his wife often had to go to neighbouring provinces to beg.

Nowadays, the family has become a prosperous grain producer.

In his spacious and bright guesthouse, the tall, bright-eyed man told how the change had taken place. As he talked, a few head of beef cattle grazed in the backyard and hens pecked in the front courtyard.

I led a miserable life ten years ago. It's really difficult to talk about it. I was as poor as a church mouse then.

Before 1978, there were ten members in my family: my mother, my wife, my son, my six daughters, and I. We lived in three thatched shacks that belonged to my father, who died when I was young. We had no furniture except for an old bed, and two worn-out quilts. We—people of three generations—had to crowd into the same bed at night. Don't laugh. It wasn't a humorous situation.

In those years we barely managed to stay alive eating rice chaff and wild vegetables.

The collective—the production team—gave each of us only 125 kilograms of food grain every year, enough for only five months.

Therefore, every year the government had to provide us with a certain amount of relief grain—usually sorghum and dried pieces of sweet potatoes. But I couldn't afford to buy it. I only earned 0.35 *yuan* (the equivalent of nine U.S. cents) a day from the team.

But I had to buy the relief grain. So I bought part of the allotment with what money I had, and sold it secretly in town at a higher price. Then, with the money I got from those transactions, I bought the rest of the relief grain.

Even so, my family still wouldn't have had sufficient food grain. Haunted by hunger, my mother and wife, together with our teenaged daughters, often went to Jiangsu, Zhejiang and other nearby provinces to beg. As a Communist Party member, I wasn't allowed to beg because I had to think of the "face" of my Party.

My family wasn't the only one begging in the village. About two-thirds of the hundred or so people in the village left their homes in autumn to beg elsewhere. A doggerel goes: "Peasants in Yandangtou go out begging when mosquitoes no longer fill the air."

I could endure the situation no longer. I discussed the situation with other leaders in the production team, and we decided to make a change. In late 1978 we distributed the collective land to farming families, according to the number of laborers.

This was done secretly, because we were afraid of being charged with "undermining the socialist collective economy" if higher authorities learned of it.

Fortunately, most families in my village reaped a good harvest the following year. This enabled us to have enough food. What pleased us even more was that Wan Li (then Secretary of Anhui Provincial Party Committee) expressed his support in the summer of 1979 when he was informed of the change. He suggested that the system be introduced on a trial basis in many other villages.

The contract system became popular quickly, first in Fengyang, and then in other parts of the county. Fengyang was the birthplace of this new system, which is now widespread.

Under the system, we, with each household serving as a basic unit, sign a contract with the production team to till a plot of land. The land still belongs to the collective, but we can use it. We can decide what crops to grow and how to grow them. After we provide the contracted amount of grain to the collective, and the state, we retain the rest, which we may sell at much higher prices to the state or on the free market. The more we produce, the more income we receive.

This is a good system for us farmers. It's greatly increased our incentive. As a result, farm production has grown real fast and things are getting better year by year.

I contracted 45 *mu* (3 hectares) of crop land from my production team in the winter of 1978, and reclaimed 27 *mu* (1.8 hectares) of wasteland the following spring. From these fields, I had a bumper harvest in 1979—7,500 kilograms of wheat and rice and 1,000 kilograms of peanuts, more than my family had ever had.

That year, I provided my contracted amount of 450 kilograms of grain to the state and the collective. I still had a considerable amount of grain remaining. For the first time, my family had more than enough to eat. We began to raise pigs, chickens and cattle.

Grain output in 1980 in my fields doubled that in 1979, reaching 15,750 kilograms. Since then it has increased year after year. In 1987, I grew 35,000 kilograms of wheat and rice, in addition to 2,500 kilograms of peanuts and 500 kilograms of rapeseed. The grain output in 1987 was 4.7 times that of what it had been in 1979, the first year of the family-contract system.

A lack of grain had been a problem for decades in the past. Now, I've a new problem—a surplus of grain. There's no grain-purchasing station near my village. To sell it, I've to transport the grain by tractor to a state-run grain station in town 25 kilometers away. The road into town is bumpy, and, as a result, it usually takes me a whole day to make the trip. I still have 12,500 kilograms of grain stored in barns.

With such a large supply of grain, my family no longer worries about having enough food. Now we can eat all we want. We've meat and egg dishes for lunch and supper every day. We often have wine to go with our meals.

I got rid of my worn-out quilts long ago. Now, I've silk ones. I've bought woolen sweaters and overcoats and leather shoes with heels for my wife and my daughters. Now they dress and have their hair "permed" like urban people. If they were in cities, you wouldn't be able to tell them apart from city women.

I've built three tile-roofed houses with a total of thirteen rooms. The old thatched shacks, where we lived for generations, have become cattle pens.

Farming technology has also improved. In 1983 I spent 6,000 *yuan* on a four-wheeled tractor and a small harvester. I've also bought all the other necessary farm implements, including ploughs and harrows. Farm work in my fields is basically mechanized.

These machines have made work easier for me. With the machines, I can finish wheat harvest in ten days. I usually have 50 *mu* (about 3.3 hectares) of wheat sown each year.

Harvesting seasons are the busiest and the happiest times for me. During the harvest season, all the members in my family help. My three elder daughters take turns driving the harvester. My son-in-law—my first daughter's husband—and I transport the crops by tractor to the threshing area. My son and other daughters come home on leave from school to help us with the harvest, and they work in the threshing area. My wife cooks at home for us. We usually start work at three o'clock in the morning, and finish at about eleven at night. We have meals in the field, not three, but five meals a day. It's exhausting work, but we're happy. Each day we bring home grain valued at 750 *yuan* (equivalent to 203 U.S. dollars).

In the coming years, I'll devote some of the land to orchards, but grain production still will remain my major business. The price of fruit is much higher than grain. At the same time, I'll branch out into animal husbandry. I've too much grain, you know, and I've to find a way to use the surplus grain to a good end. I've thought of raising animals. I'll build a piggery, a cattle farm, and a hen run. Now I've only four hogs, five head of cattle and a few chickens.

Also, I'm building a gold-dressing plant jointly with other farmers in my village. We expect to produce five kilograms of gold a year when it's put into production in 1988. Then I'll be not only a grain producer, but also a rural entrepreneur.

Poor Farmer: Deng Jianrong

I need grain, money, and water. If I have water, I'll have everything.

A majority of farmers in China have enjoyed unprecedented prosperity since 1979 when the country began to introduce the household-based contract system in agricultural production. However, China still has many poverty-stricken rural residents. According to the State Statistics Bureau, about 65.6 million rural citizens, or 6.5 percent of the total rural population, live below the "poverty line," which is now generally defined as an annual grain consumption of less than 200 kilograms and a yearly cash income of less than 200 *yuan* per person.

These poor people generally live on the Loess Plateau in the northwest, on the Yunnan-Guizhou Plateau, and in mountainous areas in the southwest. They are poor because of adverse natural conditions, family misfortunes, or lack of funds, technology, and transport facilities.

To alleviate their poverty, the state every year allocates several million tons of grain and several billion *yuan* in emergency funds for assistance programs. In addition, the state during 1984-87 provided them with relief in the form of five million tons of grain, 100,000 tons of cotton, and 500 million meters of cloth.

Deng Jianrong is one of the poor farmers. This fifty-nine-year-old man lives in Lijiabu Village in Dingxi County, Gansu Province, on the Loess Plateau. The county is one of the poorest in China.

There are five members in his family: Deng, his wife, and three sons. The couple and their elder son, twenty, a primary school graduate, cultivate eight *mu* (15 *mu* is equal to a hectare) of dry cropland that they have contracted out from the collective. The two other sons are high school students.

In his small, shabby thatched shed, Deng told how they live in this poor county.

My daughter came to visit me yesterday from Southern Jiangsu. She told me it's a good place. Everywhere there're rivers, crops, trees, and grass. And farmers are well-to-do.

But we're unfortunate to live in this god-forsaken place. The hills here are treeless, the valleys dry, and the fields grow very poor crops.

This place is more than 2,000 meters above sea level, and we've only about 140 frost-free days. We can grow only one crop a year. After we harvest spring wheat in August, the weather gets too cold to grow anything.

So, the slack farming season here lasts about six months a year. During this period, we usually make hill slopes into terraced fields. We earn forty *yuan* for the transformation of every *mu* of terraced land.

Our most serious problem isn't a lack of land but a shortage of water. We can get neither river water, nor groundwater, to irrigate our fields. We have to rely on nature for rainwater. That, however, isn't enough. The land is blighted by drought and hailstorms almost every year. As a result, it has a poor yield—we reap 120 catties of spring wheat per *mu* (or 900 kg per hectare).

Take last year for example. Water was badly needed in April but there was no rain, which delayed our spring sowing. In the autumn we had a poor harvest. I reaped only 350 kilograms of spring wheat, 50 kilograms of soybeans and 500 kilograms of sweet potatoes from my eight *mu* field. How could I feed my five-member family with such a small amount of grain? The county government had to waive my agricultural taxes, and our village had to reduce my contracted quotas.

To feed my family, I had to buy grain at the free market in the county town. I couldn't afford much, because the price was too high and I didn't have much money. I bought only 200 kilograms of wheat from the free market last year.

But my daughter now gives me twenty *yuan* every month. Both she and her husband make good salaries. Without her help, I wouldn't be able now to buy high-price grain.

In addition, the county government gives us grain each year. Last year I got 200 kilograms of emergency grain. Although we must pay for such grain, the price is much lower than that on the free market.

Even so, my family still has food problems. Every spring we have to eat wild vegetables and wheat bran. To save food, we eat only two meals a day during non-farming seasons, and meals are usually just noodles. Most of the time we can't have dishes that we'd like to eat because of the lack of vegetables and meat. Water is scarce. I don't have water to grow vegetables or raise pigs at home. It's only during planting and harvesting times that we've three meals a day of steamed bread and dishes usually of fried slices of sweet potatoes.

Providing my family with food staples in recent years, however, has become much easier than before. Now, I don't need to go several hundred miles away to beg. Before the contract system was applied in my village in 1981, I and my daughter, driven by hunger, had to beg for food in several agriculturally prosperous counties in the Gansu Corridor. We went there by train, but we had to sneak onto it. Even if we had been discovered, the attendants wouldn't have been able to fine us, because all we had was a bowl and a walking stick. At worst, they would have only thrown us off the train, which couldn't have mattered anyway either because we would have hopped on the next train.

Grain is essential to my family. Because we don't have enough, we're hungry. And because we've no surplus grain to sell, we've no money. And if a family has no money, you can imagine how difficult life can be.

I can't afford clothes for my family. The clothes my wife wears were given to her by my daughter. The ragged coat I wear now was given to me by a friend years ago.

The county government in 1984 gave my family some second-hand clothes. I was told that these clothes were contributed by urban families in Beijing and other big cities. Besides, the county government in 1986 sold me, on credit, cloth and cotton worth ninty *yuan*. My wife made two quilts. I still haven't paid off this debt.

For many years I've wanted to build a new house. But I can't, because I don't have the money. The straw shed we live in was built in 1962. It has a floor space of only 15 square meters, too small for the five of us. And, what makes it worse, is that the roof leaks in rainy weather. I have to hang a plastic sheet under the roof to prevent rain from dripping onto our *kang* (bed built of adobe heated from below). I've no money to repair the roof.

I practically have no furniture in this house. I've nothing but some pans and two large vats. I'm not afraid of being laughed at when I say that, because what I'm telling you is the truth. One of the vats is used to store grain, and the other holds water. They're perhaps the most valuable things in my shed. Oh, no. The most valuable thing is the radio my daughter brought me yesterday.

It's hard for us during the bitterly cold winters here. A few families in my village have coal-burning stoves. But I don't. I've no money to buy coal. To get fuel, I climb the hills in fall and winter to rake dead grass and dig up roots. Most people in my village do the same. This has denuded the hills and resulted in serious soil erosion.

To help us out, the county government every year gives my family some relief money. Though it's a small sum, it helps. I received twenty *yuan* last year.

In order to make money, I started a barbershop by the roadside near my village. I'm a farmer in the growing season, and a barber in the slack season. But the business at my shop in recent years hasn't been good. Several barbershops have been set up near my shop by men from other provinces. They use electric cloppers, which are better than my hand-operated one. And, they charge less than I do. Therefore most people, the young ones in particular, usually go to them.

I once thought of going into business, but I'm too old. I asked my elder son to go into business with me, and some other villagers. But he said he knows nothing about business and doesn't want to do so. I'm afraid he'll live a miserable life in this poverty-stricken area as I have.

My wife does her bit to earn money. She raises a few chickens and sells the eggs in the town. The income isn't much, however.

Lack of money in my family is because of a lack of grain, and the lack of grain is caused mainly from the lack of water. Therefore, a water shortage is the basic problem in this area.

I need grain, I need money, and what I need most, is water. I dare say, if I've water, I'll have everything.

Water shortage has brought us difficulties not only in farming but also in our daily lives. We consider water more precious than oil. When a guest comes to visit us, we'd rather give him a steamed bread than a bowl of water.

Many households in my village each have one or two pits in their courtyards about 10 meters deep. They've been built with the help of the county government to store rainwater in summer and snow in winter.

I've no pits in my yard, however, because the soil is too loose. I tried several times but failed. I fetch water on a shoulder pole and a pair of buckets from a stream each morning, but only when the water there is clean. The stream is a great distance from my shed and there're many hills on the road. It's hard to carry water from there. Sometimes I fall on the way, when my legs give way, spilling the two buckets of water. What a pity!

Pit owners in my village also fetch water from that stream with pole and buckets, or barrow-and-donkey, when there's no water in their pits. If the stream is dry because of drought, the county government brings water to us in trucks.

To save water, we use the same basin of water day after day to wash our faces and hands. We never discard the water but, instead, give it to our chickens to drink. Our clothes are easily soiled, because we work in dusty fields. But we seldom wash them, and as a result we have many lice in our clothes. We don't bathe very often. Yes, we do bathe—we take off our clothes and stand in the yard when it rains.

I've very humble wishes in life. I'd be satisfied if I had enough water, grain, clothes, a house to shelter my family, and to provide them with enough to eat. That's all I need. But unfortunately this place can't even provide me with these necessities.

I often blame myself for having been born in this poverty-stricken area and staying here.

My daughter had better luck. Although she was born here, she married a man from a rich area and left. I've wished for years that my sons would leave this region and live elsewhere.

Pearl Culturist: Yu Youfu

I hope the current policies won't change so we can stay in this business and make a good living.

Fifty-eight-year-old Yu Youfu is now quite satisfied with his present job of pearl culturing, a trade which has brought him a net income of 100,000 *yuan* in eight years.

Before he entered this trade, he never dreamed of being as rich as he is, even though his parents, like most Chinese people, gave him a name meaning a great amount of money.

Now whenever he talks about his success and fortune, he murmurs, "I'm so happy, so happy" and breaks into a broad smile.

Yu speaks slowly with a strong Zhejiang accent. Having traveled more than his neighbors, he has seen much of the world and is aware of many things outside his immediate sphere of interest.

He lives in a big house in Xiaoshan County, Zhejiang Province, but still does not feel at ease. He worries that the government's policy will change suddenly and all that he has obtained now will disappear. So now he is trying his best to help his villagers and relatives, hoping that everyone will become as rich as he is.

My village is surrounded by many small ponds and streams. In the past, we only knew that they were a source of fish and that we'd wash in them. But we never expected them to bring our families wealth.

I was the first to discover that there were pearls

in these ponds. It happened one day in 1980. That morning I went to see my mother-in-law in a neighboring county. While chatting about this and that, her relatives told me that some of their neighbors had hit it rich.

It was quite easy, they said. They cultured pearls in ponds and streams. They told me one catty of pearls could sell for more than 1,200 *yuan* and that the cost of production was very low.

At that time, we worked in the fields for nearly twelve hours a day, but our daily income was only seventy to eighty *fen*. That meant that our yearly income was, at most, 240 *yuan*.

I figured that if I cultured 300 pearl-oysters, I'd pick three catties of pearls and sell them for 3,600 *yuan*. You'd imagine how excited I was at the idea. I decided to start right away.

Of course, my neighbors said I was all "wet," and that all of this was simply a pipe dream. Some said that I would be "downstart" before becoming an "upstart."

My wife initially disagreed with me. But as I was the master of the family, and made all the decisions, I decided to try. So she in the end agreed.

Things weren't easy at first. Getting enough money was the first problem. We had only saved a little money from selling rice and duck eggs. I had to borrow a large part of what I needed from relatives.

In a month, I had gotten together about 2,500 *yuan*. I had to pinch pennies. I bought some pearl-oysters and also picked many big pearl-oysters from the river.

In February 1981, I hired an experienced worker from Jiangsu Province. With his help, I cultured 1,600 pearl-oysters. I attached each of them to very thin strings which were tied to thin sticks of bamboo, and then put the oysters into the pond.

Then I waited and waited.

I was worried those days. I wondered if the oysters would grow well under water, and how many pearls were in each of them. At the end of the tenth month I'd stand it no longer. I desperately wanted to see the results. So I brought up 300 pearl-oysters and opened them.

To my great excitement, I was able to harvest four catties of pearls. That was in October 1981, about fifteen months earlier than the normal growing period. Of course, the quality wasn't good.

Anyhow I showed them to a company which made Chinese medicine from pearls. But they were willing only to pay me 460 *yuan* per catty for half of my pearls, and 200 *yuan* per catty for the rest.

I thought my pearls were worth much more than that. So I took the pearls to my mother-in-law's village. There was a pearl dealer representing a company in the city of Wuhan in Hubei Province.

I asked for 550 *yuan* a catty, which the dealer refused to give. After some bargaining, we settled on 460 *yuan* a catty for all the pearls I had with me.

He gave me 1,840 *yuan*. I had dreamed for so long of making a big bundle of money. When this actually happened, I was speechless. I was so happy. I carefully counted the money. It was so much, and it was mine!

I dared not let anyone know of my good fortune, because I was afraid that the policy would change some day and I would be criticized as a capitalist and the money would be seized.

I took the money home and showed it to my wife. She, like me, was very happy. We then hid the money.

In April of the next year, we harvested the rest of the 1,300 oysters and got another 15.6 catties of pearls. This time we sold them for 7,199 *yuan*. My family became the first "ten-thousand-*yuan* household" in the village.

I became famous. Nearby villagers came to visit. They wanted to culture pearls and asked me to help them. I did my best.

Of course, I wasn't always successful. In 1983, I nearly went bankrupt. In June of that year, I planted 2,800 pearl-oysters in the ponds. But I only got back four catties of pearls. It was a crushing failure.

That experience taught me a lesson. I realized that I should aquire some scientific knowledge and do some reading. After that, I experimented with different ways and made careful observations. I found that the best growing period was from September to April.

Also, I found out that the pearl-oysters should be put 40 centimeters under the water. If they were put into water deeper than that, the pearl-oysters wouldn't get enough sunshine. If put in shallow water, there wouldn't be enough food for the oysters.

The following year, I gathered 70 catties of pearls, a bumper harvest. Even though the price of pearls fell sharply that year in my province, I still was able to sell them for 17,500 *yuan* in neighboring Fujian Province.

In our country, pearls are classified in five grades. The first grade sells for 10,400 *yuan* a catty, the second for 8,600 *yuan* usually. The other three grades are priced at 5,800, 1,600 and 800 *yuan* a catty respectively.

The best quality pearls are very difficult to produce. The pearls of this grade usually grow in the triangle-type oysters, which are expensive to buy and breed.

In 1986, I bought fifteen triangle pearl-oysters from the fishermen. I took great care with them. One year later, I picked four *liang* (ten *liang* equal a catty and two catties equal a kilogram) of pearls. Two *liang* of them were classified as "third-grade."

This is the highest grade of pearls I had ever produced. The price at that time was 5,600 *yuan* a catty. Each oyster netted 68 *yuan* for me.

I sold the best pearls as ornaments to jewelry stores. Usually one out of five cultured pearls are of gem-grade quality. The rest were sold to medicine shops or companies.

I never will forget May 3, 1985. That morning I discovered that the pearl-oysters in one of my ponds had been stolen. It was a devastating blow for me.

The whole family searched everywhere looking for clues. Even the policemen were called. My wife cried. It amounted to a loss of 20,000 *yuan*. We searched nearly every pond and road but found nothing.

I was very angry. I had hired a man to guard the ponds. But that night he fell asleep. Even though I paid this man 45 *yuan* a month, he had still let my pearl-oysters be stolen. I fired him without asking him to compensate the loss. Even if I had asked him to repay, he wouldn't have been able to do so.

Despite this loss, my family became rich from pearl culture. Within seven years, I earned more than 100,000 *yuan*. With this money I built two two-story houses for my two sons. Each building is about 580 square meters in floor space and cost 60,000 *yuan*.

I still have nearly 10,000 *yuan* in the bank and another 20,000 *yuan* worth of pearls in the ponds.

Now I'm going to furnish these two new houses with modern things and improve our daily life. Although it's time for my wife and me to enjoy life, I cannot.

I'm a Communist Party member. I was a team leader for more than seven years. I still feel duty-bound to help my villagers.

Nearly all the households in my village have the family name "yu". We've been told all our villagers are the descendents of the same ancestor. So we're all relatives and one big family. That's all the more reason we should help each other.

Now of the 235 households in the village, 211 have entered the pearl culturing business. Eight years ago there was only me. I'm very glad about what has happened. I helped them buy pearl-oysters and learn culture techniques. At the beginning, I even suggested that they put their pearl-oysters in my ponds, so that I'd take care of theirs at the same time.

Of course, the more people in this business, the keener the competition be. But I wasn't afraid. I knew I'd win. The best way was to cut costs.

In the first three years, I hired people from other provinces to do the technical work. They worked eight hours a day and I paid them three *yuan* a day and provided them with free board and lodging.

But now my younger son and his wife have mastered all the techniques. Each year, after they finish their own job, they go out for two to three months to help others. Now our costs have been greatly reduced. Last year, they earned 2,700 *yuan* from passing on techniques to others.

I also began to breed pearl-oysters in my ponds. Now that pearl culturing has become rather popular in my county, the price of pearl-oysters has risen tremendously. By 1985, each pearl-oyster cost one *yuan*, while in 1980 it was only twenty cents. Even so, the pearl-oysters were still very difficult to get.

Each year we had to go to different provinces around the country to find cheaper and better pearl-oysters. I once went to Boyang Lake in Jiangxi Province, 1,000 miles from my village.

We also make use of dead pearl-oysters. After the pearls are picked out, the oysters, which die, are fed to pigs, so nothing is wasted. Each year we can sell two or three pigs to the state.

I've also learned to pay attention to the market. Before I cultured pearls, I never understood of what use market information was. But now I'm most concerned with such information, just like a real merchant.

Most of the information I get is from the newspapers such as *Agriculture Science* and *Science and Technique* and *Hangzhou Daily*.

Early in 1987, I was told that the price of pearls would decline that year, and I believed it. So I asked the family to pick out all the one-year-old pearls. They sold at that time at 530 *yuan* a catty. A few months later, the price fell to 250 *yuan* a catty, less than half that figure.

I realize there're many things I need to learn. To know only how to culture pearls is far from enough.

I've become famous. My name can be heard on the radio and seen in the newspapers. I now have both money and fame, which is plenty.

Now each day after supper, visitors come to see me. We discuss all kinds of things, such as where to buy cheap pearl-oysters, how to culture better pearls, and where to get the best prices.

I'm getting old. I can't do everything, so I've delegated much of the work to my sons. I've done my duty. I feel proud, because it was I who blazed a new trail which helped the villagers to get rich.

People came to me to ask for information and I helped them. I supported my relatives and the poor households with money and materials. I lent them more than 8,000 *yuan* without asking for interest.

Now the only wish I have is that my village could make even more money from pearl culturing. I hope the current economic policies won't change so we can stay in this business and make a good living.

Dog Manager: Liang Zheng

I like to take risks. I like to do things that nobody has done before.

His name is Liang Zheng, but since the establishment of his dog-breeding corporation, people call him "the dog manager."

Since his graduation from Shanxi University in 1960, he has done many jobs.

In 1985, he established the Liang Zheng Dog-Breeding Corporation.

When I was in my teens, I used to dream that someday I'd become a pilot or a tank driver. As I grew older, I gradually became interested in education and in the end decided to become a teacher. But I never expect that at fifty I'd become a "dog manager."

When I say I'm a "dog manager," many people laugh and say that I'm joking. "No," I reply, "I'm indeed the manager of a dog corporation."

Though quite a few people in China dislike dogs, I like people to call me "dog manager." Dogs, not like other animals, have a deep affection for man and are loyal to him. In my view, "dog" is a synonym for "faith," so I guess I can be called a faithful manager.

In 1985, I was a high school teacher in Linfen, Shanxi Province. I suggested selling the campus workshop and establishing a dog-breeding corporation, the first of its kind in China.

After two years of effort, my dream of building a Chinese pets' paradise—an amusement park—came true. Entering the 47-hectare park, visitors are greeted by 500 dogs of twenty-four species, such as Chinese shapeis, shihtzus, pugs, and pekingese, all wagging their tails and barking.

In 1984, before I started the corporation, I noticed that of six animals—the horse, cow, sheep, chicken, dog, and pig—the dog was rated fifth. I chose dog-breeding and decided to establish China's first dog-breeding corporation.

To increase my knowledge of dogs and dog-breeding, I went to the Beijing Library with my daughter to look up as mush as I could. I traveled to many places in China to consult experts in the field. My research showed that dogs can be used widely, in defense, public security, scientific experiments, forest protection, hunting, and guiding the blind.

In 1985, I began working in earnest on this new enterprise. I obtained a loan of 10,000 *yuan* from a local bank and asked several unemployed young people to buy dogs for me from all over the country.

A professor at an agricultural university in Northeast China learned that Linfen had a dog company. He wrote to me saying that he was willing to sell a group of German sheepdogs to the company.

I felt as if I'd found a treasure. I immediately took a train to the Northeast and spent five days and nights bringing back the dogs by truck. Soon afterwards, I went to Guangzhou and bought over thirty Chinese shapeis, the rarest breed in the world.

The shapei is my favorite. It has wrinkled skin and is hairless. It's fierce with strangers but much more faithful to its owner than other breeds.

In three months, I had more than 300 dogs from Gansu, Sichuan, Heilongjiang, and Guangdong provinces and the Xinjiang Uygur Autonomous Region.

But, unfortunately, at that time we had no experience in dog breeding. Just as I was about to expand my enterprise, disaster struck. Within two months, 200 dogs died of disease. The corporation was on the verge of bankruptcy.

At this crucial point, I received some letters from dog lovers who expressed their great concern over the fate of my company. One of the letters was from Xiao Chuanfa, an associate professor at Shandong Agricultural University. He spoke highly of my enterprise and expressed admiration for my bold spirit in advancing canine science. He offered me two types of vaccine to help protect the remaining dogs and save the corporation.

The vaccine worked. The rest of the dogs were saved. Since then, I've understood that for an enterprise to succeed, it must enlist talented personnel.

I sent three of my young staff members to study at the Shenyang Police Dog School and engaged two postgraduates from the Nanjing Agricultural Genetic Institute, under the Chinese Academy of Agricultural Sciences as technicians in the corporation. They played a vital role in my enterprise.

To develop the dog-breeding industry and to provide a medium for the exchange of information, I established a bimonthly magazine, "The Dog-Breeding Industry in China." I serve as its editor-in-chief. At the same time, I opened China's first correspondence class for the scientific breeding and training of dogs, enrolling over 1,000 students from throughout the country. They now have become my "dog friends."

Three years have passed since the corporation began, and the number of employees has increased from the original twenty to fifty-eight, and the number of dogs from 300 to 500.

We employ both men and women, of all ages. Everyone has specific responsibilities. Forty-nine are in charge of the Linfen Chinese Pets' Paradise. They include dog raisers, accountants, cooks, storemen, poultry doctors, and a deputy manager. The other nineteen stay in the headquarters of the corporation, mainly to work on the magazine.

I arrive at headquarters at 7:45 a.m. every day. The first thing I do is deal with the correspondence from home and abroad. Then I spend two hours reading manuscripts for the magazine.

I subscribe to over ten different newspapers, to keep myself informed.

To save time, I don't go home for lunch, even though my home is close to headquarters.

In the afternoon, I spend my time doing research on canine science. Also, I do some writing and contribute articles to the magazine.

I'm a man of wide interests. I like music. I like sports. I like dancing and singing. One afternoon, I stayed home alone, singing songs from the old days.

But now, it seems I've no time to enjoy myself. My children often complain that I don't accompany them to the park on holidays. Actually, I've no holidays.

A lot of well-intentioned people ask me, "Pioneering an enterprise at such an age, is it worth it? You should stay at home, living in ease and comfort." But I cannot rest. If I had no work, I'd get seriously ill.

Some colleagues ask me how I handle the conflicts between family and enterprise. I reply that probably too often I ignore family matters. My mind is totally occupied with dogs. What I'm most concerned about is the fate of my dogs. Their deaths have become my greatest suffering.

Judging from the efforts I've made and the time I've spent, I'd be a wealthy man, according to some people. But no. My principal purpose in raising dogs isn't to make money for myself but to achieve other goals. I want to set up a Chinese dog association in the near future; become a member of an international dog club; and if possible, train a special type of dog for guiding the blind. According to incomplete statistics, there're 50 million disabled persons in China, with the blind accounting for more than a third of that total.

To my regret, in some regions people kill dogs for fear of rabies. I don't think this is right. We should take preventive measures. To guard against the disease, I regularly have all my dogs vaccinated, and my employees get preventive inoculations.

Last year, the corporation's revenue amounted to 100,000 *yuan*, much more than that of the first two years. Businessmen from Japan, West Germany, France, Belgium, and Hong Kong wrote to me for stud dogs. My book *Dog Breeding* has become a best-seller in China. However, what excites me the most is that my magazine is being sold on the open market, which offers a wide forum for expanding canine science.

My Linfen Chinese Pets' Paradise has received over 400 visitors from China and overseas. Most of them consider my operation first-class.

Many of my dogs are now playing vital roles in experiments, solving criminal cases, and protecting orchards and storehouses.

But the lack of a qualified veterinarian and a capable assistant is still a headache to me. The quality of most of our employees needs to be improved. Last year, another 120 dogs died, which was a hard blow. These dogs represent many years of painstaking labor. It's no easy job raising even one stud dog.

Some people think I'm an eccentric. A lot of people call me a legend because I have undertaken many different jobs in my life. In 1960 after I graduated from the Russian Language Department of Shanxi University, I was assigned to teach Russian in Xiangfen High School, Shanxi Province. A few years later, I was authorized to build a chicken farm at the school to combine education with practice. I built an 82-meter-long chicken shed, the longest in Asia at the time, and wrote a book entitled *How to Raise Chickens.*

After coming to Linfen, I started raising quails. In 1982, I developed a formula for preserving quail eggs, which was successfully applied and sold well in the domestic market.

I was a Volunteer in the Korean War in 1951. I've been a foreign language teacher, a spare-time roast duck chef, and a newspaper distributor. In addition to quails, I've raised chickens and ducks. But I've never done anything as satisfying as dog breeding. I like to take risks. I like to do things that nobody has done before.

Now I've passed the prime of my life. A pressing matter today is to develop canine science in China, and I hope that I can get support from people of different classes.

Now called the China Dog-Breeding Corporation, the enterprise is directly under the Linfen Prefectural Travel Service and has become a local attraction. I believe that my company can, and will, continue to prosper in the future.

Village Head: Yu Ronggen

Reform brought the farmers enough to eat. Yet even well-fed farmers didn't have much money in their pockets. As a village head, I felt it was my duty to show them a way out.

A village is the heart of China's rural community. In 1958, the year of China's unsuccessful Great Leap Forward movement, villages were transformed into production brigades, several of which formed a people's commune. The communes combined the functions of Party leadership, government administration, production, education, social welfare, and military service in the former township. The farmers were asked to grow crops under rigid conditions, and worked in the fields together.

The organization of the people's commune was dissolved in 1984. Several years after, the contract responsibility system had been adopted in rural China. At the same time, the structure of villages and townships was restored. But the villagers still needed a leader. Usually, they elected the head of the village. In most case, the village head had formerly served as the brigade leader.

Such is the case in Liaoxi Village, east of Huzhou City in Zhejiang Province, East China. Yu Ronggen, forty, has been the leader of the village with 864 people and 88 hectares of farmland since he was in his twenties. In the past, he urged the farmers to go to the fields but he couldn't help them become wealthy. Today, he is leading them to prosperity with five village-run factories he conceived.

At a height of 1.70 meters (5.6 feet), Yu is thin and doesn't look strong. But he stands straight in the cold winter wind. He has a family of five—his mother, wife, son, and daughter, and himself.

He is one of the farmer-entrepreneurs who have emerged in China in the past few years. There are now fifteen million rural enterprises in the country, one tenth of them run at the township and village levels and the rest by individual rural families or small groups of them.

When I was the brigade head, my main task was to see to it that rationally close planting was rapidly carried out, the crops grown in the proper season, and that everybody worked in the fields. I used to blow a whistle to let the farmers know it was time to go to the fields every morning.

At that time, however, farmers were eating from the "big pot" (i.e. everyone shares equally). The farmers earned workpoints, which determined their yearly income. They didn't care about output, so they didn't care about taking advantage of the varying seasons.

For example, in 1976, the transplanting of early rice was scheduled to be finished by the end of May. Actually, it wasn't completed until June 19. The transplanting of late rice in August also was twelve days behind schedule.

In order to catch the season, we tried hard to urge rush-harvesting and rush-planting. We gave them extra workpoints to do so and asked them to work at night, sometimes until one o'clock in the morning. But it was difficult to get them to work hard. Why? Because in one year a farmer then earned no more than 150 *yuan*. That was too little to make any kind of living.

The worst time was when the members gathered to decide how many workpoints one laborer should earn. Usually the appraisals were made at a meeting with all the farmers present, which was supposed to be "democratic." But everyone wanted to get more points, regardless if he or she was worth that amount. So, very often farmers quarreled with each other, and even came to blows, over one point or two at the meeting.

In those years, to be a brigade leader was really a headache. You were busy all year round but were still powerless to find a way for the villagers to earn a decent living.

I thought of fixing output quotas on a household basis. The brigade once practised this system in 1960. But it was short-lived, coming under fire and dismissed as "a road to capitalism." Those who'd once advocated the system suffered severely during the Cultural Revolution.

Therefore, although I considered the idea of fixing output quotas on a household basis again and again, I dared not put it into action. For a person in my position in a grass-roots unit, the only thing he'd do was to follow the policies and decisions from above.

I waited until 1980, when we were allowed to carry out the household-based responsibility system linking output with income. The land was divided and contracted out to individual households to farm. My family also entered into a contractual agreement to farm a plot of land.

I continued to be the head of the village. At the beginning I felt at a loss, not knowing what to do about the future. But soon I found myself acting as an agent signing contracts with the farm families on behalf of the government. I was also responsible for each household's farming and was obliged to tell them what to do and how.

Strange as it may seem, some farmers are ignorant of scientific farming, although they've farmed all their lives. When this occurs, I've to give them necessary instructions. I also have to farm my own plot of land better than others, so as to set a good example.

The reform brought farmers enough food to eat. Yet even well-fed farmers didn't have much money in their pockets. What's more, now that the farmers worked with newly fired zeal on their contracted plots, we found we'd too much labor for too little land. At least 60 percent of the labor force in our village wasn't utilized. In the past, the policy didn't allow surplus rural labor to flow into the towns. When the policy changed, we didn't have enough money to start a business, and the factories in the city nearby wouldn't hire farmers.

Farmers expected someone to show them the way out. As village head, I felt it was my duty to do so. I decided to run a factory of our own in the village. I went to twelve experienced farmers and we discussed my plan. I collected about 1,000 *yuan* from the villagers to start our first factory — a chopping block mill.

My family'd been farmers for generations. Even as a kid, I thought I'd be a farmer, toiling like my parents. I never dreamed that someday I'd deal with industry. Naturally I didn't have the experience required. But chopping blocks are easy to make, and I was sure they'd sell well, because they are a daily necessity for families, canteens, and butcher shops.

Unexpectedly, even so small a factory wasn't allowed to get started at first. Some officials thought it might create problems in the supply of logs, our major raw material. The state tightly controlled the supply of logs according to a rigid plan. Our mill wasn't in the plan, so we couldn't get the logs.

We'd to struggle for a right to exist. In two years' time, I went to the municipal government of Huzhou thirteen times, just to get permission from the authorities to set up the factory. You can't imagine how difficult it was for farmers then to start an undertaking of this sort in China! But, finally, we managed to get the wood and began producing the chopping blocks even before we got a license. We exchanged our surplus grain at the free market for logs. The first year, we made a profit of 24,000 *yuan*.

It was hard to start the chopping block mill. But it seemed nothing compared with the set-up of our down garment factory. Originally I didn't even know of such factories. I was quite uncertain when someone suggested that we run a down garment factory. So I went to other down factories to learn. Yet the people in those factories seemed to be on guard against us. They didn't want us to learn too much, except for some rough basic instruction. They didn't want new factories competing with them.

All this remains fresh in my memory and acts as a catalyst for action in the future.

We'd the funds for the new project. We took 50,000 *yuan* from the profits of our chopping block business. But the low technological level might have killed the new venture. In those days, I, a person who always slept soundly all night through, had many sleepless nights. Sometimes I even lost confidence in myself, wondering if we farmers really had the capability to run industry.

Still we were unwilling to give up our project just

like that. Fortunately, we'd an opportunity to make contacts with a large down garment factory in Hangzhou, provincial capital of Zhejiang. Through negotiations, they agreed to teach us the technical know-how in exchange for our duck down, which is available in large quantities in our village as well as nearby villages. That saved our project. Now our down garment factory has fixed assets worth 200,000 *yuan* (US$ 54,000) plus a working capital of 300,000 *yuan* (US$ 81,000). It makes not only down jackets, but also quilts.

Looking back at what I've gone through these years, I find industry isn't too difficult to learn, although it's more complicated than agriculture. Industrial production requires technical know-how, just as farming requires farming skills and a basic knowledge of soil and crops. As weather and pest information is important to farming, market information is important to industrial management.

We get our general information through newspapers and TV. As rural residents, we don't have much chance to see fashion shows, but we can watch shows in TV. In the past, I didn't believe in ads, thinking that it was nothing but boasting and that only inferior products needed to be advertised.

Later I learned that advertising can help an enterprise do well. The more ads, the greater the popularity. But you can't advertise without sound financial support. Our factory is unable to effectively promote our products because we don't have that much money to put into advertising.

Lack of money is why I didn't take a big step at the beginning. I'd my village enterprises snowball, from small to big. Now, I'm running five factories, with a total of 320 workers. Their per capita income was 1,600 *yuan* last year. That money was hard earned, since they normally worked sixteen hours a day.

My family made 6,000 *yuan* last year, four times what we made in 1978. I spent around 20,000 *yuan* building a two-story house, with a floor space of 240 square meters. I still have about 5,000 *yuan* deposited in the bank.

I enjoy running industrial enterprises. It's more challenging, and easier to get rich, compared with farming.

Farmer-Worker: Tang Jingen

If I were to move to town, I might be content for a while, but I wouldn't be happy long.

Shenjiagang, a small village of 900, is located on the Hangzhou-Jiaxing-Huzhou Plain in the lower reaches of the Yangtze River. Surrounded by rivers and ponds, it is connected to the outside by a winding concrete road 12 miles long and 3 yards wide. Tang Jingen, fifty-five, has lived there most of his life and has experienced both the "ups" and "downs" of farming.

Like thousands of Chinese farmers, Tang found himself a "surplus laborer" after the contract responsibility system was introduced to rural China at the end of 1978. Instead of moving into the cities, as surplus agricultural manpower did in the wake of the British Industrial Revolution in the eighteenth century, Tang and his fellow farmers have become "farmer-workers," who have left the farming profession but continue to live in the country.

Nationwide China's rural enterprises now employ 85 million farmer-turned-workers, whose ranks now account for 22 percent of the rural labor force and are increasing by several million a year. It is expected that another 100 million farmers will be employed by rural enterprises between now and the year 2000. The rural enterprises include factories, mines, construction, transport and commercial businesses, and service trades.

The steady transfer of rural manpower will mean more jobs and income for farmers, and the narrowing of the gap between workers and farmers and between town and countryside.

Tang is short, but sturdy. The hardships of his life have produced facial wrinkles, but a fur cap and leather boots indicate his latest prosperity. Although only semi-literate, he speaks with good logic.

I never expected to be a worker in a township-run cement plant in my late forties. I'm the first of my family to work for a salary.

Farming's been looked down upon by urban residents in China. We farmers have been called bumpkins, although the nation cannot do without us. At first I was baffled at this, but then I realized that it was poverty that made us appear to be inferior. Yet I couldn't figure out why we were so poor.

We weren't lazy. In summer, which's a busy farming season, city dwellers usually sit in the shade after four o'clock in the afternoon and begin to have their supper. But the farmers still have three more hours of work to do. After coming home from the fields, we'd be occupied with cooking, feeding pigs and washing until midnight, a time when townspeople had long since been in bed.

A day's hard work resulted in earning only three or four *jiao*, equal to the price of one kilogram of rice. Yet a worker in town could earn several times as much as a farmer did in those days. We couldn't help envy those who lived and worked in the city. But it was impossible for us farmers to move to the cities. There weren't many jobs there. In the 1960s, even school graduates in the big cities were encouraged to settle in the country, so how'd we country folks expect to become city dwellers?

Things began to change around 1979. The farmland, which used to be planted collectively, was contracted out to individual households. But there was still too many people and too little farmland, and there wasn't enough farm work to keep us fully occupied. Although we'd enough to eat, we remained very poor.

Fortunately, our township started some small enterprises, where farmers like me found a way out. Because my family was in difficult circumstances, I was fortunate enough to be hired by the cement plant in the township in 1980.

The night before I went to work, I tossed and turned in bed, unable to sleep. I was thinking what it would be like to be a worker. Early next morning, I got dressed in a new suit of blue khaki tunic and trousers to start a new job in a factory.

Everything was new to me. Though I'd been to some factories before, to move refuse, being a worker was another thing. I wasn't prepared for the strict discipline. Every part of our work was closely linked to the next "assembly-line style." People couldn't do things at their own pace. If one worked slowly, or did something wrong, he'd hold up the whole process. It was quite different from work on the farm. Influenced by traditional concepts, farmers usually go about their own way and don't bother about their neighbor's business.

My job at the plant is to pack cement. There're four of us in our team, and we pack for two hours, take a break, and then we start packing again. This's more tiring than field labor. Each of us needs to work quickly at the same speed, or we won't be able to fulfill our quotas. After two hours of labor, I feel as if all my limbs are out of joint.

However, factory work, difficult as it may be, is simpler than farming to some extent. After completing work, there're no other concerns. When I finish at four in the afternoon, I can ride back to my home to do my own business. This's in contrast to being a farmer. From planting to harvest usually is half a year. Every day during this time, you're concerned about the crops.

But I still can't relax, compared to "real" town-dwellers. Every day when arriving home, I help my wife feed the pigs and do other farm work, which usually takes several hours. I often have busy Sundays working in the fields. As a result, I'm busier than before, although I'm much better off.

My monthly income now, plus bonus, amounts to 160 *yuan*. I don't smoke, nor drink, so I can save more than 1,000 *yuan* a year. My wife and my two daughters do household sideline production, also earning about 2,000 *yuan* a year.

After four years of saving, in 1984 I built a two-storey house. The house cost me more than 10,000 *yuan*. Housing's more important to farmers than to city dwellers. There's no housing that's rented out in rural areas. Therefore, a house represents a "status symbol" to a farmer.

I'm very happy living in the new house. Without the economic reform, I couldn't have achieved this.

In the past, I'd only a shabby tile-roofed house. I worked daily, but I was in debt for thirteen consecutive years. During that time, we needed 500 *yuan* to live on, but my yearly income was only 320. When my wife became pregnant in 1960, I was too poor to give her enough to eat, let alone eggs and chickens. To make ends meet, I'd to ask my second daughter to leave school and raise pigs and sheep. It's difficult to imagine what a hard time I'd those days!

I know my present richness is the fruit of my sweat. I treasure it. But I don't have a one-track mind, nor am I miser. I enjoy ease and comfort, as everyone does. If we're free, we go to the cinema or theater for relaxation. We're proud to watch films with city dwellers. Obviously, it was impossible for us, who were so very poor, to do so in the past. And our diet has improved. Dishes of fish, shrimp, chicken, and eggs, which we could seldom afford before, except at the festivals, now are on our table often. However, I don't spend money extravagantly. I bought a double bed for more than 100 *yuan* to replace the hard one that made my bones ache, and a sofa that costs 255 *yuan* which we used to sit on when watching TV.

In our village, quite a number of families're approaching high levels of affluence. I'm merely one of the 10,000-*yuan*-householders. Compared to them, I'm only "small potatoes." Many of them made a fortune through speculation. I think these're ill-gotten gains, but sometimes I envy them. However, I feel that a man'd earn only money that was honestly made.

I'm getting old, although I feel fit. However, I don't have the energy to compete with youngsters. Now most young people don't like farming, and so those tasks're left to women and the old folk. The young're interested in doing business, which can make them wealthy quickly. As a result, much land lies unutilized and irrigation works've been neglected for years. If floods come, what's the use of having money if there's no rice on the market?

Someone once urged me to quit my job in the factory and go into business with them. I said, "No, I'd rather stay where I'm." Maybe I'm conservative.

Doing business is risky. What if I failed? What would I do?

I don't worry. I believe that as long as the present policies continue, I'll become still better off.

A good way to get rich is to be both a worker and farmer. To tell the truth, if I were to move to town, I might be temporarily content, but I wouldn't be happy long. I'm sure I'd find that vegetables weren't as fresh as before. Edible oil, chickens and eggs, which have always been our own, would have to be bought at the market. I don't think I'd like that kind of life.

Kazak Herdsman: Kadt Khan

We aren't content with living in yurts and don't want to lead the hard life our forefathers did.

Kadt Khan belongs to the Kazak minority, whose numbers total around 900,000 in China. With the reforms moving ahead in China's pastoral areas, many Kazaks, traditionally a nomadic tribe, have chosen to settle down and lead more stable lives.

Thirty-five-year-old Kadt Khan settled in 1982 in a Kazak village in Xinjiang Uygur Autonomous Region where he and his wife operate a small business and do farm work.

Kadt Khan is a short, dark man, with bright eyes. His family is considered well-off by local standards.

We Kazaks are called "people on horseback" and we live where we can find water and grass. My ancestors belonged to a nomadic tribe and led a very hard life. My peers and I are luckier because we are living in a better time. Most of us have settled down in Barkol Prairie. I finished my junior high school "on horseback," and I'm one of the few literate people in my community. So I think and do things differently than the old Kazaks. That's probably the same with all the other younger Kazaks.

I knew a beautiful intelligent girl named Jarmalyah in high school. The elderly all were pround of her, for she brought honor on her race. As our two families lived quite near, we often rode to and from school together. Sometimtes we raced our horses on the vast, grassy plains. By and by we fell in love with each other.

"Girl Chasing" is a Kazak game in which a young man asks for a girl's hand while both are riding on horses. It's also a sport that displays the riding skill of men as well as women. I still remember what happened. When we started out, we rode soulder-to-shoulder. When I told her how much I loved her, she was so shy that her face turned red and her head lowered. On the way back I was uneasy for I wasn't sure whether she'd agreed to give me her hand or not. According to custom, if a girl refuses her suitor, she'll whip him while chasing him on the way back. The suitor cannot fight back no matter how hard he's beaten. I intentionally slowed the horse's gait, ready to accept anything Jarmalyah was going to give me. She came up and lifted the whip. But all I got was a gentle tap on the back. That's the way we became engaged. Jarmalyah is now my wife.

Both my wife and I received an education. We aren't content with life in a yurt, and we don't want to live the hard life our forefathers did. We've experienced life in town and know what life is like outside our community. We want a more comfortable and cultured life.

We decided to leave the nomadic life and settled down in a village in 1980. Jarmalyah began to learn farming from the villagers and I learned to fix farm tools. However, we'd barely make both ends meet because we were both inexperienced at what we were doing. Unfortunately, Jarmalyah suffered from acute appendicitis and had to have an operation. We borrowed a lot of money and were unable to pay it back. All we had then was a shabby adobe hut and an old yurt.

One of my strong points is that I don't get discouraged when in difficulty. I felt we were educated people and should make use of the knowledge we'd acquired and become masters of our own fate. So I reduced money spent on food and cancelled a subscription to the *Xinjiang Daily*. My wife and I had read in the paper how others became rich, so we went into business. In 1982 we started the first privately owned shop in our district after we sold our cows and sheep and borrowed 500 *yuan* in government loans.

I'd never expected that we'd have so many problems, especially those created by the yoke of traditional custom. We Kazaks consider ourselves generous and don't, as a rule, get involved in business. We tend to regard bargaining as humiliating. At the start, people from our tribe made a lot of fuss about our business. They held that Kazaks shouldn't be engaged in business; my siblings also thought that business wasn't a respectable trade; the villagers didn't understand either, and they believed we were selling things at higher prices than we'd paid for at the state-owned stores. Some even said, "The couple is driven mad by poverty and want to cheat us." Even the district supply and marketing cooperative tried to stop us, saying that we were ruining its business. My wife and I had to read *Xinjiang Daily* to the villagers and point out to them the relaxed government policies and the benefits that business would bring to them.

Jarmalyah went even further. She took the paper and our business license card with her to the county and district government and told the officials there the difficulties we had encountered. Later the county government sent people here to help us run the business. Some of the villagers suspected that we were conducting a shady business. They bought a kilogram of salt from our shop and walked five kilometers to the district supply and marketing cooperative to check its weight. But when they found that we hadn't shortchanged or overcharged them, they began to trust us.

Sometimes the villagers entrusted us to buy things that weren't available in our shop. Gradually, our business began to grow.

During our first year, we netted a profit of 1,300 *yuan*. We repaid the original loan and became the most prosperous family in the neighborhood. We weren't aware that what we were doing was drawing the attention from the county government, which one day commended Jarmalyah. At the award ceremony, the county head presented her with a red flower, a great honor.

To be truthful, I'm a bit jealous. It's I who'd the idea of running a business, and the one who's done most of the work. But when the recognition came, the honor went to Jarmalyah. She now is the head of the district private business labourers' association. After all, women are liberated now.

In the past few years I've often gone to Hami and Urumchi to purchase goods, while Jarmalyah has remained at home selling things. In addition, we purchase livestock products from herdsmen, which we then take to the county market to sell. Through these efforts, our family income has increased graduallly. Last year, my family had a net income of 10,000 *yuan*. Following our example, 13,000 people in our district have started businesses. And many of the old customs of our ancestors have been broken.

I was glad that Jarmalyah was becoming famous, but to be frank, I felt a bit hurt. A man shouldn't be dependent on his wife. I wanted to do something on my own. So I started to open up wasteland for farming. Jarmalyah supported my plan.

I began my project in 1987. I contracted 2.7 hectares of wasteland from the government and invested 13,000 *yuan* in digging a well, the water from which was to be used for irrigation. That year I grew wheat and lucerne in the field. I harvested 6,000 kilograms of wheat. I was overjoyed when I scooped up the yellow grain and looked at it. I was so excited that I rode my horse on a wild gallop across the grassland.

Now we're one of the wealthiest families in the village. We've built a new four-room house, bought a TV set and sofa, and have new furniture, just as city dwellers do. Even the bedding is new. My father told me that Kazaks of his generation had never dreamed of living as well as we do.

I don't think our hearts have been hardened as we've tried our best to help villagers who're having a hard time. I've donated 15,000 *yuan* to help poor households in the village. I don't get a cent of interest from this.

A man named Munamp was killed in a road accident and his family was hard up for money. I gave his family 160 *yuan* for burial expense. Mahammap, another man in the village, was deeply in debt, and I gave him 200 *yuan*.

Last year, I was admitted into the Communist Party and was named an "advanced person" in the district.

Jarmalyah is a warm-hearted woman. She helps private owners run their businesses. She's been chosen as an "advanced private labourer" in the county and the prefecture for several years.

Farmer-Turned Book Trader:
Zhao Guopei

Selling books isn't a way to make a lot of money, but the respect I get from my readers and customers gives me great satisfaction.

He is thirty-seven years old and of average height. He married a country girl in 1980, and now has a daughter. Inspired by the policy of encouraging prosperity for farmers, he turned to book selling in 1983. Occasionally, he writes poems and short stories. So far, he has published about 100 poems and two short stories, which he says proudly are "quite popular."

I'm not ashamed to admit that I'm a farmer, pure and simple, although now I'm a book trader. I'm pleased whenever neighbors back in the village call me "our own book trader." Nearly all my customers are farmers.

I was born in a small village 25 kilometers from Beijing. My parents got up early in the morning and worked late in the fields to support the family. I've two brothers and two sisters.

According to Mom, I liked reading even as a child. I'd save every cent of candy money that I got from my grandfather. Every weekend when my father went to town to sell vegetables, I'd give him all the money I'd saved and he'd bring me back wonderful picture-books. I'd immerse myself in these books for days.

In 1966, I had to quit shortly after I entered high school because of the outbreak of the Cultural Revolution. As my grandfather was considered a landlord, I was regarded as a social outcast. I was sent back to my native village to be "re-educated" through labor —or, in other words, to "purify" my thinking by tempering my body.

Fifteen years of hard work in the fields did toughen my body. Also, I should feel grateful for that period of life because it is now the source of inspiration for my creative writing.

At that time, few people in our tiny village were able to read and write, so I stood out as an intellectual. I was editor of the village wall-newspaper and speech writer for village heads. They thought I was tractable and planned to make me the village clerk. But one thing that happened accidentally changed the course of my life.

The day Chairman Mao Zetung died in 1976, I was taking a break with two other farmers in the fields. When the news was broadcast, I said casually to the two farmers that Mao was wrong to start the Cultural Revolution.

I didn't realize that the two were informers until some policemen came and took me away that same night. I was jailed for fifteen days for having "slandered the great leader."

I lost everything. I never got promoted because of that. My girl friend, whose father was head of the county, wanted nothing to do with me because her parents shunned me now.

I remained a farmer. Occasionally I wrote some

poems in the evening after working in the fields. Almost all my poems were and are about the rural life in China. When I'd some of them published, they were well received. This, of course, pleased me.

In 1980, I married a farmer's daughter. She's really a virtuous wife. She treats me well and loves me deeply. But when I try to talk to her about my poems, she doesn't understand them at all. She hasn't had a chance to go to school.

Now, farmers are encouraged to engage in business. In the early 1980s, many farmers left the fields and went to town to try their luck.

What could I do? As I liked reading the most, and bookstores in rural areas were few, I asked myself: "Why couldn't I start one? Farmers in my village had to travel a long way to buy newspapers in the next closest city."

I started from scratch, by displaying my books on a plastic sheet in front of my house. Most of my customers were my neighbors.

When people in other villages got to know about my bookstand, many asked me to bring books to their villages to sell. So I got two big baskets of books and placed them on the rack of my bike. In this way, I started a mobile bookstore.

Usually on Sundays or on country fairs, I'd take my books to the marketplace where farmers gather to buy or sell. Often at such times, I can sell a large number of books.

Sometimes, I order textbooks on behalf of village schools from publishing houses, and deliver them to the schools without charge.

Selling books doesn't make much money for me, just about 200 *yuan* (76 U.S. dollars) a month. Sometimes I prefer to take a loss rather than earn if it's for a good cause. When it happens that customers don't have enough money with them for a book, I'll let them have it.

Some of my friends tried to persuade me into turning to some profit-making business. They thought book trading was worthless. I answered that as it was my own life, I had a right to do what pleased me and that the respect I get from my readers and customers gave me great satisfaction.

One day, a young man hurried to my home. He desperately needed a certain book to study for an examination, but he'd failed to find it in any of the bookstores in the city. I also had sold out my supply of that particular book. However, I happened to have kept one copy for myself. I gave it to him. The young man was so moved that with his hands clasped he bowed to me—a traditional Chinese way of expressing thanks.

By selling books, I learn a lot about people, since I'm with them all day long. I know what kind of books they need most and this can be very informative.

Since we've the one-child policy, farmers are now very generous in spending money for their children's reading materials. They also buy magazines about films and television. Cookbooks are popular among rural women.

As my bookstand expanded, so did my reputation. Furthermore, I also had more of my poems published. So my wife began to be suspicious of me. I often found her weeping while alone. One night in bed, she told me she was afraid of losing me. Seeing that I'd letters and visitors every day, she felt I'd cause to look down on her since she couldn't read or write.

She'd examine all my letters to see if there were women's photos in them. I knew that her jealousy was out of love for me, and I told her I wasn't at all annoyed. I asked her to keep my letters in good order so that I could refer to the addresses on the envelops if I needed. This was a joke and she laughed at it.

I'm a faithful husband, unlike those who forsake their wives and children when their social status rises. I told my wife to put her heart at ease. I'm a son of a farmer, and will always be. I certainly hope that someday I'll become a great poet, but even then, I'd still like to be called the "poet of farmers."

Part Nineteen

Military Service

Engineer at a Satellite Launching Base: *Sun Jicheng*

Whenever I watch a satellite launched successfully into the sky, I'm filled with elation.

Sun Jicheng took part in the launching of China's first missiles in the early 1960s and its first satellite in 1970s; the recovery of China's first satellite in 1975; the first launching of an intercontinental missile across to the Pacific in 1980; and the launching of three satellites carried by one rocket in 1981.

He is now a senior engineer in the test and technical department of the China Jiuquan Satellite Launching Center. He is in charge of the telemetering system. Having only graduated from junior high school, he has gone a long way from being a soldier to an expert in satellite launching.

This fifty-five-year-old man has an honest face and sharp, trusting eyes.

I was born in a small town in Liaoning Province. I graduated from junior high school in 1950. At that time, I was relatively uneducated and had no real purpose in life. New China had just been founded. The People's Liberation Army was instrumental in overthrowing the corrupt rule of the Kuomintang government and enjoyed a very good reputation. So I joined the army.

A year later, I went to Korea as a CPV (Chinese People's Volunteers). I had several narrow escapes during the war when bombs exploded near our shelters or blasted away the barriers. I didn't believe I'd die because when I was a child a fortune-teller said I'd have a long life. We returned to China triumphantly in 1955. I remained in the Shenyang Military Area Command as a radio operator.

In 1958, China began to set up its first missile launching base (the predecessor of the Jiuquan Satellite Launching Center). Our command was asked to select a number of personnel with specialised knowledge to take part in the work. The job was unknown to us then. Candidates had to go through extremely rigorous political and physical examination. Those selected were the most qualified. I was excited to be selected then—and I'm excited even recalling it now.

I came to Jiuquan in Gansu Province in Northwest China with my battle buddies. There were also scientists and technicians from all parts of the country. We were shocked to find that where we were going to live and work was a vast stretch of bleak and barren desert. When the weather was bad, the wind blew so hard that it picked up stones, and caused sandstorms. But we weren't frightened. Living in tents, eating solid food, and enduring the severe cold, we remained in high spirits.

At the base, I was assigned to work on telemetering. I wasn't happy with the news because I knew nothing about it. In fact, no one in China knew about it then. We invited Russian experts to give us training. I was appointed chief of our group. However, when the Russian experts learned that I only had a secondary education, they wouldn't even allow me to touch the machines, saying that only college graduates were qualified to use the machines. As they wouldn't teach me, I had to learn and operate machines on my own. But I finally mastered the know-how.

When I came to the base, I was only twenty-five years old and unmarried, which made my parents concerned. So they busied themselves finding a girl friend for me. But the work I was doing then was secret. We were cut off from the outside world. Our letters were delivered by the base's special post office. For reasons of secrecy, I didn't tell my parents what my job was. All their efforts to arrange a marriage for me were wasted since they couldn't visit me then. Thanks to my comrades, I got to know a nurse who was also working at the base. She wasn't particularly attractive physically but had many virtues nonetheless. We got married. She has given me much support. I owe half of my achievements to her.

I've spent thirty years working at the base, during which time I've devoted my best years to the country's astronautics industry. Apart from rare occasions on special assignment, I've spent most of my time in the desert, having had no opportunity to work in the city. Although I have perhaps missed many things, I don't regret it. Working here isn't boring to me since I've become accustomed to it. And I feel that I've been leading a full life, never frittering away my time.

Since the first launching of a missile in the early 1960s, I've taken part in hundreds of test missile launchings and the launching of twenty-one satellites. Whenever a satellite was launched safely into space, I was elated.

I'm a founding member of this "space city" (Jiuquan). People regard me as an expert in telemetering. I'm not extraordinary but merely the first one to come to the test and technical department. "The longer I work, the more experience I get," I usually say to them. Even a man with a dull brain would learn something if he worked long enough. If equipment is in need of repair, I can find what needs to be done and fix it in a couple of minutes.

I was promoted to engineer in 1978 and senior engineer not long ago. In defense scientific circles, I'm the only senior engineer without a university degree. I feel I've obtained what I deserve and reached the goal I've been striving for.

In recent years, I've pioneered ten technological innovations, including a telemetering rate indicator that was used in the launching of the first satellite. The invention received an award at a scientific meeting sponsored by the State Science and Technology Commission and received high praise from the National Defense Commission on Science, Technology, and Industry. I've won third-place citations four times.

After we finished successful launching, my colleagues wanted to commend me for my efforts. But I refused to be awarded. I felt the state had given me enough honors and that it was more important to encourage other young people.

As far as I'm concerned, a man can increase his own personal value through diligent study. An old Chinese saying goes: "A golden house can be found in books." But a man can find his prospects and value in books, I might say. Although I came to the base, I started on my own to study college courses, including higher physics and mathematics. On holidays and weekends, my colleagues would help their wives do house chores or go on outings with their children. However, I spent all my spare time in the reference room or library. My wife was unhappy about this, and, as a result, we quarrelled on occasion. I sometimes wept in private recalling the things I had said to her. However, nothing could prevent me from studying. And in this way I taught myself Japanese and English.

I think of myself as modest. I don't feel embarrassed in the least about learning from my subordinates even now that I'm a senior engineer. This is one of my good qualities, I think.

But I also have a bad habit: I complain too much. This probably is one of the obstacles to my getting a promotion. Many of my present superiors were once my subordinates. But I know my own limitations and acknowledge that I may not have the makings of a chief. So I'm willing to be a ladder on which young people can climb up. I'm always pointing out or trying to resist what I don't think is right, even if it means offending my superiors. Despite my complaints, I myself observe the discipline and carry out tasks seriously. I think of myself as a qualified soldier, which is why I can win respect from both superiors and subordinates.

We at the base are paid twice the rate of those outside. We live in low-rent state housing. I earn more than 400 *yuan* a month, which is what a Chinese cabinet minister makes. However, we can't buy all we need here since the logistics department is short of products. And I've to put aside money for my sons' marriages someday.

Mentioning my sons, I feel guilty. I used to be at the testing site most of the time and, thus, had no time to tutor them. Perhaps that is why they didn't pass the college entrance examinations. My wife says that I'm selfish and can do nothing except work. She probably is right. But I think anyone who wants to accomplish something must also give up something. I don't know how to make it up to my sons. And I'm feeling more and more guilty about it. My elder son has joined the army and the younger one is still at home looking for a job. They are all at the base with us. But since girls are rarely seen here, I worry about my sons' being able to find wives.

My wife has asked me to move to the city. I think the authorities could arrange it for us. But in Jiuquan every tree was planted by us, and every building built by us. Everything here is lovely to me. I'd be sorry to leave here. The tall launching tower is like my "other half." I couldn't bear leaving it. When I was younger, not worrying about what would happen later, I once vowed that I'd live here until I died. However, now that I've succeeded in my career and made a name for myself, questions about my future crop up. One thing I do know is that I'd like to be engaged in other satellite launchings before I decide whether to leave or not.

Part Twenty
Religion

Imam: Wu Baozhen

Thanks to the Allah for helping me get over so many hurdles, and also thanks to the government for creating a good living environment for us Muslims. I hope I can make contribution to the government and my fellow Muslims.

Islamism, with a history of 1,300 years in China, has the largest number of adherents among the five major religions still practiced in China (Buddhism, Taoism, Christianity including both Catholicism and Protestantism, and Islamism). Twelve of the country's fifty-five ethnic minorities, or a total population of 14 million, believe in Islamism. In 1987, there were 23,000 mosques for Chinese Islamic believers, representing half of all the places of worship in China, including churches and temples.

Wu Baozhen, seventy-four, is the imam of the Nanguan Mosque, the largest in Yinchuan, capital of Ningxia Hui Autonomous Region, in Northwest China. With the financial help of the state, he made a pilgrimage to Mecca in 1987.

Wu has two wives, thirteen children, and numerous grandchildren. (He is not sure of the exact number of the latter.) He uses Islamic preachings to teach his offsprings to unite together and live and work in peace. At the same time, he also exhorts his Islamic believers to love their country and abide by the law as well as to contribute to the country's economic construction.

I was born in an Islamic family in Shaanxi Province. My father was an imam. He died suddenly when he was thirty-two, and I was two and a half years old. My mother married another man the same year, leaving my five-year-old sister and me to my grandparents, who were in their eighties.

My grandfather was a butcher but earned little from selling beef. We'd a very hard time. Worse yet, my grandparents died when I was seven, and my sister was taken away as to become someone else's child bride. I was left an orphan with nobody to take care of me. Thanks to the Allah, the imam in the neighborhood mosque accepted me as a disciple. And the Muslim brothers there gave me food and clothing.

I studied the classics in the mosque until I was twelve. All I wanted to do at that time was to become an imam. And towards that purpose I set out to acquire more knowledge. Together, with two brothers, I walked all the way to Gansu, where we became disciples of an old imam named Luo Jinsi at Changjiahe Mosque. People there had a very hard life. The staple food was a kind of buckwheat with a very bitter taste. The wheat couldn't be made into noodles. It was cooked as porridge, which was hard to swallow because of its bitterness. One person left because he couldn't withstand the hardships. But the rest of us remained. The next year, Imam Luo was invited to teach in Pingliang, but we were rejected because of our youth. Thanks to the Allah again, we met a kind-hearted imam named Ma Haji who introduced us to a mosque in Hai*yuan* County in Ningxia, where

I studied Islamic classics for three years until I became an imam at the age of sixteen.

Later I went to a big mosque in Ningxia's Tongxin County, where I was trained under Great Imam Zhou Shengqing. Because I was still young, I liked to play, so some imams thought I was a good-for-nothing. But I was quite confident of myself because I did my assignments well. Imam Zhou understood me and said I was talented and quick-minded, and had a good comprehension of the classics. He liked me and never reprimanded me.

Some people became imams so they'd eat fried cakes free of charge and earn an easy living. I did it for other reasons. I got help from the Allah from the time I was very small and therefore was able to understand His purpose very well. And I spread Islamism with enthusiasm. The Muslims had brought me up and so I wanted to repay the kindness of the Allah.

To help my Muslim brethren, I often walked along hilly paths with luggage on my back to conduct funeral rites and wedding ceremonies for them, as well as did missionary work in villages. My feet sometimes hurt so badly that I wept, but I never gave up. Through persistent effort, I acquired eloquence in speech, gained experience in conducting religious services, and became famous locally.

In the following years, I was invited to teach at various mosques in the region. By 1960 I became a reputed imam in Ningxia Autonomous Region. After Liberation in 1949, I was elected a deputy to local people's congress and member of the Political Consultative Conference in Gu*yuan* County. I enjoyed political power as well as economic subsidies from the state.

In 1961, I was appointed deputy director of Ningxia Islamic Association and moved to Yinchuan, capital of that autonomous region. And that promotion brought me both good and bad luck. In October I became a post-graduate student at the China Institute of Islamism. At that time, the left had assumed control of the country and Sino-Soviet relations were bad. It was a difficult time for me.

When I was in my second post-graduate year, I went back to Gu*yuan* County to attend a seminar with other imams. Some of my former fellow imams said jokingly: "You got a promotion, but we're still eating fried cakes."

I said: "Some people back from a visit to the Soviet Union said that imams in Soviet rural areas are still eating not so good fried cakes although that country has supposedly reached socialism." The words were later taken as evidence of my supposed anti-Soviet attitude. I was called back from the China Institute of Islamism and fired from my post as deputy director of Ningxia Islamic Association. I was criticized at meetings, and later was sent to work in a labor camp for three years. I was repeatedly criticized in public and suffered a lot during the Cultural Revolution. Once I was so frustrated that I tried to electrocute myself. Obviously, I failed.

Later I became a dressmaker. I didn't dare do missionary work, nor did most Muslims dare to take part in religious activities. It seemed that right was wrong, and wrong was right.

However, I was an imam, one who'd lived in the old society. I believed that the Chinese Communist Party didn't intend to bar Muslims from believing in Islamism. You know, in the first few years after

Liberation, the Party sent army troops to protect mosques at the same time it advocated freedom of religion. Sure enough, after the overthrow of the leftists in the state leadership, the Party's religious policy was once again restored. In 1979, I was able to teach at a mosque in Gu*yuan* County.

In order to raise the calibre of imams in mosques in the Ningxia Autonomous Region, the Islamic Association ran a training course in 1982. I was invited to explain Koran to the imams. The same year, the government announced my rehabilitation and restored my subsidies. I was once again appointed a standing member of the Islamic Association of the Autonomous Region. In July 1985, I was invited to serve as the chief imam in Nanguan Mosque, the largest in Yinchuan City. I was also named deputy head of the Ningxia Institute of Islamism. Now I get 114.5 *yuan* a month from the state, and 130 *yuan* a month from my mosque, plus alms from Muslims. So I'm quite well-off, thanks to the blessings of the Allah.

It's hard for old people to get excited, but I cannot help doing so because so many exciting things have happened to me in the last couple of years. Last year, the government gave me 12,000 *yuan* to make a pilgrimage to Mecca, fulfilling a lifelong dream.

As for my marriage, mine is really an exceptional case. The Constitution only allows monogamy. But I've two wives—a fact that has a historical explanation. According to Islamism, a Moslem may have four wives. I married my two wives before Liberation in 1949. Of course today, religious practices must be in accordance with state law, which means a Muslim cannot have four wives.

I was actually a poor imam without the money to

get married. But because I earned a good reputation teaching in mosques, one of my fellow imams liked me and asked me to marry his younger sister, and they didn't ask for betrothal gifts. That was in 1936. I'd no money and no house of my own, so I had to live at my in-law's. When we got married, my wife, whose name is Ke Daying, was only thirteen. The next year she bore me a daughter. I've six sons and two daughters by my first wife. It's a Muslim practice to marry early. And in the past, marriages were usually arranged by parents. My marriage was decided after only one meeting with my future wife. This's quite different from today's customs.

My second wife, Jin Yumei, is twenty years younger than I'm. she's now fifty-four. In 1948, while I was teaching in a mosque in Gu*yuan*, a pious Muslim, who admired my work, offered his daughter in marriage to me. I married that year. We've four sons and a daughter, who lives with me.

My two wives treat me very well. They're both loyal to me. In accordance with the Islamic practice, I also treat them impartially. So they've never quarreled. However, bigamy is contrary to the state Constitution. So in 1950, a government work team advised that one of them divorce me. But neither wanted to. So I had to separate them into two families. The government has never interfered since then. Now my first wife lives in a nearby county while my second wife lives with me. My first wife often visits us. And I, too, find time to see her at her home. I've thirteen children and scores of grandchildren. I don't know exactly how many grandchildren I have. Eight of my sons and all three daughters are married. All my children are economically independent and all but one are farmers. That son works as a surgeon in an army hospital in Gansu Province. Two of my sons live with me. One is studying at the Ningxia Institute of Islamism, the other is at senior high school. My first grandson, Wu Jinhai, is twenty-two and has two children. He's now studying the Koran with me.

There is an Islamic saying that "not many are able to attain the age of seventy." I'm seventy-four and am lucky to be able to live in comfort in this good society. Thanks to the Allah for helping me to get over so many hurdles, and also thanks to the government for creating a good living environment for us Muslims, I hope I can make contributions to the government and my fellow Muslims for the rest of my life.

Although I'm getting on in age, I still do evangelical work whenever I'm asked to. I've got too many children, which now I realize creates many economic problems for my family as well as for the state. Now I've got proof from the Koran that the Allah agrees to fewer children and use these words to promote family planning. I tell my fellow Muslims to have fewer, but better children. While explaining the Koran, I encourage Muslims to abide by the law, to love their country as much as they love their families, and to contribute to the country's economic construction. And my efforts are paying off. I'll continue my work until I stop breathing.

Taoist Priest: Zhou Jinfu

I've chosen to become a Taoist. I find it extremely satisfying.

At a time when high-school graduates crowd colleges and universities, a small group of young Chinese choose to believe in a Divine Being. Those with religious beliefs were unfairly victimized and ostracized during the ten-year turmoil of the Cultural Revolution. But thirty-one-year-old Zhou Jinfu was more fortunate when he decided to become a Taoist priest in 1977. He experienced no discrimination. Now staying in Baiyunguan Temple, which is located in western Beijing, Zhou, like 5,000 other Taoist priests and sisters in the country, is enjoying religious freedom.

I became interested in Taoism in my junior high-school days. I think it had a lot to do with the family environment in which I was brought up. My mother is a devout Taoist, and the five boys in my family have all been influenced by and believe in this religion. I'm the youngest in the family. Even as a child, I wanted to learn about Chinese culture and traditions. I read lots of Taoist classics, such as those by Lao Zi and Zhuang Zi, two great thinkers and philosophers in ancient China whose theories are regarded as the bulwark of Taoism. At the same time, I also read Hegal and Bacon.

I decided to become a Taoist priest in 1977 when many of my classmates were busy preparing for the college entrance exam. I met with no resistence, either from the school, local township, or from my family. In fact, my mother gave me a lot of encouragement. My father was noncommittal about my choice. However, he believed that being a monk meant being well-behaved and mentally well balanced. He let me make my own decision. Therefore, I became a professional Taoist.

I first went to Wudang Mountain, which isn't very far from my hometown. It's one of the four holy mountains of Taoism, a religion rooted in China with a long history. And it also represents an important part of Chinese culture. I felt that inheriting this rich heritage and tradition was not only an obligation, but also a privilege for every Chinese. I was really lucky to be able to choose religion as my life-long pursuit.

I went to Wudang Mountain at a time when the *kungfu* movie "Shaolin Temple" created such a sensation in the country and thousands of young people swarmed to religious temples, where they believed they'd learn real martial art.

I chose to go to Wudang Mountain because I'd gone there several times during my junior high school days and become fascinated with Taoism. I knew quite a lot of Taoist priests, so it wasn't difficult for me to become a priest there. However, it wasn't (and still isn't) easy to be accepted. You had to carry all kinds of documentation, such as those from your former high school, the local township, and county. Besides, you were also supposed to bring written permission from your parents. I met all these requirements. After I'd settled down at Wudang Mountain, I started to do physical exercises and farm work, such as planting vegetables. This was in addition to reading and memorizing Taoist classics. It was a totally rewarding experience for me.

My knowledge of Taoism is very poor compared with those old priests who've devoted their whole life to the study and research of the religion. To fill in the vacancy, I left Wudang in late 1980 and went to Tongbo Mountain in Henan Province to visit a leading Taoist priest named Tang Chongliang, who was more than 100 years old at the time. He shared with me some of the secret herbal prescriptions of traditional Chinese medicine, in addition to Taoism. "Life lies in activity," he taught me. I found this to be quite true. One has to pay attention to the condition of his mind. When I'm absolutely at peace, I feel that everything in the universe belongs to me. It's so good.

I left Tongbo Mountain in 1983 after my Taoist teacher passed away. I then went to Changchun Temple in the city of Wuhan, in Hubei Province. In 1984, I was sent by the temple to participate in a special class for the study of Taoism. This lasted six months. I went back to Wuhan after finishing the course.

I came to Baiyunguan Temple in Beijing last June. We Taoist priests are very free. We can choose to stay at any temple we want. I left Wuhan because I couldn't get used to the humid weather there. Besides, I don't like to eat rice. Here at Baiyunguan, we're responsible for taking care of the temple and making sure that the entire temple is clean. Sometimes, visitors ask you something about the temple, or Taoism. Then you need to offer some explanations. When some pilgrims burn joss sticks, those in charge of the temple strike the wooden fish, which is a percussion instrument made of a hollowed wood block, originally used by Buddhist monks to beat rhythm when chanting sutras. By hitting the wooden fish, we can help the pilgrims communicate with the Divine. I can't tell you how this communication is conducted. I think this is something one can only sense, rather than express in words.

In the morning, we chant Taoist classics for forty minutes, and then we have our breakfast. Lunch is at 11:30. Bean products, noodles, steamed bread, and rice are our everyday fare. All of them are purchased at markets. The money to buy them comes from donations of pilgrims.

Every priest at Baiyunguan Temple gets about seventy *yuan* a month as living allowance, of which thirty *yuan* is usually spent on food. The rest of the money is spent on books. There're about fifty priests here in the temple. On the first and fifteenth of each month, we've better and free food, because these two days are Taoist festivals.

Taoism falls into two schools. One is the Zhengyi (Right Meaning) school, and the other is the Quanzhen (Pure Truth) school. I'm devoted to the first one. This school forbids the priests to marry, or to eat meat.

Our everyday chanting, or reading, of Taoist classics stresses self perfection and the improvement of one's mind. The purpose of this is so one can understand many things by oneself, rather than having to be instructed by someone else. Although there're many books of Taoist classics, lots of questions lie behind the written words or between the lines. I think that's the reason why Taoist priests are so few in number. It requires lots of brainwork. Just like the magical breathing exercises, you can only learn to do by persistent practice accompanied with real mental efforts. It's not easy. The breathing exercise is very popular nowadays, but there're very few people who are really experts on it, because people fail to comprehend the subtlety of the exercise. In fact, it's Taoism roots. If people studied this religion, they'd find the breathing exercise easier to do.

Taoism emphasizes filial obedience to one's parents or elders. Every two years, I'm permitted to visit my parents at the temple's expense.

Taoism is unlike Buddhism in that it doesn't require all believers to change their family names. I refer to those who've gone through a formal ceremony to become Buddhist monks. Last May, I left the temple in Wuhan where I lived for some time, and went back home to visit my seriously ill mother. My brothers insisted that I go back to my Taoist pursuit. I came to Baiyunguan Temple here in Beijing, and my mother passed away soon after. I regret that I didn't stay with my mother for a longer while.

Here, I share an eighteen-square-meter room with another young priest. We've heat in the winter, and reading desks. There's a communal reading room and a TV room as well. Taoism requires all to recognize reality, and be conversant about state affairs. So we read many newspapers and magazines. I personally like to watch *kungfu* films, or movies with characters wearing ancient Chinese costumes. And we watch the news roundup every day, in addition to TV dramas.

After I came here, I realized that to be a Taoist isn't easy. You've to be able to well versed in chess, music (play a musical instrument or two), painting, and calligraphy. All these artistic skills are considered very important in assessing one's capability. Besides, you should have an elementary grasp of medical science, since the religion holds that you'd be able to help those in misery or illness.

Every Tuesday, Thursday, and Saturday night, we read Taoist classics for an hour and a half. Some think it's a burden to have to obey the religious rules of behavior. But I've never had such a feeling. Taoism emphasizes self-discipline and obedience out of one's own willingness. There's no compulsion.

Although I've studied Taoism for years, I still find it hard to understand. It's not superficial. The joy's that the more you learn, the more convinced you become. To be more qualified as a priest, I spend my free time reading and thinking about the classics. On weekends, I go to bookstores. Most of my possessions are books, and I'm very proud of that. Everyone's different and I've my own goal in life.

We still have our troubles apart from Taoism. Sometimes when you're on duty in the temple, people will try to embarrass, or even humiliate you. I'm angered by such impoliteness and ignorance. All of us are the same, and shouldn't look down upon others. Fortunately enough, I can tolerate all these things. I think that a Taoist priest is quite like a scientist in that they've to be above earthly concerns. At the same time, I think the temple's opening to the outside is quite necessary, since it enables the clergy to meet and communicate with the lay people. And this also helps us to adapt ourselves to the changes and development of society.

I was brought up in New China, and I might have entered a college instead of a temple. But I've chosen to become a Taoist priest, and I find it extremely satisfying.

Christian Minister: Qin Honghong

We're passing on the Lord's message to people. It's like bringing life to the earth.

You would not be able to guess her occupations solely on the basis of her appearance.

Dressed in blue jeans and a grey sweater, Qin Honghong, thirty-seven, says not one person guesses that she is a physical-education coach and a minister of the Gangwashi Christian Church in downtown Beijing.

After being closed for more than a decade during the Cultural Revolution, three churches in Beijing resumed services in the late 1970s. Pastors returned to churches but many were elderly. With more than a congregation of 700, the Gangwashi Church had four pastors and two ministers like Qin Honghong. Qin graduated from Nanjing Union Theological Seminary in 1986.

It wasn't my own choice to become a pastor. The Lord selected me to pass His passage on to the people. I come from an atheistic family. Both my parents are in the military, and are atheists. They didn't know about my feelings until I wrote to tell them that I was enrolled at the seminary. The letter must have concerned them a great deal. They sent me a long telegram asking me to return immediately for "construction." I couldn't go home, for the school was about to open. Then three months later, they wrote me saying, "We love you the same as we always have.

We won't try to change your mind. Where you find meaning and contentment in life is your own decision."

I remember when I was a child, my family lived in a garden-like setting on the outskirts of Chengdu. My mother says I was very emotional. I cried every time I was told a sentimental story. While I was still a child, my father was labelled a "counter-revolutionary rightist" and taken away. We moved into a shack. I knew something terrible had happened. But I never asked why, or revealed my own feelings.

My two brothers, my sister, and I were sent to the countryside at the end of the 1960s. I worked for ten years with local farmers in a mountainous village. I think that also was preparation for my present life. Moses spent forty years in the wilderness before he started to serve the Lord.

My parents tried every means to get their children out of the country. But when I finally got permissions to return to Beijing, I wanted so much to go back. The country people were simple and kind, although they were poor. The complexity of city life was something I couldn't handle easily.

It was a time when people had just been liberated from a decade of turmoil and depression. They'd recovered something they'd lost during the Cultural Revolution, but still were guarded about their personal relationships. I used to feel that everyone was my enemy and was trying to persecute me. As a shop assistant, I never smiled at customers. Sometimes I was so lonely and helpless that I even thought of committing suicide.

The Lord was pushing me to the extreme and

testing my perseverance. But I thought very little about the Lord, although I passed by a church every day on my way to work. Once I happened to go into the church. I took a seat in the back. The pastor had a strong Shaanxi accent. I'd hardly understand him when he was praying. But when the choir began to sing some hymns, I broke into tears and cried all the way through the service. I was overwhelmed to see that a light had been turned on in my own private dark room. And I'd found the place where I belonged.

My life began to change after I began to go to church regularly. By talking to pastors and making friends with other believers, I got to know the Lord and His people. Six months later, I decided to apply to study at Nanjing Union Theological Seminary, which had just reopened. I knew I'd be admitted. The night before I took the entrance examination, I dreamt of a face as big as the sky looking down at me and saying, "You have been chosen."

About sixty percent of my classmates came from Christian families. The rest of the students like me, who had only "accidentally" found the Lord, had to start from the very beginning. Our subjects included Bible study, history of Christian thought, a brief account of Jesus' life, and contemporary Western theology.

Study is necessary, but contemplation is even more important. The Lord is inside everyone. If only you look for Him, you'll find Him. As I began to look more deeply into myself, I came closer to the Lord.

After four years at the seminary, I'd solved most of my personal problems. But I became really aware of my mission only after I began my work at Gangwashi Church. Everytime I stood on the platform, or talked with people, I expressed my gratitude to the Lord for His salvation. He's tested me in many ways. And He gives me a voice that is soft, yet strong enough to pass on His message to other people.

We've about 700 people who regularly come to services. There're over 1,000 on Sundays. They come from all walks of life. We baptise about twenty-five people a year on the average. Most of them are encouraged by their Christian families. People without a religious background are more cautious and it requires a major decision on their part. Some are even afraid that they aren't qualified to come to church. We tell them the Lord accepts all those who come to Him. Consequently, most church goers are self-confident and are good workers.

We've a full schedule: two services on Saturday evening and Monday morning, a prayer meeting on Wednesday morning and a Bible study meeting on Tuesday evening. The other minister and I rotate presiding over services with the four pastors.

As we are young, compared to the pastors, who all are over sixty-five, we also organize special meetings for young people. A college English teacher is invited to give lessons on English Bible study on Monday evening. A youth prayer meeting on Wednesday evening is usually attended by sixty to seventy young believers. But the highlight of the week is on Thursday evening when the young people gather to have discussions on religious beliefs. But the topics also can include sensitive social issues such as bureaucracy, crime, abortion, and divorce.

Some young people come to me with personal problems. Others come out of curiosity. The church is clean and quiet, which they enjoy that.

We also encounter "very stubborn guys" who question the Bible and have no intention of believing in the Lord. But we remain friends. I often go to concerts and art exhibitions with young people. But I won't schedule anything on Sunday because that's the time to meet people in church.

As I live inside the church compound, there can be visitors from morning until night. One may drop in to pray as early as five in the morning and as late as eleven. Usually I get up at six. After morning prayers, I do breathing-exercises for half an hour. People start telephoning and coming at around eight. We talk to people and pay visits to hospitals.

Occasionally I go to Beijing suburbs to assist in establishing new churches there.

I'm busy all the time. My husband is also busy in Nanjing engaged in post-graduate study in theology. We were classmates. I didn't have to choose a Christian believer as my life partner, but he's the most attractive and resourceful man I've ever met. I'm not sure if we're going to have children. We'll be happy either way. We're passing on the Lord's message to people, and it's like bringing life to the earth.

Part Twenty-One

Sports and Sundry

Woman Judoist: Gao Fenglian

Sometimes I find it difficult to find training partners of my own sex because of my size and strength; even men are daunted by my physique.

Gao Fenglian was selected by millions of Chinese sports fans as one of China's ten foremost sports figures in 1986 and 1987. Her performances have won her eight national gold medals and sixteen international golds as a judoist.

Born to a farmer's family in Inner Mongolia, Fenglian grew up in the fields helping her parents with farm work. She did not have a chance to go to school.

She grew fast and soon developed a powerful physique which drew the attention of a judo coach who happened to be on a mission to search for talents to form a regional judo team.

Despite her imposing figure (She weighs 116 kilograms and is 1.86 meters high), Gao Fenglian, twenty-four, is easy-going, soft-spoken, and even a bit shy at times.

People often ask me: Did you feel excited when you captured a world title or a gold medal? I say: No, not really. I was happy, but not excited, because I thought it was just the result of lots of hard work. It's like harvest in autumn after all the back-breaking ploughing, sowing, and hoeing in spring and summer. My excitement came later when I saw how pleased my coaches were with my results. They told me that my achievement was a victory for all Chinese judoists. "You have fulfilled the dream of several generations of judoists in China," they said.

Judo is a pretty new sport in China, particularly for women, not like table tennis, basketball, volleyball, and football, which are very popular. Before me, no judoist in China had ever been picked as one of the top ten sports personalities in the nationwide poll held every year.

At first I didn't realize my success would mean so much to people outside of my family. It makes me happy to find that my success has brought pride, excitement, and hope to the entire judo community in our country.

But I know such an honor won't last long. It comes at a time when you are in your best form, which is short. I'm twenty-four now. I don't know how long my prime time in sports will be. I hope it will last long so that I can take part in more international competitions and win more medals.

But, you know, competition is tough and you are challenged all the time by up-and-coming young people. I've got to obey the law of nature. Once a newcomer surpasses me and I can find no way to turn the tables, my career as a judoist is over. Then I've got to leave the judo mat, no matter how much I want to stay.

My biggest hope is to win an Olympic gold medal. It's a pity women's judo won't be listed as an official competitive event at the Olympiad until 1992. It's only a demonstration event at the Olympic Games in

Seoul. Perhaps the 1992 Olympic Games are beyond my hoping for, because by then I'll be twenty-eight. God knows, whether I'll still feel up to the heat of the competition then.

I tell you it's really hard in fierce international competitions to beat all your opponents to capture a title. And the pre-tournament training is tedious.

I'm in the over-72-kilogram category, the heaviest class. You've to train with a partner much stronger than you if you want to improve quickly. And sometimes I've difficulty finding a match among people of my own sex. So very often men judoists are assigned as my training partners because of my size and strength. Sometimes two male coaches take turns competing with me in training sessions. Those two or three hours of training are like hell. My judo uniforms are often soaked in sweat and I feel so tired after each session that the only thing I want to do is sleep a whole day. But I must get up on time and begin another session. Of course I repeatedly tell myself to get over my self-complacency and weakness.

Training for a judoist is far tougher than farm work. Two hours' judo training tires you more quickly than a whole day of labor in the field. Judo exercises demand bursts of energy; farmwork just requires endurance.

I was born in a farming family in Xinfeng Village in Linhe County, Inner Mongolia. I'm the third of five children in my family. When I was a child, my parents expected me just to be a good farmhand. So they didn't send me to school. Instead, I was taught to do all kinds of farm work at a very early age. At eight, I began to help out in the fields. I also looked after my younger brother and sister. During the busy farming season, I worked in the fields all day long.

Over the years, I grew very tall and strong, taller and bigger than any of my sisters. Nobody knows why. Once my elder sister joked: "We saved all the food for you. That's why you became so big and strong." That wasn't exactly true, although my sisters often left work for me to do because I was the strongest. But my parents protected me if ever my elder brother and sister tried to bully me.

I guess my farm work during my teens helped me to develop powerful muscles. In 1980, when I was seventeen, my physique was so conspicuous that I was selected by a sports school in Inner Mongolia to be trained in throwing events—discus and shotput.

One year later, after doing well in these events, I was spotted by the coach of the Inner Mongolia judo team. He asked me whether I'd like to try and I accepted the offer. After just a month's training, I was chosen to compete in China's first women's judo invitational tournament held in Shanxi Province, even though it was only a small-scale contest. My first performance was lousy. Among the six competitors in the over-72-kilogram category, I came last. I hadn't got the knack of the sport, my coach said. After that tournament, my regional judo team was disbanded and I went back to work on my family's contracted plot of land.

But I returned home a different person. The first taste of competition fired my interest in judo and the trip to Shanxi Province was an eye-opener. I saw my potential as a judoist and knew that I'd do far better in judo with proper training. And I hated the idea of spending my whole life on the farm. I told myself that perhaps I'd do more for my family, my country and myself through sports. So I went to my former judo coach, Dong Yacheng, in 1983, and I was lucky enough to run into a good opportunity, because at that time the State Physical Culture and Sports Commission was organizing a thirty-member national women's judo team. Coach Dong recommended me. I was then nineteen, fully grown, 1.86 meters tall and weighed over 110 kilograms. They accepted me and I became a full member of the Chinese national judo team. That day was July 20, 1983, a turning point in my life.

Since I never went to school, I have no idea what a school teacher is like. I figure school teachers must be like my coaches. In my mind, coaches, in some ways, are better than parents because they give almost all their time to helping better athletes. My coaches not only teach me sports skills, but also shows me how to be a good citizen and how to gain the willpower to overcome shortcomings.

I'm tall, big, and strong, for sure, but my legs used to be rather weak and my movements were clumsy. My coaches spent more time on me than on the others to help me to practise the same movements and strengthen my legs.

My coaches, two men and one woman, are very strict with me. They don't let me go until they're satisfied with my movements. Sometimes, I feel so exhausted that I'm on the point of giving up, even like crying. It's the coaches who pull me up and make me finish the training schedule.

I won my first world title at the fourth World Women's Judo Championships held in Maastricht, the Netherlands, in October, 1986. When we arrived there a few days before the championships began, Meng

Zhaorui, one of my male coaches, wanted me to get accustomed to the new surroundings and urged me to throw him with all my strength in a simulated match with me. He said that in this way he'd judge for himself my competitive capabilities. In fact, I was so powerful that I nearly injured him! But he made me determined to do my best to win first place. I don't like to fail my coaches.

Nineteen eighty-seven was a disastrous year for me despite the fact that again I won several gold medals in international competitions. In one training session in Kunming, southwest China, in March, I injured my neck and was hospitalized for two months. In June, I came down with bronchitis. And a week before my team left for Essen, in Federal Germany, for the fifth World Championships in November, I injured my right leg. It was terribly painful and I wanted to pull out, but my coaches insisted. So I gritted my teeth and went on with the training. Then, surprisingly, I regained my top form and won two gold medals in the over-72-kilogram class and the overall category.

Now I'm still nursing several injuries which cause me pain from time to time. But that's OK. There're many ace sportsmen and women who've injuries of one kind or another.

Naturally, my life isn't all training and competition. I've leisure-time activities. After burning a lot of energy during daily training sessions, I usually do something which I can just sit and relax—read, work in my diaries, watch TV or videos, or play chess.

I'm no longer illiterate. I've learned to read and write since I joined the national judo team. He Guoxiang, my coach, a very gentle woman with two children, has helped me a lot. She was my first teacher. I often write letters to my parents in Inner Mongolia and also keep a diary chronicling my training and competitions.

What am I reading? I don't like love stories because most of the characters are stereotypes. I enjoy legends and crime stories, especially martial arts stories which I find stimulating. I like the dare-devil heroes in *kungfu* films and novels who hate evil and who uphold justice. I admire such characters.

Now that I'm much better off materially, I feel I must assist my parents, sisters and brothers and other relatives financially. I don't need money myself that much. Every time I go home, I buy gifts for my family, especially for my nephews and nieces.

People live much better in China these days. Some people, especially the young, are wearing very fashionable clothes. I also like beautiful clothes. I go to clothes shops regularly, but find it difficult to buy ready-made fashion clothes that fit me, because I'm too big. So I always wear sports clothing. I've no time to have my clothes tailored.

Do I have a boyfriend? No, I don't. My mother used to tell me that it was time to find a boyfriend. My teammates, most of whom have boyfriends now, often nag me to look for one, too. But I think that sort of thing can wait. For me, it may not be easy to find a boyfriend. I don't consider myself good-looking, and I'm tall and big. Many young men are too concerned about the appearance of girls, not their personality and ability.

I'm not sure what I'll do after I retire from the competition mat. It's unlikely that I'll take up a coaching job. I've little formal education and I'm not good at expressing myself effectively. Besides, my smaller judo movements are clumsy, so I wouldn't be able to demonstrate such movements to others.

Some people have suggested that I write an autobiography. I'm interested but not now. Maybe I'll ask someone to be my ghost writer. A person always has many things to do. First things first. For now, I want to reach my summit in sports—an Olympic gold medal.

Roving Carpenter: He Xuewen

I come to Beijing to earn money and have a more interesting life.

The thirty-six-year-old He Xuewen is a carpenter from the Huangshan Mountain region in Anhui Province in Central China. Unhappy with country life, He left his hometown and came to Beijing four years ago. Now he finds it easy to make a living in Beijing. He said after he has earned enough money he will build a big house for his family. Also, he would like to put enough money aside for his son to go to college someday.

I came to work in Beijing for two purposes: to earn money, and to have a more interesting life. My home's located at the foot of a mountain which's sparsely populated. As a carpenter I had to have ample work throughout the year. But you weren't able to find customers all the time because in our area there seem to be more carpenters than clients. Besides, doing replicas of outdated furniture there drives you crazy. So when I learned that Beijing lacked carpenters, I decided to go to the capital. It was a place I'd seen only on films.

When I first arrived in Beijing I was entirely lost. I didn't know where to go. A stranger I met suggested I go to a small hotel in east Beijing where I paid four *yuan* a day for lodging. That was a quarter of all the money I'd at that time. I was fortunate to get something to do the next day. I worked hard to make a wardrobe in two days for a lady who paid me thirty *yuan*. Later I was told that I'd gotten too little for such work.

I've made many acquaintances with other carpenters, most of them're also from Anhui. I feel very comfortable when we talk in our native tongue. It's bad to be unable to speak Mandarin because you'll be at a disadvantage in bargaining with Beijingers. Now I can speak it fairly well. I often go to the market near Hujialou (in east Beijing) and await potential customers.

Before establishing my reputation as a carpenter, I'd trouble at first finding clients. Later, my strength and professional skills made me competitive.

Sometimes I'd so many contracts that I didn't know who I'd work for first. I did my best to keep the loss of potential customers to a minimum.

I've an eleven-year-old boy. He's in the first-grade at a local primary school. I miss him very much. I earn about 500 *yuan* a month, six times the average income of an ordinary worker in Beijing. Each month, I send home two hundred *yuan*, about a quarter of which goes to my parents-in-law.

I earn 600 *yuan*, and more, during the busy period but less than 200 when it's off-season.

Before 1980, I'd to send sixty *yuan* a month to my production brigade as a contribution, regardless of the amount I earned.

Since the introduction of the responsibility system in the countryside, however, things're quite different. Farmers who've left their hometowns to work somewhere else needn't contribute any of their earnings to the production teams they belong to. So now I can determine how to spend all my money.

I pay ten *yuan* a month for housing and about thirty for food, little compared to what most Beijing residents pay for the same things.

Beijing people pay more attention to the quality of furniture than prices. So I can get high prices, although I seldom bargain with them. I guarantee good-quality furniture. That's enough. Generally speaking, I receive good treatment from my customers. Some of my customers're quite warm-hearted and treat me as if I were a relative. They invite me to sumptuous dinners and serve me quality cigarettes and jasmine tea. Occasionally I meet clients who treat me like a country bumpkin. Well, I'm the wrong person to be treated that way. I'll do shoddy work if that happens.

I was born and reared in Huangshan (a scenic spot in Anhui Province). It's called "the most marvelous mountain under heaven." I like Huangshan very much but I like Beijing even more.

I've spent about 100 *yuan* each year touring Beijing's scenic spots and places of interest. I'm never tired of visiting these beautiful sights. But I think Beijing's food's too expensive.

During Spring Festival (Chinese lunar New Year), I returned home for a family reunion. They considered me an "expert" on Beijing. The fellow villagers look on me as a master carpenter, rich both in money and information.

Sunday Engineer: Ren Shiyao

My experience as a Sunday engineer also helps me in my principal work.

Sweeping social changes tend to give rise to new things, which call for new terms to come into existence. "Sunday engineer" is a new term which has appeared in China in recent years. It refers to those engineers and technicians working in state-run institutions who use Sundays and other holidays to go to the countryside to help township- and village-run enterprises solve technical problems.

Fifty-four-year-old Ren Shiyao, a senior engineer teaching at the Shanghai Jiaotong (Communications) University, is one of such Sunday engineers. Working in cooperation with some of his colleagues, he has helped save a township enterprise in a nearby county from the brink of bankruptcy and turned it into a flourishing, profit-making enterprise by developing new line of products.

The appearance of Sunday engineers has, to a degree, alleviated the acute shortage of engineers and technicians among the roughly one and half million township and village enterprises. These enterprises are eager to recruit Sunday engineers and pay generous remuneration.

Ren thinks that his activities on Sundays have not only brought him extra money, but also benefited him intellectually.

The township and village enterprises, on the other hand, regard their Sunday engineers as "gods of wealth" for the enormous wealth they halp create. To express his appreciation for the work that Ren and his three colleagues have done, the manager of the Shangyu Draft Fan Plant had a group portrait of the four painted and hung on the wall of the canteen. "I want everybody in my plant to appreciate the contributions of our Sunday engineers," the manager said.

Ten years ago, the Shangyu Refractory Material Plant had difficulty selling its products, and the plant was about to close down. Thirty-year-old Xu Cangen, manager of the plant, was very disturbed but could do nothing about it. At that time, I was recuperating in Shangyu County, my hometown. One evening, he came to see me. He asked me to help save his plant. I was teaching fluid mechanics in a college and had some knowledge of ventilating mechanisms and heat exchanges. So I advised him to produce cooling tower draft fans, which were badly needed at that time.

Xu accepted my advice, and I became their technical consultant. Xu bought some production tools such as pincer pliers, iron and wooden hammers, with the remaining 2,000 *yuan* of floating capital that the plant had. With these simple tools, Xu and his workers produced China's first D-80cm cooling tower draft fans in three shabby rooms at the bottom of a hill.

After I recovered from my illness, I returned to Shanghai, and continued as a "Sunday engineer" at the plant. It was a five to six hour train journey from Shanghai to Shangyu. Every Saturday evening, after I'd finished my work at the college, I would jump on my bicycle and rush to the railway station. It was late when I reached the factory. Early the next morning, I began work, and that evening, I returned to Shanghai by train. At the train station in Shanghai I parked my bicycle wherever I could in an alleyway. It was an old bike and I didn't care what happened to it. Once I forgot to lock it, and the bicycle was taken by the police to a lost-and-found office.

The Shangyu Draft Fan Plant has more than 300 workers who are all farmers from nearby villages. They are skilled in farm work, but are not very good at operating machines. I had to teach them how to operate them. In the summer, I wore only a sleeveless shirt and shorts when instructing them. Usually I was drenched in sweat. However, I was pleased that the farmers mastered the skills very quickly. A number of middle and small sized cooling tower draft fans were soon put into production. Xu formally announced the establishment of the Shangyu plant by hanging up the factory nameplate. In 1984, Shanghai Jiaotong University, where I work, also cooperated with the plant and they jointly established a production body consisting of research, designing, manufacturing, management, and technology services. Then, a technology development group and a draft fan research institute also were organized. As a senior engineer at college, and the first "Sunday engineer" at Shangyu plant, I was considered a key member of these new organs. It was in 1984 that my colleagues Fan Qitai, a senior engineer, Zhang Zhongchao, a professor, and Zhu Shiti, an associate professor, also joined the ranks of "Sunday engineers" at the plant.

I'm busy at college. Each week, I have two classes. At the same time, I have several scientific research project underway as well as many social activities. Many of my colleagues say to me, "Engineer Ren, it's hard to find you." I tell them, "It's easy. I have a beeper. You only dial a BPS number if you want to reach me." Although I'm busy with my own work at school, I'm devoted to "Sunday engineer" responsibilities at the plant. Every weekend, I shuttle between Shanghai and Shangyu. Once, after we got off the train, we hitchhiked aboard an open tractor to get to the plant. On the way, it began to rain heavily. We got drenched from head to toe. One of us joked, "Heaven will help us wash the dirt off our body."

Industrious work results in good gains. With our technical assistance, the Shangyu plant is developing new products every year, and its economic situation is steadily improving. Its more than 150 specifications for four series of cooling tower draft fans sell well domestically. The Diaoyutai State Guest House, Zhongnanhai Huai Ren Hall and the Great Hall of the People in Beijing and the Park Hotel in Shanghai all are using our draft fans. Because our products have reached the advanced international level, they are expected to fourteen countries and regions. In 1987, the output value of the plant reached 20 million *yuan*, and the annual profit was nearly 4 million *yuan*. Ten years ago, when the plant was founded, the output value was less than 10,000 *yuan*. As a major enterprise in Shangyu, the draft fan plant has fostered more than thirty village factories.

Early this year, the United Nations Science and Technology Development Center sent a film group to Shangyu to shoot a TV documentary entitled, "*Chinese County and Village Enterprises' Way to Success*." The film will be shown in Third World countries, and is a great honor for us.

My experience as a "Sunday engineer" also helps me in my regular occupation. In the past, I had little touch with reality. My lectures were principally based on books, and weren't interesting. The students didn't like them. One time, some students told me after class, "We won't attend your lectures if you continue this way."

Now, I give lectures that combine theory with practice. My lectutes are more interesting and the students like them. I've brought some senior students to the plant to do their graduation projects.

Many people ask me, "How much money do you get from the Shangyu plant, which is doing so well?" That is hard to answer, because when I started, the goverment had no regulations on how much a "Sunday engineer" should get a month. My principal intention was to save the factory. Money wasn't my primary consideration. For six years, I didn't get one cent. After the factory recovered, I got 30 *yuan* a month as a "technology consultancy fee." I kept 10 and turned over 20 to my university. Since the latter half of 1986, my consultancy fee has gone up to 50 *yuan*. I keep 35. At the end of the year, the university gives me a bonus of 1,000 *yuan*, in recognition of the work I've done at the plant.

My family isn't a very wealthy one. Actually we are rather poor compared to my colleagues. My wife and I together earn 200 *yuan* a month. Besides providing for ourselves, we also have to support two children, and both of our mothers. In addition, I spend some money on health food. I've suffered from hepatitis and pulmonary tuberculosis, and am not in good health.

I'm very satisfied when I see that my knowledge has helped county and village enterprises. Workers at the factory have said many times, "Considering Mr. Ren and his colleagues' contribution to our factory, several thousand *yuan* a month isn't too much." But I think China is still a poor country. The time hasn't come when we can lead a life of such affluence.

形形色色的中国人

刘炳文 熊蕾 编

*

外文出版社出版

(中国北京百万庄路 24 号)

邮政编码 100037

外文印刷厂印刷

中国国际图书贸易总公司发行

(中国北京车公庄西路 21 号)

北京邮政信箱 399 号 邮政编码 100044

1990 年(36 开)第一版

(英)

ISBN 7－119－01160－X/Z・474(外)

00890

17－E－2479P

Mensajeros de la oscuridad

Novela
Crimen y Misterio